T0330248

Modelling in Ecological Economics

CURRENT ISSUES IN ECOLOGICAL ECONOMICS

Series Editors: Sylvie Faucheux, *Professor of Economic Science* and Martin O'Connor, *Associate Professor of Economic Science, C3ED, Université de Versailles–Saint Quentin en Yvelines, France,* John Proops, *Professor of Ecological Economics, School of Politics, International Relations and the Environment, Keele University, UK* and Jan van der Straaten, *Retired Senior Lecturer, Department of Leisure Studies, Tilburg University, The Netherlands*

The field of ecological economics has emerged as a result of the need for all social sciences to be brought together in new ways, to respond to global environmental problems. This major new series aims to present and define the state-of-the-art in this young and yet fast-developing discipline.

This series cuts through the vast literature on the subject to present the key tenets and principal problems, techniques and solutions in ecological economics. It is the essential starting point for any practical or theoretical analysis of economy-environment interactions and will provide the basis for future developments within the discipline.

Titles in the series include:

Greening the Accounts
Edited by Sandrine Simon and John Proops

Nature and Agriculture in the European Union
New Perspectives on Policies that Shape the European Countryside
Edited by Floor Brouwer and Jan van der Straaten

Waste in Ecological Economics
Edited by Katy Bisson and John Proops

Environmental Thought
Edited by Edward A. Page and John Proops

The Ecological Economics of Consumption
Edited by Lucia A. Reisch and Inge Røpke

Modelling in Ecological Economics
Edited by John Proops and Paul Safonov

Modelling in Ecological Economics

Edited by

John Proops

School of Politics, International Relations and the Environment, Keele University, UK

Paul Safonov

Department of Business Computer Information Systems, St. Cloud State University, Minnesota, USA

CURRENT ISSUES IN ECOLOGICAL ECONOMICS

Edward Elgar
Cheltenham, UK • Northampton, MA, USA

Published by
Edward Elgar Publishing Limited
Glensanda House
Montpellier Parade
Cheltenham
Glos GL50 1UA
UK

Edward Elgar Publishing, Inc.
136 West Street
Suite 202
Northampton
Massachusetts 01060
USA

A catalogue record for this book
is available from the British Library

Library of Congress Cataloguing in Publication Data

Modelling in ecological economics/edited by John Proops, Paul Safonov.
       p. cm. (Current issues in ecological economics)
     Includes bibliographical references and index.
     1. Environmental economics—Methodology. 2. Environmental economics—Econometric models. I. Proops, John L.R., 1947–   .
II. Safonov, Paul. III. Series.
HC79.E5M626   2005
333.7'01'1—dc22

2004058449

ISBN 1 84376 222 6

Printed and bound in Great Britain by MPG Books Ltd, Bodmin, Cornwall

Contents

Figures

Tables

Contributors

Stefan Baumgärtner, Department of Economics, University of Heidelberg, Germany

Jeroen C.J.M. van den Bergh, Department of Spatial Economics, Free University, Amsterdam, The Netherlands

Luis Cruz, Department of Economics, University of Coimbra, Portugal

Malte Faber, Department of Economics, University of Heidelberg, Germany

Mario Giampietro, Unit of Technological Assessment, INRAN, Rome, Italy

Marco A. Janssen, Center for the Study of Institutions, Population, and Environmental Change, Indiana University, USA

Kozo Mayumi, Faculty of Integrated Arts and Sciences, University of Tokushima, Japan

Giuseppe Munda, Department of Economics and Economic History, Autonomous University of Barcelona, Spain

John Proops, School of Politics International Relations and the Environment, Keele University, UK

Paul Safonov, Department of Business Computer Information Systems, St. Cloud State University, Minnesota, USA, and Institute of Control Sciences, Russian Academy of Sciences, Moscow, Russia

David I. Stern, Department of Economics, Rensselaer Polytechnic Institute, New York, USA

Preface

This volume is a further contribution to the Current Issues in Ecological Economics series, which aims to provide comprehensive and authoritative overviews of a range of areas of within ecological economics.

This book arose from our concern that while many and various modelling approaches are being used and developed in ecological economics, there was no single source to which researchers in the field could turn. Instead, lengthy searches of the literature, particularly the journal *Ecological Economics*, was necessary to gain insights into modelling methods and their applications. In particular, we felt that those beginning research in this area had no guidelines on what modelling techniques were appearing in the current ecological economics literature, nor any way of appraising the areas where these techniques can be applied, their strengths and limitations, etc.

When we began to design the book, we were immediately struck by the broad range of modelling methods already being used, ranging from thermodynamics, through evolutionary concepts, structural modelling, multi-criteria analysis, to agent-based modelling. Our task then was to identify recognized experts who could provide authoritative overviews of these methods, and we were fortunate that those we approached were willing to undertake the demanding tasks we set them, in terms of word limits, structure, completeness, etc. We are indebted to all of them for their efforts in producing this volume.

Each chapter was commissioned and written specially for this book, and as a consequence we hope, and believe, that it offers an authoritative overview of current approaches to modelling in ecological economics.

John Proops and Paul Safonov

1. An Introduction to Modelling in Ecological Economics

John Proops and Paul Safonov

1.1 MODELLING IN ECOLOGICAL ECONOMICS

Ecological economics has emerged as a thriving (trans-)discipline over the past twenty years, and its research concerns are well represented in the (highly cited) journal *Ecological Economics*, published by Elsevier Science. A review of this journal's contents suggests that research in this area can be classified into four main areas (though many articles contain elements of more than one category):

- Conceptual analysis, exploring issues relating to (e.g.) environmental ethics, environmental epistemology, etc. (See Page and Proops (2003), in this series, for an overview of this area.)
- Empirical studies, using data to test ideas and draw policy conclusions.
- Policy analysis, focused on ways in which environmental policies may be formulated, institutional barriers to decision making, etc.
- Modelling, using mathematical or other methods to represent interactions of the components of the world of environmental interest.

This book focuses on the final category, modelling, and offers an overview of current and emerging methods of applying mathematical, computational and conceptual methods to environmental issues. As alluded to above, one characteristic of ecological economics is the overlap of concepts, empirics, policy and modelling, so the chapters that follow are never solely technical. Instead, they reflect the nature of current ecological economics in always relating to wider concerns and activities.

Before reviewing the contents of the chapters, it is worth noting that none explicitly deals with 'neoclassical' modelling in ecological economics. This is for three reasons. First, there is quite a strong strand within ecological economics which explicitly rejects the neoclassical approach (i.e., of assuming optimizing behaviour by strictly self-interested agents, etc.). Second, this

1

approach to modelling has already received extensive treatments in the literature (e.g., the classic text by Dasgupta and Heal (1979)). Third, the range of applications of the neoclassical optimizing approach is so vast that it would be nearly impossible to do justice to it in a single chapter.

1.2 THE CONTENTS OF THE BOOK

The eight substantive chapters of this book cover a range of current modelling approaches which are either in current use within ecological economics, or which are beginning to be used and could benefit from a wider audience. The approach in several of the chapters (e.g., Chapters 2, 3, 4, and 9) is mainly mathematical in content, though we have urged authors to limit the level of the complexity of the mathematics to no more than is necessary to allow a grasp of the modelling principles involved.

The two chapters on thermodynamics (Chapters 5 and 6) focus more on the conceptual aspect of modelling rather than its technical aspects. They seek to show the scope for, and limitations of, thermodynamic methods in ecological economics and their divergent approaches embrace the current and extensive literatures on such diverse issues as far-from-equilibrium systems, exergy analysis, and production theory. The chapters on multi-criteria evaluation (Chapter 7) and agent-based modelling (Chapter 8) involve the currently least well-established methods within ecological economics, but they show that these methods deserve attention for their significant theoretical and practical applications.

1.2.1 Chapter 2 – Evolutionary Models

While the concept of evolution is quite central to ecological economics (e.g., Norgaard, 1984; Faber and Proops, 1998), there is so far a rather sparse literature on applications of formal evolutionary modelling to environmental issues. This chapter offers an overview of a range of evolutionary concepts and methods that are beginning to be utilized, or that might usefully be applied.

Jeroen van den Bergh begins by noting that, as with several other modelling approaches discussed later, evolutionary modelling takes a disaggregated approach, reflecting the multiple actors and influences in economy-environment interactions. He reviews the development of evolutionary theory in the social sciences, especially evolutionary economics, with its foundations in the work of Schumpeter.

There is then an overview of current evolutionary approaches, including evolutionary game theory and multi-agent models (which are dealt with in more detail in Chapter 8). In particular, he contrasts the evolutionary approaches taken in environmental economics and ecological economics, especially with respect to considerations of sustainable development and ecosystem management, arguing for the need for evolutionary approaches to generate historically relevant long-run models.

The conclusion is that evolutionary thinking is the next logical step for ecological economics, with its emphasis on dynamics, diversity of scale and the use of bounded rationality.

1.2.2 Chapter 3 – Input-Output Models

Input-output analysis is also a (highly) disaggregated approach to modelling, extremely well suited to the multi-sectoral representation of economy-environment interactions, and quite widely used already in ecological economics.

Luis Cruz, John Proops and Paul Safonov begin with an introduction to the structure of the basic I-O model, noting that it easily allows the relating of quantities of goods to their 'dual' prices, thereby naturally offering a basis for representing national accounts (a widespread use of input-output models).

The basic input-output model is then extended to include interactions with nature, and a variety of such approaches that have been developed over the past half-century are reviewed and compared. More recent applications of input-output methods are discussed, such as to 'green' national accounting, the analysis of waste and the calculation of 'environmental footprints'.

Historically, a rather distinct input-output literature has emerged concerned with 'energy analysis', imputing energy use to the production of goods and services. This literature is reviewed, noting the way this approach has developed separately but in parallel to the 'environmental' analysis.

Finally, there is a discussion of the way input-output models may be made dynamic (also discussed in Chapter 4), through including savings-investment, giving rise to increased capital stocks and productive capacity.

1.2.3 Chapter 4 – Neo-Austrian Models

As need above, input-output models can be made dynamic. A related approach is that of neo-Austrian modelling, which while less disaggregated than the general input-output approach, perhaps offers a more convenient and theoretically well-founded approach to multi-sectoral modelling for long-run economy-environment interactions.

Malte Faber and John Proops note that the neo-Austrian method is rather like a 'construction kit' for modelling, using the adaptable notion of the 'production process' rather than the more familiar neoclassical formulation of the 'production function'. The approach is argued to be oriented towards empirical work, particularly able to cope with changing production techniques, and corresponding changes to resource use and waste production.

There is a brief historical review of the development of the nineteenth century Austrian approach to capital theory, leading to the emergence of the more soundly formulated neo-Austrian method in the mid-twentieth century.

The basic neo-Austrian model is outlined, stressing the role of capital accumulation in causing the (multi-sectoral) restructuring of the economy over time. It is shown how the neo-Austrian model can be represented in the input-output form, allowing the exploitation of the quantity-price duality methods of that approach.

Finally, it is shown how the basic neo-Austrian model can easily be extended to include various types of economy-environment interactions for dynamic modelling (of both quantities and prices). The issues discussed include: natural resource extraction and pricing; waste generation; recycling; waste treatment; green accounting; trade and the environment.

1.2.4 Chapter 5 – Entropy in Ecological Economics

While Chapters 2 to 4 dealt with modelling in the technical (i.e., mathematical) sense, this chapter (and, to some extent, Chapter 6 also) concerns modelling as the application of concepts, in this case the concepts from thermodynamics.

Kozo Mayumi and Mario Giampietro offer an overview of the development of thermodynamic concepts and how they can and are being applied in ecological economics. They begin with a discussion of the entropy concept, from Carnot's initial work on energy transformation, up to the recent (and contested) interpretation of entropy in terms of information. They point out the relationships and inconsistencies between these various approaches, but note that most are rather pessimistic in tone (e.g., the notion of the ultimate 'heat death' of the universe).

However, they then note that since the mid-twentieth century, there has been a change in the interpretation of the role of entropy in systems, beginning with the work by Prigogine on open-system thermodynamics, with an emphasis on the emergence of complexity (i.e., 'becoming'). They note that these two separate applications of the entropy concept are mirrored within the wider ecological economics literature, with some authors being notably optimistic (the 'cornucopians') while others interpret thermodynamics as having more pessimistic implications for human and natural systems (e.g., Nicholas Georgescu-Roegen).

The authors stress the importance of the entropy concept as a tool for metaphorical reasoning, and offer a review of recent applications of the entropy concept within ecological economics, including such issues as resource depletion, coevolution (cf. Chapter 2) and the thermodynamics of sustainable development.

1.2.5 Chapter 6 – Thermodynamic Models

This chapter is also about thermodynamics, but while Chapter 5 stresses the far-from-equilibrium approach of Prigogine, and its conceptual implications, Stefan Baumgärtner's contribution stays closer to 'classical' thermodynamics.

After a brief review of the emergence of thermodynamics, up to its application by Georgescu-Roegen, the importance of both the First and Second Laws of thermodynamics for understanding economy-environment relations is noted, in particular in showing the difference between the standard economic 'circular flow' model of economic accounting, compared to the material energy linear through-flow approach from natural science. The basic principles of thermodynamic systems are described and applied to 'exergy' (i.e., free energy) analysis.

The use of analogies and isomorphisms between thermodynamics and economics are noted, and the failed attempts to use entropy, energy and exergy to achieve theories of value (cf. the labour theory of value) are discussed. A more fruitful approach to modelling is seen to be the use of thermodynamic constraints on human action, through the transformations of energy and matter, showing the relationships between resource use and waste production, with its strong implications for production theory.

Finally, it is noted that the exergy concept is being fruitfully applied to the modelling of real production process (i.e., those being undertaken in finite amounts of time), with its implications for analyses of notions of economic efficiency and sustainability.

1.2.6 Chapter 7 – Multi-Criteria Evaluation

Multi-criteria evaluation (MCE) is a method by which decisions can be made in the light of competing and even conflicting information, and this general approach is clearly relevant to ecological economics, with its stress on problems of knowledge and rationality.

Giuseppe Munda argues that because of its flexibility and transparency, MCE can be used to resolve (*inter alia*) environmental conflicts, by making clear how the ranking and compensation of various criteria used in society lead to alternative decisions. Thus the aim is not so much to derive *the* decision as to show how alternative decisions depend on alternative assumptions.

There follows a comprehensive review of the technique and the related issue of its application, paying particular attention to the following aspects: incommensurability of criteria; the role of participation; the weighting of criteria in decision making; the need for methodological consistency; problems of compensability; informational requirements for MCE. Finally, there is a review of the desirable properties for Social MCE.

1.2.7 Chapter 8 – Agent-Based Models

In this chapter, Marco Janssen offers an overview of a developing type of modelling, which involves the computational simulation of social agents as evolving, autonomous and interacting. In particular, the chapter addresses how this approach can be applied to ecological economic systems, where human agents interact with their environment and with each other.

The benefits of this method are stressed when compared with the standard equation-based methods of, e.g., game theory, particularly noting its ability to deal with situations involving bounded rationality and complex social systems. A range of approaches to the agent-based approach are discussed, including cellular automata and reactive and goal oriented agents.

There is overview of the current applications of the agent-based method in ecological economics, and there is stress on the use of method for analyses involving institutions, communication, and monitoring and sanctioning systems, in maintaining cooperative behaviour. The potential applications of the method are noted, including to common-use resources, land use, integrated modelling and participatory decision approaches (cf., Chapter 7).

1.2.8 Chapter 9 – The Environmental Kuznets Curve

The final chapter, by David Stern, combines a methodological analysis of the widely used Environmental Kuznets Curve (EKC) with a plea that ecological economics take more seriously modern econometric techniques in its empirical analyses. The EKC is the (much contested) inverted U-shaped relationship between environmental damage and income per capita, and it is argued that many of the explorations of the EKC are marred by poor econometric practice, in part explaining why various authors come to such different empirical conclusions.

There is an overview of the development of the EKC notion, deriving from the Brundland Report, and noting the standard explanations for the EKC phenomenon, including the effects of scale, output mix, input mix and the state of technology. The various models that give rise to the EKC shape are discussed, and the role of trade and the relocation of manufacturing are also assessed. Next here is a review of the econometric criticisms that can be levelled at much of the EKC literature (supported by an appendix on current econometric methods and terminology). It is concluded that almost all of the statistical analyses which identify the standard inverted U-shape are econometrically flawed.

Finally, an alternative analytical framework is offered for understanding pollution-income relationships, based on the decomposition of the causes of emissions into a variety of casual factors, which can impact in a different ways, according to time and place.

1.3 WHAT ELSE? ... OR CHAPTERS THAT COULD HAVE BEEN IN THIS BOOK

Having set the goal for this monograph we intended to embrace as full as possible a range of approaches and techniques used in modelling of ecological economic processes. However, it is not feasible to combine all relevant material in one book, so we thought we should mention other important methods in the discipline which, for one or another reason, unfortunately, stayed outside the scope of this work.

A substantial contribution to ecological economic modelling was made by the group of Robert Costanza, namely, in building integrated approaches to dynamic ecological economic modelling and applying systems dynamics to spatial ecological economics models (see, e.g., Voinov et al., 1999).

Models of industrial metabolism (e.g., Ayres 1994), comprise another important method, which helps analysing physical flows in environmental-economic systems.

Certainly, other modelling approaches exist that deserve mention, and we refer interested readers to other publications, such as Faucheux et al. (1996) and van den Bergh (1996), that give more examples, and contain substantial review of methods used in modelling of ecological-economic interactions.

REFERENCES

Ayres, R.U. (1994), 'Industrial metabolism: theory and policy', in B.R. Allenby and D.J. Richards (eds), *The Greening of Industrial Ecosystems*, Washington DC: National Academy Press.

Bergh, J.C.J.M. van den (1996), *Ecological Economics and Sustainable Development: Theories, Methods, Applications*, Cheltenham: Edward Elgar.

Dasgupta, P. and G. Heal (1979), *Economic Theory and Exhaustible Resources*, Cambridge: Cambridge University Press.

Faber, M. and J. Proops (1998), *Evolution, Time, Production and the Environment*, Heidelberg: Springer Verlag.

Faucheux, S., D. Pearce and J. Proops (1996), *Models of Sustainable Development*, Cheltenham: Edward Elgar.

Norgaard, R. (1984), 'Coevolutionary development potential', *Land Economics*, **60**, 160–73.

Page, A. and J. Proops (2003), *Environmental Thought*, Cheltenham: Edward Elgar.

Voinov, A., R. Costanza, L. Wainger, R. Boumans, F. Villa, T. Maxwell and H. Voinov (1999), 'Patuxent landscape model: integrated ecological economic modeling of a watershed', *Environmental Modeling and Software Journal*, **14** (5), 473–91.

2. Evolutionary Models

Jeroen C.J.M. van den Bergh

2.1 INTRODUCTION

A typical feature of studies in the area of ecological economics is a disaggregated approach to integrated modelling that does not conflict too much with reality. Evolutionary modelling is a prime example of this, because it is based on populations of heterogeneous individuals. Neither evolutionary modelling nor evolutionary theory have seen much application to environmental issues. This is somewhat surprising given that evolutionary biology and ecological economics have their origins in population ecology, characterized by notions such as competition and carrying capacity. It is also surprising in view of the fact that evolutionary economics has developed into a respected branch of economics. This suggests that the combination of economics and ecology in integrated modelling could in principle start from an evolutionary approach. This chapter aims to examine such a line of research.

Since evolutionary theory and methods are not yet part of the standard knowledge of environmental and ecological economists, to begin with, evolutionary theory, evolutionary economics and evolutionary modelling will be briefly discussed. Subsequently, several areas within ecological-economics where evolutionary models might be fruitfully applied will be considered. In summary Section 2.2 considers evolutionary theory and evolutionary economics, and Section 2.3 builds on this to explore a range of approached to evolutionary modelling. Section 2.4 examines evolutionary approaches in environmental and ecological economics and Section 2.5 offers some conclusions.

2.2 EVOLUTIONARY THEORY AND EVOLUTIONARY ECONOMICS

The fundamental mechanisms of which all evolutionary processes consist can be regarded as together composing an 'accordion model'. This model applies equally to genetic and non-genetic evolution. It emphasizes that evolution works upon populations of individuals through opposing forces. One force is the creation or generation of variation (or variety or diversity), through various mechanisms, such as genetic mutations and technical innovations. It can be considered to foster a disequilibrating and often random effect. A second force is selection, which reduces variety. It can be considered to cause an equilibrating and directive effect. Instead of being a law, like gravity, selection is a taxonomy of closely related but different processes, which constitutes an 'umbrella term'. For instance, natural selection covers such different mechanisms as competition for food, sexual competition, predator pressure, and scarcity of space or resources, whereas economic selection includes, among others, market competition, mergers and takeovers, financial requirements, laws and public regulation, and consumer opinions.

The mechanism of opposing forces is both simple and powerful, and its result is the continuous generation and selection of diversity. Understanding and modelling its dynamics means taking account of diversity and changes therein. In other words, evolution implies that without understanding diversity in a system there can be no understanding of system dynamics. The most important possible consequence of sustained evolution – where the relevant time period depends on the type of system: biological, social, economic or technological – is that structure and complexity emerge along a non-equilibrium dynamic path of change. This is nowadays best – most simply and clearly – illustrated by experiments with computer simulation models, which show that surprisingly complex structures can be generated with rather simple models of interactive innovation and selection mechanisms. Such experiments have even given rise to a new field in computer science: namely, 'evolutionary computation' (Bäck, 1996).

Evolutionary thinking is slowly but definitely permeating economics. The roots of this process go as far back as Veblen (1898), but it is the legacy of Joseph Schumpeter that has been most influential of all early evolutionary economic reasoning. Schumpeter questioned the static approach of standard economics, and showed a great interest in the dynamics of economies, in particular the capitalist system, in all of his major works (starting with Schumpeter, 1934). Schumpeter saw economic (capitalistic) change as the result of revolutionary forces from within the economy, which destroy old processes and create new ones: 'creative destruction'. This allows for discrete or non-gradual changes, through clusters of derived innovations following a major invention. Another important notion derived within his dynamic perspective is that of (what was called later) Schumpeterian versus equilibrium (neoclassical) competition, where Schumpeterian competition denotes a competitive advantage that is brought about by process or product innovation.

Since the 1950s, there has been a slow increase of publications on economic evolution. This can be partly explained by the success of evolutionary biology, the limits of neoclassical economics, and the search for evolutionary underpinnings of the optimizing behaviour as assumed by neoclassical economics (Alchian, 1950).

The most cited work since the 1950s has been that of Richard Nelson and Sidney Winter, which culminated in their book *An Evolutionary Theory of Economic Change* (1982). Not only has this work influenced evolutionary economists in the neo-Schumpeterian tradition, but it has also been regarded as the most important evolutionary text by mainstream economics. The reason is that a formal, axiomatic approach to evolutionary economics is proposed, involving theoretical models and empirical, statistical applications.

Neo-Schumpeterian theories of technical change, integrated with elements of Nelson and Winter's work, currently dominate the evolutionary approach in economics (Dosi et al., 1988). These study phenomena at the firm level (technological innovation), the market and sector level (competition and diffusion, structural change), and at the macro-level (growth, long waves and international trade). Innovation is considered to cause asymmetry in technology among firms, sectors and countries, leading to exchange and trade. Comparative advantages are not fixed but change due to innovation and diffusion.

Within the neo-Schumpeterian literature on technological evolution, the notion of path dependence has received much attention. This is based on the idea that changes in population systems are characterized by increasing returns. These can be based on various phenomena, such as learning-by-using, bandwagon demand side effects (imitation), network externalities (e.g., telecommunication), informational increasing returns (if more adopted, then better known), and technological interrelatedness or complementarity (Arthur, 1989). Increasing returns are important in competition among alternative technologies. Who gets a larger market share, by coincidence, has an advantage and can grow relatively quickly and at the cost of others. In standard economic terminology, one can translate this as 'the existence of multiple equilibria'. The paths towards the equilibria are important, which is typically the study area of evolutionary economics. Consequences and characteristics of increasing returns are that inefficient equilibria can arise and a certain (inefficient) technology can be locked-in. A consequence of path-dependence is that the adoption process is very unstable and sensitive to initial events (historical coincidences or accidents). Ample empirical support exists for lock-in and path-dependence due to increasing returns. Well-known examples of locked-in and suboptimal technologies are the QWERTY keyboard, the VHS video system, the fossil fuel engine, and the Windows operating system.

Various other, authentically evolutionary, approaches have been proposed – perhaps with less impact (so far), but not necessarily less relevant. A diversity of approaches addresses the interface between evolutionary economics and organization theory (Hannan and Freeman, 1989; Carroll and Hannan, 2000). The most important recent proposal concerning the direction evolutionary economics should follow is without any doubt Potts (2000), closely following Kauffman (1993). Potts presents a kind of axiomatic foundation of evolutionary economics. In his view, economic systems are complex 'hyperstructures', i.e., nested sets of connections among components. Against this background, economic change and growth of knowledge are in essence a process of changes in connections. In line with the idea of changing connections, Potts calls for a new microeconomics based on the technique of discrete, combinatorial mathematics, such as graph theory, to study the change of microeconomic connections. This can be seen as a fundamental discussion of the need for multi-agent or population models. It allows the study of complexity and its change, heterogeneity, modularity and decomposability.

A different current 'school' of evolutionary thought in economics is becoming increasingly influential, namely evolutionary game theory (Friedman, 1998). This method was originally used to support insights of sociobiology. A more detailed discussion of this will follow in the next section. It is important to note here that evolutionary game theory is an incomplete theory from an evolutionary perspective, because it emphasizes selection processes while neglecting innovation processes.

2.3 EVOLUTIONARY MODELLING

2.3.1 Typology and Purpose

Evolutionary theory has been translated into a number of formal modelling approaches, used foremost in biology, economics and informatics (evolutionary computation). Both biology and social science, characterized by living organisms, groups, culture, economies and technology, are complex compared with physical systems. This explains why simple models have had less predictive success than in physics. The presence of evolution implies the need for different modelling purposes as well as approaches. Core characteristics of all evolution are a population structure and boundedly rational agents.

A population approach can be operationalized in three different ways. One is by means of aggregate variables, as is common in evolutionary game theory. This assumes that diversity is limited, or can be simplified, to sub-populations, each of which are assumed to be internally homogeneous, i.e., consisting of identical units or individuals. A second approach is a probabilistic one, namely to describe population distributions and changes therein. A third approach is the most disaggregate or thorough micro-approach imaginable. It takes the form of multi-agent systems, in which each individual is explicitly described and can be assigned unique features. The agents can be defined in a setting of entirely random interactions ('gaseous cloud') or systematic interactions through a network structure or a spatial grid ('lattice'). Note that the traditional multi-agent (general equilibrium) and multi-sector (macroeconomic) models in economics are essentially different from multi-agent population models, in that the former are based on complementary and representative agents or activities and lack population dynamics through selection and innovation.

In spite of the simple opposition between aggregate (evolutionary game type) and disaggregate (multi-agent type) models presented above, a wide range of specific techniques can be identified. These include genetic algorithms, neural networks, cellular automats, fuzzy sets, and deterministic chaos models. As can be expected from a relatively young research area, and given the fact that evolutionary modelling crosses a range of academic disciplines, there is a wide range of terms that are not always precisely bounded. Below, first two opposing types of modelling are discussed, and subsequently we turn to specific models found in economics and biology.

2.3.2 Evolutionary Game Theory

Game theory went from economics to biology and came back in the form of evolutionary game theory (Maynard Smith and Price, 1973; Maynard Smith, 1982; Selten, 1983). This is part of non-cooperative game theory. Evolutionary game theory is analytical, and can be so due to the fact that it adopts an aggregate approach to describing evolutionary economic phenomena (Samuelson, 1997). Usually, two groups are distinguished, reflecting minimal diversity, and allowing for a description of population dynamics with a single difference or differential equation. Since groups are considered to consist of identical individuals, evolutionary game theory is a compromise between representative agent and fully-fledged evolutionary models. A related feature is that interactions among individuals, and between individuals and the environment, are only described implicitly and jointly: for instance, through a replicator equation and an abstract fitness function (Taylor and Jonker, 1978). A replicator equation formalizes the idea that individuals with above-average (below-average) fitness will increase (decrease) their proportion in the population. Note that the aggregate character of a replicator equation makes it impossible to distinguish between selection as exit from the system, as individual learning, or as imitation.

Three assumptions characterize evolutionary games. In the first place, behaviour is characterized by rules, norms, imitation, trial-and-error, mistakes, or analogy with similar situations. Second, the context is non-cooperative and there is no influence on others' actions. And third, situations should be frequently occurring, so that learning and selection work. This means one-shot games are excluded. However, repeated games among a given set of players are not relevant. Instead, individuals from a large population are randomly paired. All taken together, the game should be played many times by individuals randomly drawn from large populations.

The most important and characteristic concept in evolutionary game theory is an evolutionary stable state or strategy (ESS). The definition is as follows: given fitness function $f(r,s)$, state s is an ESS if $f(s,s) > f(x,s)$ or $f(s,s) = f(x,s)$ and $f(s,x) > f(x,x)$. An ESS is able to resist all intrusions of 'mutations' either because they are less fit in general or when they are widespread in the population. The conditions can be seen as combinations of NE and stability-type requirements. ESS is often interpreted as stability of the equilibrium, defined in terms of the dynamic adjustment equation.

The results of evolutionary game theory remain very abstract and theoretical. Two general findings are as follows. First, pure strategies are more often selected by stability criteria instead of mixed. This supports the intuitive idea from game theorists, and the findings of experimentalists, that players often do not have an incentive to randomize strategies. Second, the infinitely repeated prisoner's dilemma game has no single ESS, and the most successful strategy depends on the initial pool of available strategies. Tit-for-tat (start with cooperation and then follow the strategy that the opponent played in the previous round; e.g., Axelrod, 1984) is often a good strategy, but GRIM may also be (cooperate until the first instance of defection, after which always defect). According to Maynard Smith and Szathmáry (1995, p. 261) the evolutionary importance of the prisoner's dilemma has been overestimated. They make a distinction between sculling and rowing games. These games reflect different types of functions – complementary or substitutable – and associated benefits of cooperation. In sculling games, all individuals simultaneously row on both sides of a boat, while in rowing games individuals row on different sides. The sculling game is an example of the familiar symmetrical prisoner's dilemma, whereas the rowing game is perhaps a more general description of complementary, specialized interactions among humans. Examples of related payoff matrices are ((3,3) (0,5); (5,0), (1,1)) and ((3,3) (0,1); (1,0), (1,1)), respectively. These show that whereas in the prisoner's dilemma defection is rational, since it is the best strategy whatever the other player plays, in the rowing game cooperating and defecting are ESS, with cooperating having higher payoffs. Likewise, cheating has a higher cost in the rowing game than in the sculling game.

The dominant type of game studied in the literature is symmetric bimatrix games. Strategically there are three types:

- Prisoner's dilemma: has a unique equilibrium in pure strategies which is ESS, namely defection.
- Hawk-Dove game: has three equilibria, of which one in mixed strategies is ESS, and two in pure strategies not.
- Coordination game: has three equilibria, of which two in pure strategies are ESS and the mixed strategy is not ESS.

Many other games build upon these results, and can in fact be seen as combinations of them. Gintis (2000) presents a very complete array of examples of games.

Evolutionary game theory poses the existence of asymptotic equilibria. This follows from no attention being given to a structural process of diversity generation, due to which selection completely dominates system dynamics. In other words, the interaction between innovation and selection, typical of evolution in reality, is missing. The result is an incomplete view of the complexity and outcome of economic evolution, as is reflected in the name 'equilibrium selection', which evolutionary game theorists themselves have given to typify their approach. In a way, the approach can be seen to downplay non-equilibrium, which is common of real world evolution.

2.3.3 Multi-Agent Models: Real Micro

With the advent of the personal computer, evolution can be studied with multiagent modelling – also referred to as microscopic modelling (Levy et al., 2000), artificial society models (Epstein and Axtell, 1996), social simulation (Gilbert and Doran, 1996; Troitzsch et al., 1996), or modelling of complex adaptive systems (Holland, 1992; Janssen, 1998). This is a (numerical) computational approach to the study of interactions among large numbers of adaptive agents. Epstein and Axtell (1996, p. 4) refer to the multi-agent models as 'laboratories', because they can 'grow' social structures in the computer and create an artificial history.

Some of the important questions when designing a multi-agent model are as follows:

- What are the agents or microscopic elements? This reduces to questions such as: 'What is the appropriate scale to represent and understand a system?' 'Which units make decisions?' and 'Which parts of the system are more tightly connected than others?' A necessary condition is that at the chosen scale variability is present and subject to change.

- What are the elementary behavioural characteristics of agents? From the perspective of ecological economics this involves physical-biological features, such as (industrial) metabolism (energy and material use and creation of waste).
- How do agents interact? This relates to cooperation (ultimately forming groups or organization), competition, trading and price negotiation, and influencing each other.
- Do agents move? What makes them move, how quickly and far can they move?
- Do agents appear and disappear, and how? This comes down to asking if they are selected, can exit or enter, and can be born or die.
- In what medium do agents interact and move: spatial grid, a network or a non-spatial cloud? Related to this and the issue of interaction is the question of whether interaction is purely local, or also can occur beyond local ranges (as in social-economic systems).
- How many agents need to be modelled? (And what are the large number properties of the resulting system?)

In ecological economics, systems modelling is widely practiced. At first sight, multi-agent modelling may seem to be a special case, and indeed it is about modelling systems. However, traditional systems modelling is associated with non-evolutionary systems. Extending traditional systems models with cellular automata or diversity below population level – thus allowing one to add selection and innovation – will give rise to multi-agent models. From an analytical perspective, one can regard traditional dynamic systems models as a set of differential equations. Multi-agents systems are, however, more irregular and complex.

Schelling (1969, 1978) is regarded as the first application of multi-agent modelling to social-economic phenomena. He made a spatial model of local interactions among agents who prefer some fraction of their neighbours has the same 'colour' as themselves. Although computational power at the time was very limited, he could show that the result is segregated neighbourhoods.

The well-known Sugarscape model developed by Epstein and Axtell (1996) covers many issues that are relevant to ecological economics, including economic trade, cultural change, exploitation of renewable resources and the impact of pollution. In addition, it is a showcase for what can be achieved with evolutionary multi-agent models. Sugarscape refers to sugar as the renewable resource and scape as the landscape. Individuals are characterized by sex, metabolic rate and vision (myopia), which are fixed for life, and differ between individuals. Preferences, wealth, cultural identity and health can change. Agents are born and can die. In certain versions of the model birth can result from mating. Behaviour is assumed to be boundedly rational, expressed by myopia in space and time. The natural environment provides the sugar which the agents need to survive. Sugar is needed for metabolism. In some versions another good, namely spice, is available, which allows for trade and substitution in the welfare function.

Space is essential and modelled as a landscape. It is a real medium in which interaction and movement occur. Agents both operate on and interact with space. The resource (sugar) is initially unevenly distributed over space, and the dynamics of the sugar growth is modelled as a cellular automaton. The state of resources and the environment are defined on each grid. The grid also allows one to trace the development of the geometries of networks of communication, relationships (friends, family) and trade.

Evolution is multilevel and occurs in three ways:

- Selection changes the distribution of fixed characteristics: 'society learns'. Note that selection operates without a fitness function being explicitly specified. Fitness can be calculated as an outcome but is not ex ante assumed, as in more aggregate evolutionary types of modelling.
- Behavioural rules are adapted due to experience or interaction with other individuals (imitation/culture): individuals learn.
- Transmission of genetic traits occurs via sex.

Some results of Sugarscape are as follows:

- Carrying capacity becomes evident: the environment can only support a certain number of people.
- Migration occurs: due to seasons, or exhaustion of resource.
- Selection changes the distribution of fixed agent characteristics. It resembles closely survival as in biological selection. Selection favours low metabolism and less myopic individuals.
- The distribution of wealth is often highly skewed, due to differences in capabilities and initial position.
- Spatial concentration occurs, or sub-populations emerge. The resulting congestion causes the carrying capacity to go down. The inclusion of pollution as an externality also leads to less concentration.

A version of Sugarscape with two commodities introduces real economics, namely trade and negotiated local prices. Agents trade at non-equilibrium prices. Internal valuation is based on the marginal rate of substitution (MRS) of spice for sugar (the marginal value of sugar in spice units). The MRS is based on a combination of metabolism (biology) and preferences (culture).

Local trade leads to an approximation of a local Pareto optimum. As a result, trade increases the carrying capacity of the system. But social inequality can increase. Furthermore, continuous preference change stimulates trade since possessions may no longer satisfy wants, in turn destabilizing prices. Local trading prices cause total trade to be smaller than demand and supply under perfect coordination and a (single) equilibrium price. Finally, local trading prices may statistically converge or not: no ex ante equilibrium can be assumed.

Due to its numerical approach, multi-agent modelling is capable of addressing a wider variety of assumptions than is common in economics, namely also those that do not allow analytical treatment. Of course, the insights obtained with numerical analysis are less general. This can be partly overcome by extensive sensitivity analysis or accurate estimation of parameters on the basis of reliable empirical data. Nevertheless, the latter two solutions are often not possible in practice.

2.3.4 Models in Evolutionary Economics

This section discusses a few essential aspects of evolutionary models applied to economic issues in more detail.

Nelson and Winter's general theory
The three basic concepts of Nelson and Winter (1982) are organizational routine, search and selection environment: they affect the performance of the firm and its changes. A decision rule on output and input is:

$$\frac{X_i}{K_i} = D(P, d_i) \tag{2.1}$$

with X_i a vector of outputs, K_i a capital input, P a vector of output and input prices, d_i a vector of decision rule parameters, and i denoting the firm. Aggregation over firms gives:

$$\frac{X}{K} = \frac{\sum_i D(P, d_i) K_i}{K} \tag{2.2}$$

with variables without index equivalent aggregates. Now decomposing the change in the output-capital ratio between times 0 to T:

$$\left(\frac{X}{T}\right)^{T} - \left(\frac{X}{T}\right)^{0} =$$

$$\sum_{i} \left[D(P^T, d_i^T) - D(P^0, d_i^T) \right] \left(\frac{K_i}{K}\right)^{0} \qquad \textit{Firms moving along the decision rule}$$

$$+ \sum_{i} \left[D(P^0, d_i^T) - D(P^0, d_i^0) \right] \left(\frac{K_i}{K}\right)^{0} \qquad \textit{Decision rule evolving through search}$$

$$+ \sum_{i} D(P^0, d_i^T) \left[\left(\frac{K_i}{K}\right)^{T} - \left(\frac{K_i}{K}\right)^{0} \right] \qquad \textit{Selection of firms changing the distribution of capital}$$

$$+ \textit{remainder term} \qquad\qquad\qquad \textit{No disjunct decomposition}$$

This model is elaborated in Nelson and Winter (1982, Chapter 9) in the context of their evolutionary model of economic growth.

A model of innovation and imitation
Iwai (1984) presented a general model of innovation and imitation. The model describes the change in the frequency of unit costs $f_t(c_i)$ of production methods co-existing in a particular industry, where $c_n < c_i < c_1$; i.e., with c_n the unit cost of the best practice method. The cumulative frequency function is then:

$$F_t(c) = \sum_{i=k}^{n} f_t(c_i) \text{ for } c_k < c < c_{k-1} \tag{2.3}$$

The dynamics follow Schumpeterian competition; i.e., each firm continuously tries to reduce the unit production cost employing two strategies, namely innovate or imitate. The dynamics of technology and industry are thus the interaction of these strategies.

The probability of imitation, adoption or copying a particular production method (obviously with lower unit cost than its present one), is assumed to be proportional to the frequency of firms which employ that method at the time. The proportionality parameter μ can change over time due to actions (R&D, investment) by the firm. This can be shown to generate logistic (S-shaped) growth, through a set of differential equations:

$$\frac{dF_t(c_i)}{dt} = \mu F_i(c_t)[1 - F_t(c_t)] \text{ for } i = 1, \dots, n \tag{2.4}$$

Here $[1 - F_t(c_i)]$ is the relative frequency of firms amenable to imitation; i.e., with unit costs higher than c_i. $F_i(c_i)$ reflects the relative frequency of firms that can be imitated; i.e., with unit costs lower than c_i. The relative frequency of a certain inefficient method ($i < n$); i.e., the difference between two adjacent logistic curves, initially expands by absorbing firms with even less efficient methods, but ultimately approaches zero, when all firms have adopted the most efficient method (n).

The latter equilibrium (all firms 'at n') will not be attained since innovation is a disturbing force. The innovation (i.e., first implementation) by a certain firm of a cheaper method with cost c_{n+1} ($< c_n$) and probability ξ is the beginning of a process of creative destruction. Imitation of the new technology will create another logistic growth pattern. If innovation occurs by the 'most efficient firm' then another logistic curve is added, starting at initial frequency $1/M$ (M is total number of firms). If a less efficient firm with cost c_i 'jumps' immediately to the new method, then logistic curves 'in between' ($i+1, \ldots, n$) experience a discrete jump. If the unit cost of best practice due to innovation is as follows:

$$c_{min}(t) = \exp(-\lambda t) \tag{2.5}$$

with λ the rate of decline of minimum unit costs, then innovation time T can be written as a function of unit cost:

$$T(c) = -\frac{\ln(C)}{\lambda} \tag{2.6}$$

Now the impact of the parameters on the distribution of methods or cost levels in the industry (population of firms) can be examined: imitation/adoption rate μ, innovation probability ξ, and rate of decline of minimum unit costs λ. Combining all of the previous results into a long-run distribution (density) function leads to alternating phases of widening and narrowing distributions of characteristics; i.e., interaction between equilibrating and disequilibrating forces (innovation: λ, ξ) and equilibrating (adoption: μ) forces.

Path-dependence and lock-in due to increasing returns
All evolution in a large number of dimensions implies path-dependence but does not necessarily lead to lock-in. Arthur (1989) proposes a simple model to illustrate path-dependence and lock-in. Two types of agents (consumers) are assumed who can choose between two types of goods. Agent type 1 has utility a_1+rn_a for good a and b_1+rn_b for good b. Agent type 2 has utility a_2+rn_a and b_2+rn_b for goods a and b, respectively. Here a_i and b_i denote the utility of good a and b, respectively, without network or externality effects; r

denotes the intensity of these effects; and n_a and n_b the number of adopters of goods a and b, respectively. Now, even if $a_1 > b_1$, i.e., agents of type 1 in principle prefer good a above b, due to network effects they may decide to buy good b. This occurs when $a_1 + rn_a < b_1 + rn_b$, or $(n_b - n_a)r > a_1 - b_1$, which means for a sufficiently large number of adopters of good b (n_b) or a sufficiently large network or externality effect (r). A similar result can be stated for consumer 2 in combination with good a. This implies that beyond a certain number of adopters of a certain good, a or b, all new decisions will be in favour of that type of good; i.e., a lock-in results. The question is then what determines the path towards the surpassing of the adopters-threshold. It is the order in which agents with a particular preference 'arrive'. If this follows a more or less random process, then the ultimate lock-in – in this case dominance of consumption of good a or b – is entirely random.

The NK model

Kauffman (1993) proposed the famous NK model. It describes complex decisions, such as evolutionary change, as combinatorial problems, which can be regarded as one way to operationalize bounded rationality. A concrete application is to the design of products. Frenken (2001) applies it to economics, particularly innovation trajectories, illustrated by the early development of the steam engine.

The term NK denotes the total number of dimensions (N) of the problem and the number of dimensions that on average determine the function of the system in each dimension (K). The value of K can thus be seen as a measure of the interdependence of dimensions; i.e., the complexity of the problem. $K = 0$ means minimal complexity, and $K = N - 1$ maximum complexity. If in each dimension at least two discrete options are available, then the total number of decisions or systems is at least 2^N.

The dimensions can be thought of as components in products, subprocesses in production, individuals in groups, organizations in market networks. Kauffman initially focused on applications to biology and chemistry, such as molecules in networks of chemical processes, and genes and proteins in living organisms.

The model further consists of evolutionary notions, namely fitness. Two levels are defined, namely fitness per dimensional choice and average fitness of combinations of choices over all dimensions. This allows, for instance, for examining whether a continuously ascending path in terms of overall fitness exists that results from single mutations; i.e., changes in choices within only one dimension. The NK model can further be used to illustrate path-dependence and evolution as going through, or even ending in, local optima.

2.3.5 Models in Evolutionary Biology

Here we will very briefly, without all possible nuances, mention aspects of evolutionary models in biology. Although much of evolutionary biology has proceeded without the use of mathematics, a great deal of effort has gone into formalizing basic concepts. Many of these are the result of fusing genetics and ecology, resulting in evolutionary ecology (see Roughgarden, 1979; Maynard Smith, 1989).

Selection by competition
Maynard Smith (1989) presents the following model to formalize the idea of selection by competition in an asexual population with individuals of two types; i.e., two subpopulations that have different intrinsic growth rates and carrying capacities, which depend on a single scarce resource.

$$\frac{dx}{dt} = r_1 x \left[1 - \frac{(x+y)}{K_1} \right] \tag{2.7}$$

$$\frac{dx}{dt} = r_2 y \left[1 - \frac{(x+y)}{K_2} \right] \tag{2.8}$$

Studying this system leads to the insight that the species associated with the largest carrying capacity will survive and the other one will be eliminated. With a more detailed (more micro) model, that explicitly describes birth and death rates, it can be shown that also differences in intrinsic growth rates (r_i) have an impact on the selection outcome. The resulting model is:

$$\frac{dx}{dt} = \frac{r_1 x}{(1+x+y)} - d_1 x \tag{2.9}$$

$$\frac{dy}{dt} = \frac{r_2 y}{(1+x+y)} - d_2 y \tag{2.10}$$

Analysis of this model shows that the type with the largest r_i/d_i, with d_i the death rate of subpopulation i, will survive at the cost of the other.

Combined genetic-population dynamics
Evolutionary ecology is about genetic and population dynamics. Roughgarden (1979, Chapter 17) states that these can be integrated by relating the two parameters of density dependent population growth (i.e., intrinsic growth rate r and carrying capacity K) to individual reproduction and fitness. The fitness

can be linked to the growth of sub-populations according to density dependent growth:

$$W_i = 1 + r_i - \frac{r_i N}{K} \text{, with } i \text{ denoting a sub-population.}$$

Average fitness is $W^* = p^2 W_{AA} + 2pq W_{Aa} + q^2 W_{aa}$. The change of p over time
can be described in continuous time as replicator dynamics (frequency-
dependent selection): for allele A it is:

$$\frac{dp}{dt} = \left[\frac{(pW_{AA} + qW_{Aa})}{W^*} - 1 \right] p \qquad (2.11)$$

Of course, since $p+q=1$ we have:

$$\frac{dq}{dt} = 1 - \frac{dp}{dt} \qquad (2.12)$$

Finally, the change in the population can be written as the sum of growth of
sub-populations (with alleles AA, Aa and aa):

$$\frac{dN}{dt} = N_{AA} W_{AA} + N_{Aa} W_{Aa} + N_{aa} W_{aa}$$
$$= p^2 NW_{AA} + 2pqNW_{Aa} + q^2 NW_{aa} = W^* N \qquad (2.13)$$

(Note that it is also possible to formulate the model in discrete time, which
perhaps is more realistic given discrete generations, although overlapping
generations suggest that continuous time may not be such a bad choice.) It
can be shown that this model leads to an equilibrium at which fitness is
locally optimized.

Things can be made much more complex by introducing mutations that
allow r_i and K_i to change. Note in this respect the distinction between
r-selection and K-selection. The first denotes density-independent selection
due to mortality keeping a population far below its carrying capacity, while
the second denotes density-dependent selection of a population that approaches its carrying capacity level.

Coevolution
The simultaneous, interactive evolution of multiple species in an ecological
community is known as coevolution. Roughgarden (1979) presents formal

models of coevolution. These are multiple, linked cases of the above discussed 'combined genetic-population dynamics'. Formally we have for S
interacting populations:

$$\frac{dN_i}{dt} = W * N_i$$

$$i = 1, ..., S \qquad (2.14)$$

$$\frac{dp_i}{dt} = \left[\frac{(p_i W_{AA} + (1 - p_i)W_{Aa})}{W *} - 1 \right] p_i$$

The W_i (and W^*) reflect absolute (average) fitness that may depend on the
own population as well as those of other species: $W_j = f_{Wi}(N_1, ..., N_S)$, with
$j = AA, Aa, aa$; note that this relationship reflects interspecific frequency
dependent selection. For two species the possible relationships are – (competition), ++ (mutualism) and +– (predation, parasitism and herbivore-plant
interaction). The interactions between species can now occur in various
ways: evolution in one species can affect the population size in another; or it
can affect the gene frequencies in another. The population size effect feeding
back to the own population size can be regarded as a pure ecological effect;
the gene frequencies effect feeding back to the own population size is known
as evolutionary reciprocation. Roughgarden (1979, p. 473) shows that this
generally is smaller than the ecological effect. This type of model can be used
to address several other interesting issues, related to optimization of fitness,
stability of communities, and reinforced feedbacks due to repeated selection
for fitness (known as the 'arms race' or the 'Red Queen hypothesis').

Group selection

Altruism and cooperation have received much attention from an evolutionary
perspective, and are the main focus in the evolutionary study of behaviour.
This is an overlapping area of research between ethology, evolutionary
ecology, (social and evolutionary) psychology and behavioural economics
(van den Bergh and Stagl, 2003). In a theoretical sense it is dominated by
evolutionary game theory. Sociobiology indeed formalized much of its main
insights with this method (Maynard Smith, 1982). It has fostered the idea that
all altruism in most animals derives from reciprocal and kin selection; group
selection clearly has had less credibility. Roughgarden (1979) and Gintis
(2000) present models suggesting that group selection can work..

Gintis (Section 11.7) presents a model in which the payoff matrix is
$((b - c, b - c), (-c, b), (b, -c), (0, 0))$ reflecting that cooperating produces a
payoff b for the partner at a cost c. Cooperating individuals in this case are
altruists as they sacrifice for the benefit of others. This is a prisoner's di-

lemma in which defection is the dominant strategy. If $r>0$ is defined as the probability of 'assortive interaction' (i.e., identical strategies meeting each other), Hamilton (1963) regarded the degree of kinship (biological relatedness) as a proxy for r. In an economic context, however, the variety of r among groups will depend on group-specific institutions that promote cooperation and altruism. Examples of these are schooling, religion, political features (voting systems), free press and democratic history. It can be shown that if $br \geq c$ then cooperators can 'invade' a population of selfish individuals, or altruism is viable.

2.4 EVOLUTIONARY APPROACHES IN ENVIRONMENTAL AND ECOLOGICAL ECONOMICS

2.4.1 Introduction

Evolutionary approaches in the study of environmental problems and public policy responses are relevant for three main reasons. First, environmental problems often mean a loss of diversity of options, which hampers resilience of systems and limits possible future development paths. This is best illustrated by the loss of biodiversity. Second, many environmental problems are difficult to resolve because undesirable, second-best technologies are locked-in as a result of historical accidents and increasing returns to scale. The most significant examples are the complete dependence of modern economies on fossil fuels, the dominance in both passenger and freight transport of cars with fossil fuel combustion engines, and agriculture which is dominated by practices that involve large-scale production based on intensive use of fossil fuels, artificial fertilizers, pesticides, herbicides and fungicides. Third, many resource based sectors, such as agriculture, fisheries and forestry, affect not only the size of renewable resources and ecosystems, but also their internal (genetic) diversity. This undermines the long run profitability of activities.

Despite the relevance of evolutionary thinking to environmental and ecological economics, the diffusion of it has been very slow. Nevertheless, in the last few decades a small number of studies has tried to introduce evolutionary aspects in environmental economic analysis. Some of these are discussed below, where emphasis is given to modelling aspects.

Boulding (1978, 1981, *inter alia*) has most clearly and consistently emphasized the analogy between ecology and evolutionary biology on the one hand and economics on the other. This is exemplified by a focus on concepts like homeostasis and population. He also emphasizes the relevance to evolutionary economics of the distinction between genotype and phenotype. Ayres (1994) is a very original synthesis in book form of evolutionary ideas about virtually any aspect of reality, including economics and environment. Faber and Proops (1990) have combined elements of evolutionary thinking with the neo-Austrian approach, which emphasizes the temporal features – notably roundaboutness – of economic processes. This allows them to derive structural changes or transformation process, such as from simple production (agriculture) to more complex and more roundabout production (industry). Like Boulding, they stress the relevance of genotype versus phenotype, and try to find analogies of this distinction in an economic context. Allen (1997) discusses evolutionary modelling of environmental-economic systems in a spatial setting.

Table 2.1 summarizes the essential characteristics of evolutionary approaches to environmental economic problems and confronts these with ecological and traditional environmental and resource economics. It turns out that evolutionary approaches are closer in spirit to ecological economics. Two areas of application of evolutionary modelling are discussed in detail: the transition to sustainable development and ecosystem management.

Table 2.1   Differences in emphasis between evolutionary, ecological and traditional environmental and resource economics

Evolutionary Environmental Economics	Economics Economics	Traditional Environmental and Resource Economics
Evolutionary potential	Optimal scale	Optimal allocation
Variety	Equity	Efficiency
Evolutionary stable strategies	Sustainable development	Sustainable growth
Adaptive limits	Limits to growth	Growth of limits
Path-dependence	Irreversibility	Reversibility
Very long run	Long run	Short/medium run
Concrete causal processes	Concrete causal processes	Abstract statics/dynamics
Population/distribution indicators	Physical and biological indicators	Monetary indicators
Bounded rationality	Myopic and social behaviour	Rational behaviour
Fitness counts	Environmental ethics	Utilitarianism
Open system (energetically)	Open system	Closed system

2.4.2 Evolutionary Modelling of Historical Transitions and Sustainable Development

The transition of the current era of environmentally destructive growth to a sustainable development is the most important and potentially fruitful area for evolutionary modelling. The standard economics perspective of gradual economic growth in equilibrium is not shared by evolutionary economics. The evolutionary theory of growth is based on the notion of differential growth, which can be seen as a change in the frequencies of all possible individual characteristics. An important element of evolutionary growth theory is that there is no such thing as an aggregate production function (van den Bergh and Gowdy, 2003). Instead, a micro-approach is adopted in which – in principle – individual firms are described. In effect, evolutionary theories propose to avoid an aggregate production function and instead describe diversity of production relationships at the level of individual firms. Various formal evolutionary models of growth have been proposed (Conlisk, 1989; Silverberg et al., 1988; Silverberg and Verspagen, 1994).

An important element of evolutionary growth models is that new capital follows from profit being redistributed, so that relatively profitable types of capital accumulate relatively quickly. This can be regarded as selection, such that a technique with a relatively high fitness spreads quickly. This is often modelled through replicator dynamics. In order to complete the evolutionary dimension of the model, selection is complemented by a mechanism of innovation, usually modelled as a stochastic variable in the spirit of the general model of innovation and imitation by Iwai (1984).

Evolutionary theory can, in comparison with economic growth theory, be regarded to extend the time horizon of analyses beyond decades and even centuries, which seems required by the objective of sustainable development. The need for a distant time horizon is especially relevant for research on climate change and biodiversity loss, as these are bound significantly to affect both natural and cultural-economic evolution. Nevertheless, climate change research is one of the few areas where (optimal) growth models have been actually 'applied' (Nordhaus, 1994), leading to severe criticism (e.g., Demeritt and Rothman, 1999).

In economics, growth is usually isolated from biological-social and even technological reality. Moreover, it is regarded essentially as a-historical, describing an extremely aggregate process that is driven by reversible mechanisms. However, not only sustainable development requires a major historical transition, but also history itself is full of such transitions. Evolutionary growth theory, with its emphasis on variable diversity, means a step in the direction of an historical analysis, and in fact will allow the merger of rigorous modelling and historical data. The remainder of this section will argue that in order to create an accurate historical context for economic growth, one needs to include evolutionary mechanisms – variety, selection and innovation – as well as environmental and resource dimensions.

Economic-environmental evolutionary history starts as far back as the transition of the hunter and gatherer societies to agriculture, sometimes referred to as the Neolithic revolution, which is hypothesized to have been stimulated by climate change, sufficient variation of flora and fauna, and our innate capacity to exchange (Diamond, 1997; Ofek, 2001). Social-cultural development accelerated, because agriculture allowed for division of labour and specialization. Agriculture also meant settlements and concentration of people in certain areas, which gave rise to human alterations of the environment. The second major phase, set in motion by the Industrial Revolution, has ultimately led to an environmental crisis during the second half of the twentieth century. From an environmental perspective, the twentieth century is exceptional in human and natural history, illustrated by a large number of indicators. During the twentieth century the world population quadrupled, the global economy expanded 14-fold, energy use increased 16 times, and the 'control' of world biomass increased to about 40 per cent. From an evolutionary perspective it is not difficult to regard the extreme and rapid change of the environment as a case of a species, namely *homo sapiens*, being maladapted.

Few complete models are available to understand and study the immense changes such as those described. Several authors have tried to produce evolutionary frameworks (e.g., Gowdy, 1994; Mulder and van den Bergh, 2001). These have been argued to be consistent with the theory of punctuated equilibrium (Somit and Peterson, 1989; Mokyr, 1990; Gowdy, 1994), although so far this is no more than a loose conceptual connection. A very general type of model is based on the notion of coevolution. This was originally proposed to integrate elements from evolutionary biology and ecology, namely to refer to the evolution of species interactions. Currently, however, coevolution is used in a much wider sense. It has been employed to refer to interactions of the following kind: biological-cultural, ecological-economic, production-consumption, technology-preferences, and human genetic-cultural (Lumsden and Wilson, 1981; Norgaard, 1984, 1994; Durham, 1991; Gowdy, 1994). The following typology of coevolution by Durham (1991) is of great use in enriching our understanding of economic-environment interactions:

- *Genetic mediation (interactive mode):* Genetic changes affect cultural evolution.
- *Cultural mediation (interactive mode):* Cultural changes affect genetic evolution.

- *Enhancement (comparative mode):* Cultural change reinforces natural evolution.
- *Opposition (comparative mode):* Cultural change goes against natural evolution; i.e., cultural and biological evolution are (negatively) additive.
- *Neutrality (comparative mode):* Cultural change is independent of biological evolution or selection.

Although this focuses on genetic-cultural interactions, it can serve as the basis for a generalization to other types of coevolution, such as the interaction between evolutionary economic and ecological systems. Note that coevolution is, however, often used in a loose manner, without including aspects of populations and diversity. In this case, the term 'interactions' of subsystems rather than coevolution would be preferable.

The idea that environmental factors may have influenced crucial changes during the cultural-social history of humankind has yet to influence economic growth theory. Diamond (1997) summarizes the large literature that has tried to support the theory that the availability of animal and plant species stimulated early domestication and thus agriculture and settlements. He notes that sufficient diversity of agricultural experimentation was only possible in continents with the major axis being east-west oriented, as this would allow for a spread of agricultural technologies among regions with similar climates. This he considers as an important reason for the early 'economic success' of Eurasia. Diamond's theory thus explicitly relates early economic development to geographical and resource factors. His ideas are surprisingly close to notions of the spatial diffusion of technology, which are so common in neo-Schumpeterian theories of technical change.

Wilkinson (1973) has developed an ecological theory of economic development that aims to link the Industrial Revolution to natural resource factors (see also Common, 1988). It recognizes a number of human strategies to respond to resource scarcity, such as new techniques, new resources, new goods, and migration. Wilkinson's ideas imply an environmental perspective on the origins of the Industrial Revolution at the end of the eighteenth century. This started with agriculture and iron smelting, which used large amounts of timber for energy purposes, in turn giving rise to a significant loss of forest cover in England. The resulting shortage and related high price of wood stimulated the use of coal. In an early phase, this focused on coal strip-mining at the surface; later, deep mines were explored. This created an important problem, namely that groundwater needed to be pumped out. This allowed the first large scale application of the steam engine. In turn, widespread use gave rise to various refinements of the steam engine and competing alternative models. In a next phase, spin-offs to other sectors occurred, especially the textile industry and transport through ships and trains led by steam locomotives. From a self-organization perspective, the critical mass of communicating 'populations' of scientists and pragmatic inventor-engineers in England at the time was probably crucial as well for the Industrial Revolution to occur, and to do so in England.

Faber and Proops (1990) propose a neo-Austrian approach with evolutionary elements, to replicate changes as observed during the Industrial Revolution. (For fuller details on the neo-Austrian modelling approach, see Chapter 4.) They allow for irreversibility of changes in the sector structure of the economy, for uncertainty and novelty, and for a teleological sequence of production activities (roundaboutness). The long-term relation between environment, technology and development is then characterized by three elements:

- The use of non-renewable natural resources is irreversible in time, so that a technology based on it must ultimately cease to be viable.
- Inventions and subsequent innovations lead to both more efficient use of resources and substitution to resources previously not used.
- Innovation requires a stock of capital goods with certain characteristics to be built up.

The authors construct a multi-sector model with the production side formulated in terms of activity analysis, which allows one to study the effect of invention and innovation on a transition from a situation with simple to more complex or roundabout production activities. For instance, food production has become more roundabout, moving from agriculture with labour, through agriculture with labour and capital, to a large food processing industry with many intermediate deliveries. This approach can simulate economic and environmental history from a pre-industrial agricultural society to an industrial society using fossil fuels and capital.

2.4.3 Evolutionary Modelling of Ecosystem and Resource Management

At the level of ecosystem and resource management, various issues play in relation to evolutionary economics. The dynamics of ecosystems involves reversible dynamics such as population growth and ecosystem succession, and irreversible changes due to selection, and more fundamental evolutionary changes. Ecological economics is very much influenced by the notion of resilience, which is an extended stability concept. Resilience is often linked to biodiversity: more diversity enhances the stability of systems (however, this is still debated). At the moment resilience is even examined as an analogy for the functioning of social systems, such as bureaucracy, politics, economy, etc. (see Levin et al., 1998).

An important type of impact of human resource use on ecosystems and populations of living organisms is through selective pressure exerted by managment and harvesting practices. The general nature of the problem is that resource harvesting affects not only the quantity of the resource but also its quality, or composition in genetic terms. Examples can be found in agriculture (use of pesticides, herbicides, etc.; monoculture), fisheries (mesh size, season of fishing), ecosystem management (groundwater level, fire protection), and health care (antibiotic use selects for resistant strains of bacteria). These are all special cases of biodiversity loss. Munro (1997) studied the example of the use of insecticides that raises the fitness of resistant insects relative to their susceptible competitors. He sought the optimal use of insecticide given the dynamics of systems. The perspective can be that of an individual farmer, or more realistically a policy maker trying to understand the optimal dosage of insecticide. He extends the standard model of optimal use of a renewable resource and the model of optimal pesticide use, with an abstract representation of the problem as a dynamic negative externality with irreversible features. He makes use of the 'combined genetic-population dynamics' model of evolutionary ecology in Section 2.3.5. It is found that a fixed dosage that makes the resistant individuals fitter than the susceptible ones initially leads to a decrease of both the pest population size and the proportion of resistant individuals, but beyond a critical point the population as a whole recovers and finally returns to its original level, composed entirely of resistant individuals. So initially insecticide use is effective but finally completely ineffective. Such a strategy is consistent with certain types of myopic decision making, where the discount rate is high or it is assumed that the genetic composition of the population is constant over time. Genuine optimization under perfect foresight about the evolutionary consequences of insecticide use and not-too-high discount rates shows that both pesticide use and R&D on it will be too high under myopic decision making.

Much attention has recently been given to an evolutionary perspective on the risk of overexploitation of common-pool resources, such as fisheries (Ostrom, 1990). One finding is that externally imposed rules and monitoring can reduce and destabilize cooperation or even completely destroy it. Instead, a sustainable use norm can evolve by communication among the resource users. External regulation is only desirable if monitoring and sanctioning can be well developed. This self-organization process in the most fundamental and general form is still not entirely understood: the influence of the size of the group is unclear; instability in the evolutionary equilibrium can arise when certain parameters change, such as the resource price; equilibrium can also break down when sanctions decline, harvesting technology becomes more productive (technical progress), or the price of the resource increases. Other risks to evolved norms are migration, external economic and political disturbances, and natural disasters influencing the resource. These issues can be examined with multi-agent/cellular automata models (Noailly et al., 2003a) or evolutionary game theory (Noailly et al., 2003b; Sethi and Somanathan, 1996).

2.5 CONCLUSIONS

Evolutionary thinking is a logical next step in environmental and ecological economics. This chapter has illustrated that the building blocks are available for this, and that we can already learn from a small number of applications. The methodological approach of ecological economics is very close in spirit to that of evolutionary economics – witness core features such as a focus on causal and explicitly dynamic processes, recognition of the relevance of diversity at all scales, and regarding agents as boundedly rational.

An important choice in evolutionary modelling concerns the level of aggregation. Most aggregate and abstract are analytical approaches such as evolutionary game theory. The most disaggregate approach, which can be termed 'real micro', is based on multi-agents systems, possibly in a spatial or network structure.

In the context of environmental problems, the transition to sustainable development is the most urgent task for analytical and applied modellers. Any serious analysis of long-term growth is bound to be unreliable if it excludes feedback from natural resource scarcity, environmental problems and environmental regulation. An evolutionary perspective adds to this the insight that long-term economic history and future is very much based on coevolution; i.e., interactions among biological and cultural evolutionary systems with internal diversity. Energy scarcity and the risk of climate change may have an important influence on the next transition towards a sustainable development, in which renewable energy will have to play a central role. Evolutionary modelling can help to clarify our understanding of what needs to be done in terms of policy aimed at unlocking current systems, fostering the transition, and avoiding new lock-ins.

The main advantages of evolutionary modelling relative to other approaches are that it enables the integration of natural and social science insights – witness Sugarscape – and the synthesis of history and theory. Both advantages should kindle enthusiasm for evolutionary modelling in ecological economists.

REFERENCES

Alchian, A. (1950), 'Uncertainty, evolution and economic theory', *Journal of Political Economy*, **58**, 211–22.

Allen, P.M. (1997), 'Evolutionary complex systems and sustainable development', in J.C.J.M. van den Bergh and M.W. Hofkes (eds), *Theory and Implementation of Economic Models for Sustainable Development*, Dordrecht: Kluwer, pp. 67–99.

Arthur, B. (1989), 'Competing technologies, increasing returns, and lock-in by historical events', *Economic Journal*, **99**, 116–31.

Axelrod, R. (1984), *The Evolution of Cooperation*, New York: Basic Books.

Ayres, R.U. (1994), *Information, Entropy and Progress: Economics and Evolutionary Change*, Washington: AEP Press.

Bäck, Th. (1996), *Evolutionary Algorithms in Theory and Practice: Evolution Strategies, Evolutionary Programming, Genetic Algorithms*, Oxford: Oxford University Press.

Bergh, J.C.J.M. van den and J.M. Gowdy (2003), 'The microfoundations of macroeconomics: an evolutionary perspective', *Cambridge Journal of Economics*, **27** (1), 65–84.

Bergh, J.C.J.M. van den and S. Stagl (2003), 'Coevolution of economic behaviour and institutions: towards a positive theory of institutional change', Working paper, Amsterdam: Free University.

Boulding, K.E. (1978), *Ecodynamics: A New Theory of Societal Evolution*, Beverly Hills: Sage Publications.

Boulding, K.E. (1981), *Evolutionary Economics*, Beverly Hills: Sage Publications.

Boyd, R. and P.J. Richerson (1985) *Culture and Evolutionary Process*, Chicago: University of Chicago Press.

Carroll, G.R. and M.T. Hannan (2000), *The Demography of Corporations and Industries*, Princeton NJ: Princeton University Press.

Common, M.S. (1988), *Environmental and Resource Economics*, Harlow: Longman.

Conlisk, J. (1989), 'An aggregate model of technical change', *Quarterly Journal of Economics*, **104**, 787–821.

Demeritt, D. and D. Rothman (1999), 'Figuring the costs of climate change: an assessment and critique', *Environment and Planning A*, **31**, 389–408.

Diamond, J. (1997), *Guns, Germs and Steel: The Fates of Human Societies*, New York: Norton.

Dosi, G., C. Freeman, R. Nelson, G. Silverberg and L. Soete (eds) (1988), *Technical Change and Economic Theory*, London: Pinter Publishers.

Durham, W.H. (1991), *Coevolution: Genes, Culture and Human Diversity*, Stanford CA: Stanford University Press.

Epstein, C. and R. Axtell (1996), *Growing Artificial Societies: Social Science from the Bottom Up*, Cambridge MA: The MIT Press.

Faber, M. and J.L.R. Proops (1990), *Evolution, Time, Production and the Environment*, Heidelberg: Springer-Verlag.

Frenken, K. (2001), *Understanding Product Innovation using Complex Systems Theory*, PhD Thesis, University of Amsterdam and University of Grenoble.

Friedman, D. (1998), 'On economic applications of evolutionary game theory', *Journal of Evolutionary Economics*, **8** (1), 15–43.

Gilbert, N. and J. Doran (eds) (1996), *Simulating Societies*, London: UCL Press.

Gintis, H. (2000), *Game Theory Evolving: A Problem-Centered Introduction to Modeling Strategic Interaction*, Princeton NJ: Princeton University Press.

Gowdy, J. (1994), *Coevolutionary Economics: The Economy, Society and the Environment*, Dordrecht: Kluwer.

Hamilton, W.D. (1963), 'The evolution of altruistic behaviour', *American Naturalist*, **96**, 354–6.

Hannan, M.T. and J. Freeman (1989), *Organizational Ecology*, Cambridge MA: Harvard University Press.

Holland, J.H. (1992/1975), *Adaptation in Natural and Artificial Systems: An Introduction Analysis with Applications to Biology, Control, and Artificial Intelligence*, 2nd edn, Cambridge MA: The MIT Press.

Iwai, K. (1984), 'Schumpeterian dynamics, part I: an evolutionary model of innovation and imitation', *Journal of Economic Behaviour and Organization*, **5** (2), 159–90.

Janssen, M. (1998), *Modelling Global Change: The Art of Integrated Assessment Modelling*, Cheltenham: Edward Elgar.

Kauffman, S.A. (1993), *The Origins of Order: Self-Organization and Selection in Evolution*, Oxford: Oxford University Press.

Levin, S., S. Barrett, S. Anyar, W. Baumol, C. Bliss, B. Bolin, P. Dasgupta, P. Ehrlich, C. Folke, I.-M. Gren, C.S. Holling, A.-M. Jansson, B.-O. Jansson, K.-G. Mäler, D. Martin, C. Perrings and E. Sheshinsky (1998), 'Resilience in natural and socioeconomic systems', *Environment and Development Economics*, **3** (2), 222–35.

Levy, H., M. Levy and S. Solomon (2000), *Microscopic Simulation of Financial Markets: From Investor Behavior to Phenomena*, New York: Academic Press.

Lumsden, C. and E.O. Wilson (1981), *Genes, Mind and Culture*, Cambridge MA: Harvard University Press.

Maynard Smith, J. (1982), *Evolution and the Theory of Games*, Cambridge: Cambridge University Press.

Maynard Smith, J. (1989), *Evolutionary Genetics,* Oxford: Oxford University Press.

Maynard Smith, J. and G.R. Price (1973), 'The logic of animal conflict', *Nature*, **246** 15–18.

Maynard Smith, J. and E. Szathmáry (1995), *The Major Transitions in Evolution*, Oxford: Oxford University Press.

Mokyr, J. (1990), 'Punctuated equilibria and technological progress', *American Economic Review, Papers and Proceedings*, **80** (2), 350–54.

Mulder, P. and J.C.J.M. van den Bergh (2001), 'Evolutionary economic theories of sustainable development', *Growth and Change*, **32** (4), 110–34.

Munro, A. (1997), 'Economics and biological evolution', *Environmental and Resource Economics*, **9**, 429–49.

Nelson, R. and S. Winter (1982), *An Evolutionary Theory of Economic Change*, Cambridge MA: Harvard University Press.

Noailly, J., J.C.J.M. van den Bergh and C. Withagen (2003a), 'Spatial evolution of social norms in a common pool resource game', Working Paper, Amsterdam: Free University.

Noailly, J., J.C.J.M. van den Bergh and C. Withagen (2003b), 'Evolution of harvesting strategies: replicator and resource dynamics', *Journal of Evolutionary Economics*, **13** (2), 183–200.

Nordhaus, W.D. (1994), *Managing the Global Commons: The Economics of Climate Change*, Cambridge MA: The MIT Press.

Norgaard, R.B. (1984), 'Coevolutionary development potential', *Land Economics*, **60**, 160–73.

Norgaard, R.B. (1994), *Development Betrayed: The End of Progress and a Coevolutionary Revisioning of the Future*, London: Routledge.

Ofek, H. (2001), *Second Nature: Economic Origins of Human Evolution*, Cambridge: Cambridge University Press.

Ostrom, E. (1990), *Governing the Commons: The Evolution of Institutions for Collective Action New York*, Cambridge: Cambridge University Press.

Potts, J. (2000), *The New Evolutionary Microeconomics: Complexity, Competence, and Adaptive Behavior*, Cheltenham: Edward Elgar.

Roughgarden, J. (1979), *Theory of Population Genetics and Evolutionary Ecology: An Introduction*, New York: MacMillan.

Samuelson, L. (1997), *Evolutionary Games and Equilibrium Selection*, Cambridge MA: The MIT Press.

Schelling, T.C. (1969), 'Models of segregation', *American Economic Review, Papers and Proceedings*, **59** (2), 488–93.

Schelling, T.C. (1978), *Micromotives and Macrobehaviour*, New York: Norton.

Schumpeter, J.A. (1934), *The Theory of Economic Development*, Cambridge MA: Harvard University Press.

Selten, R. (1983), 'Evolutionary stability in extensive two-person games', *Mathematical Social Sciences*, **5**, 269–363.

Sethi, R. and E. Somanathan (1996), 'The evolution of social norms in common property resource use', *American Economic Review*, **86** (4), 766–88.

Silverberg, G. and B. Verspagen (1994), 'Collective learning, innovation and growth in a boundedly rational, evolutionary world', *Journal of Evolutionary Economics*, **4**, 207–26.

Silverberg, G., G. Dosi and L. Orsenigo (1988), 'Innovation, diversity and diffusion: a self-organization model', *Economic Journal*, **98**, 1032–54.

Somit, A. and S. Peterson (1989), *The Dynamics of Evolution: The Punctuated Equilibrium Debate in the Natural and Social Sciences*, Ithaca NY: Cornell University Press.

Taylor, P. and L. Jonker (1978), 'Evolutionary stable strategies and game dynamics', *Mathematical Biosciences*, **40**, 145–56.

Troitzsch, K.G., U. Mueller, N. Gilbert and J.E. Doran (1996), *Social Science Microsimulation*, Berlin: Springer-Verlag.

Veblen, T. (1898), 'Why is economics not an evolutionary science', *The Quarterly Journal of Economics*, **12**, 373–97.

Wilkinson, R. (1973), *Poverty and Progress: An Ecological Model of Economic Development*, London: Methuen.

3.   Input-Output Models

Luis Cruz, John Proops and Paul Safonov

3.1 INTRODUCTION

Input-output (I-O) analysis, sometimes called 'interindustry modelling', was first proposed by Leontief (1936, 1951/1986), as a tool for economic planning. I-O has been widely used in almost every country, often as the underlying procedure for maintaining national accounts.

With the rise of environmental awareness from the 1960s, I-O methods began to be adopted as a method of integrating economic activity with the environment, and since then there has been an explosive growth in this literature. Sadly, there is not yet a single book-length work which surveys all of the many environmental applications of I-O, and in this chapter we can do little more than offer an overview. However, it will be our aim to indicate the main strands of development over the past forty years, and in particular to note the recent work in the literature.

The reasons that I-O methods have proved so popular in environmental work, and recently in ecological economics, are probably three-fold. First, it is a multi-sectoral method, so a range of economic and ecosystem activities can be represented simultaneously, including their interactions. Second, the I-O method allows *all* direct and indirect effects to be calculated in a relatively simple and efficient way. Third, the mathematics involved in I-O analysis is not complicated, and demands little more than a grounding in simple matrix algebra. As a result, a rich literature has developed, some of which is theoretical in nature, though most is more practical in orientation.

In this chapter we introduce, rather briefly, the I-O method and its matrix representation, and then move on to its applications to environmental issues. We also, in a separate section treat at some length the parallel, though distinct, literature on I-O methods applied to the way economies use energy. Finally, we outline the latest developments in dynamic I-O modelling of economy-environment interactions.

In more detail, the remainder of this chapter is structured as follows. In Section 3.2 the basic I-O model is outlined, and represented in matrix form.

In particular, it is stressed that the I-O model allows the treatment of both quantities and prices, using the 'Leontief Inverse' matrix. Section 3.3 offers an overview of four principal types of I-O models involving the environment, while Section 3.4 outlines some further applications. Section 3.5 treats the extensive literature on energy I-O models, while Section 3.6 introduces some dynamic I-O applications. Section 3.7 offers some conclusions.

3.2 OUTLINE OF INPUT-OUTPUT ANALYSIS

There are various introductory texts for I-O analysis, but perhaps the most comprehensive is Miller and Blair (1985). A reasonably comprehensive introduction to I-O and environmental issues is Proops et al. (1993).

To illustrate the I-O modelling method, we begin with a simple two sector example. Each economic sector produces a single good, using inputs of produced goods from other sectors, and labour. We suppose that the goods produced have two alternative destinations:

- They can go to consumers, where they are consumed (Final Demand).
- They can be used as inputs by one or both manufacturing sectors (Inter-mediate Demand).

We represent the interrelationships between the producing sectors in an I-O table, as in Table 3.1.

Table 3.1   An input-output table for a two sector economy

	Sector 1	Sector 2	Final Demand	Total Output
Sector 1	x_{11}	x_{12}	Y_1	X_1
Sector 2	x_{21}	x_{22}	Y_2	X_2
Labour	L_1	L_2		

Here:

- x_{ij} represents the the flow of goods from sector i necessary for production by sector j.
- Y_i is the output from sector i to final demand (i.e. to consumers).
- X_i is the total output from sector i (i.e., $x_{i1} + x_{i2} + Y_i = X_i$).
- L_i is the labour input needed for production by sector i.
  (NB: Here 'labour' is shorthand for inputs such as labour itself, capital and natural resources.)

We should stress that these variables represent physical quantities, not monetary values (which will be introduced below).

We now follow the activity analysis approach (Koopmans, 1951), and assume that for each sector, the inputs to the sector are proportional to the outputs from the sector; i.e.:

$$\frac{x_{11}}{a_{11}} = \frac{x_{21}}{a_{21}} = \frac{L_1}{l_1} = X_1; \qquad (3.1) \qquad \frac{x_{12}}{a_{12}} = \frac{x_{22}}{a_{22}} = \frac{L_2}{l_2} = X_2 \qquad (3.2)$$

The coefficients $\{a_{ij}\}$ and $\{l_i\}$ are known as the 'technological coefficients', and for any particular static model are taken to be constants. In particular, the $\{a_{ij}\}$ signify the amount of product i necessary to produce one unit of product j, and are often referred as 'input-output coefficients'; the $\{l_i\}$ are known as labour intensities.

Substituting the above relationships into the relationship between inputs and outputs give two 'output equations':

$$a_{11}x_1 + a_{12}x_2 + Y_1 = X_1 \qquad (3.3)$$
$$a_{12}x_1 + a_{22}x_2 + Y_2 = X_2 \qquad (3.4)$$

This pair of simultaneous equations can be solved for the total outputs $\{X_i\}$ if we specify the technological coefficients $\{a_{ij}\}$ and the final demands $\{Y_i\}$.

3.2.1 Matrix Representation

The two simultaneous equations above can be written in the standard element form of matrix notation as:

$$\begin{bmatrix} a_{11} & a_{12} \\ a_{21} & a_{22} \end{bmatrix} \begin{bmatrix} x_1 \\ x_2 \end{bmatrix} + \begin{bmatrix} y_1 \\ y_2 \end{bmatrix} = \begin{bmatrix} X_1 \\ X_2 \end{bmatrix} \qquad (3.5)$$

We can further simplify this using the standard condensed matrix form, where:

$$\mathbf{A} \equiv \begin{bmatrix} a_{11} & a_{12} \\ a_{21} & a_{22} \end{bmatrix}; \quad \mathbf{x} \equiv \begin{bmatrix} X_1 \\ X_2 \end{bmatrix}; \quad \mathbf{y} \equiv \begin{bmatrix} Y_1 \\ Y_2 \end{bmatrix}$$

This gives:

$$\mathbf{Ax} + \mathbf{y} = \mathbf{x} \qquad (3.6)$$

Factoring this equation gives:

$$(I-A)x = y \tag{3.7}$$

Here I is the identity (or unit) matrix, with ones on the main diagonal, zeros elsewhere. If the matrix $(I-A)$ is non-singular (i.e., it can be inverted), then we can write:

$$x = (I-A)^{-1}y \tag{3.8}$$

This is the fundamental equation of I-O analysis, and holds for a model with any number of sectors. The matrix $(I-A)^{-1}$ is known as the 'Leontief Inverse', in honour of its inventor.

From the above, it will be apparent that we use the following notation:

- Vectors are represented by bold face, lower case letters (e.g., x); vector elements are represented by the corresponding upper case letters, with a subscript (e.g., X_i).
- Matrices are represented by bold face, upper case letters (e.g., A); matrix elements are represented by the corresponding lower case letters, with two subscripts (e.g., a_{ij}).

3.2.2 Decomposing Direct and Indirect Effects

We can think of the inter-industry trading in terms of the *direct* and *indirect* effects of the elements of final demand. To satisfy a certain level of final demand (y), that vector of goods must be produced. However, to produce y, there must be a corresponding production of intermediate inputs Ay. Now, this in turn requires a further (second round) of indirect inputs $AAy = A^2y$, and so on. So, to produce the final demand y, the total output is given by:

$$x = y + Ay + A^2y + A^3y + \ldots = (I + A + A^2 + A^3 + \ldots)y \tag{3.9}$$

However, it can be shown that: $(I-A)^{-1} = I + A + A^2 + A^3 + \ldots$ So the standard Leontief inverse relationship between final demand (y) and total output (x) can be decomposed into the direct effect (y) and the indirect effects, as follows:

$$x = \underset{Direct}{y} + \underset{Indirect}{(A + A^2 + A^3 + \ldots)y} = \underset{Direct}{y} + \underset{Indirect}{[(I-A)^{-1} - I]y} \tag{3.10}$$

3.2.3 Introducing Prices

To introduce prices into the I-O model, we suppose that each good x (pro-duced or non-produced) has a unique price, p_x. We introduce these into the input-output table of Table 3.1, to give Table 3.2:

Table 3.2   An input-output table for a two sector economy, in value terms

	Sector 1	Sector 2	Final Demand	Total Output
Sector 1	p_1X_{11}	p_1X_{12}	Y_1	p_1X_1
Sector 2	p_2X_{21}	p_2X_{22}	Y_2	p_2X_2
Labour	wL_1	wL_2		
Total Output	p_1X_1	p_2X_2		

We have also defined the price of labour as w (i.e., the wage rate), with the product of labour input and wage rate for each sector (wL_i) being known as the 'value-added' for that sector. We have also introduced a new row of *Total Output*. As the table is now in value terms (i.e., price×quantity), we can calculate the values of outputs *and* of inputs, rather than simply the quantity of outputs. Of course, for accounting balance the value of each sector's inputs must equal the value of its outputs.

If we now focus on the inputs (i.e., columns) in Table 3.2, we see we can formulate two new (input) equations, in value terms:

$$p_1x_{11} + p_2x_{21} + wL_1 = p_1X_1 \tag{3.11}$$
$$p_1x_{12} + p_2x_{22} + wL_2 = p_2X_2 \tag{3.12}$$

We can also substitute from the production relations above for the X_{ij}, to give:

$$p_1a_{11}X_1 + p_2a_{21}X_1 + wl_1X_1 = p_1X_1 \tag{3.13}$$
$$p_1a_{12}X_2 + p_2a_{22}X_2 + wl_2X_2 = p_2X_2 \tag{3.14}$$

These equations simplify to:

$$p_1a_{11} + p_2a_{21} + wl_1 = p_1 \tag{3.15}$$
$$p_1a_{12} + p_2a_{22} + wl_2 = p_2 \tag{3.16}$$

In matrix form these become:

$$\begin{bmatrix} p_1 & p_2 \end{bmatrix} \begin{bmatrix} a_{11} & a_{12} \\ a_{21} & a_{22} \end{bmatrix} + w \begin{bmatrix} l_1 & l_2 \end{bmatrix} = \begin{bmatrix} p_1 & p_2 \end{bmatrix} \tag{3.17}$$

We can now write this in condensed form as:

$$\mathbf{p'A} + w\mathbf{l'} = \mathbf{p'} \tag{3.18}$$

This can be reorganized to give:

$$\mathbf{p'} = w\mathbf{l'(I-A)}^{-1} \tag{3.19}$$

This equation shows how the prices for an I-O model can be derived from the technological coefficients and the price of the non-produced inputs, again using the Leontief inverse matrix.

3.3 ENVIRONMENTAL INPUT-OUTPUT MODELS

Extensions of the application of I-O models, to include the environment, date back to the late 1960s. Cumberland (1966) is usually recognized as the first to include environmental effects in an extended I-O model, adding rows and columns to the traditional table, in order to identify environmental benefits and costs associated with economic activity, and to distribute these by sector.

Miller and Blair (1985, p. 236) consider that environmental I-O models can be categorized into three basic types, to which we also add a further, first, category:

- ecological I-O models, where only relationships between natural elements of ecological systems are considered; i.e., the I-O model is applied to non-economic relationships;
- generalized I-O models, which have as a main feature the augmentation of the technological coefficient matrix with additional rows (to represent the generation of pollutants) and columns (to represent pollution-abatement activities);
- economic-ecological models, which have as a central characteristic the extension of the interindustry framework to include ecological sectors (creating an 'ecosystem submatrix'), allowing the consideration of flows within and/or between economic and ecological systems; and
- commodity-by-industry models, which are identifiable by the consideration of environmental factors as commodities in a commodity-by-industry

table (with additional rows for ecological inputs and columns for ecological outputs).

We now examine each of these categories in turn.

3.3.1 Ecological Input-Output Models

Ecological I-O models use the standard I-O representation of flows between sectors, but substitute ecosystem components (e.g., species) for the usual industrial sectors; they were first suggested in the 1970s (Hannon, 1973).

This approach allows the construction of 'natural' I-O tables in terms of 'natural' units, exactly analogous to the quantity table in 'economic' quantity units above (Table 3.1). However, the chief application of such ecological I-O models is to the determination of 'natural prices' (e.g., Amir, 1989; Hannon, 1998). Some basic aspect of nature (e.g., sunlight) is taken as the 'value-added' component, analogous to the use of labour in Table 3.2, and then the usual I-O calculation allows the calculation of the 'natural' prices.

While this is a potentially important method of valuation, so far the literature has dealt with the approach in mainly theoretical terms. This is for two main reasons. First, it is not clear what constitutes the appropriate 'value-added' component(s) for ecological I-O systems. Second, as noted below, obtaining the technological coefficients for ecological systems (i.e., the **A** matrix) is far from straightforward.

3.3.2 Generalized Input-Output Models

Early work by Leontief (1970, 1973) and Leontief and Ford (1972) augmented the standard I-O model through the introduction of additional rows (representing pollution generation) and additional columns (indicating pollution-abatement activities), which were included in the technical coefficients matrix.

With this approach, alterations of the output level of pollutants can be explained, or even anticipated, by modifications in the final demand (for specific goods or services) and/or in the technical structure (of specific sectors) (Leontief, 1970, p. 266). Thus, this approach retains a close proximity to empirical work, as is shown by its practical application to the US economy, for example in Leontief and Ford (1972).

3.3.3 Economic-Ecological Models

Among examples of economic-ecological I-O models are those developed by Daly (1968) and Isard et al. (1972). Both incorporated environmental activities into the I-O framework, employing material flows within and between both economic activities and environmental processes.

They used I-O tables divided into four quadrants (hence giving a matrix with four submatrices). One of the quadrants is the traditional inter-industry table, representing the exchange of economic commodities within the economic system. The items exchanged in the other three quadrants are ecological commodities, where: one quadrant represents interrelations within the ecological system; another represents the flows (outputs of pollutants) from the economy to the environment; and the final one represents the flows (inputs of resources) from the environment to the economy.

While Daly used the assumption of an industry-by-industry model (i.e., single-product industries), Isard recognized that this assumption is incompatible with the secondary production of ecological outputs, and adopted a different accounting scheme (commodity-by-industry), allowing the consideration of multiple commodities (economic and ecological) produced by a single industry.

To overcome the problems in the determination of the technical coefficients for the submatrices representing non-economic flows, and above all for the 'ecological' submatrix, Isard proposed the estimation of these (fixed) technical coefficients directly from technical data. However, problems of the availability of data for the cells in the ecological system's submatrix appears to be the main drawback in Isard's model.

3.3.4 Commodity-by-Industry Models

One of the most distinctive examples of the commodity-by-industry model is presented in Victor (1972). This approach limits the scope of the fully integrated economic-ecological models, accounting only for flows of ecological commodities from the environment into the economy (raw materials) and of the waste products from the economy into the environment (i.e., it does not include interactions within the environment).

Victor considers a commodity-by-industry model in which he makes the analysis of ecological flows conform to the principles of consistent I-O accounting, by adopting the materials balance concept (Richardson, 1972, p. 231). Victor uses a hybrid model, where the flows within the economic system are expressed in monetary terms, while the flows between it and the environment are quantities measured in the appropriate physical units.

The main achievement of Victor's model is that it provides an I-O framework to integrate economic and ecological data, in a form that is empirically workable (or, at least, more applicable than that proposed by Isard). Indeed, one of its particularly important characteristics is that it allows the relating of ecological commodity inputs and outputs with the final demand for economic commodities. However, Victor's scheme continues to present some problems of implementation because of data availability concerning the ecological flows.

3.4 FURTHER APPLICATIONS

3.4.1 National Accounting and the Environment

All things considered, it was seen that the kind of extensions to the basic I-O model discussed above support scenario-based approaches. The scope of the scenarios is limited, however, both by the type of model used and by the database.

Concerning the need for broadly conceived databases to meet the challenge of extending traditional I-O applications, there has been some progress, through the construction of 'Satellite Accounts', with the purpose of expanding the scope and the analytical capacity of the national accounts to specific areas of social and/or environmental concern.

A critical contribution for this advance was the development by Stone (1970, 1986) of the Social Accounting Matrix (SAM), which is a data framework to represent income distribution in a generalized I-O format. This can also be extended to include inputs from and outputs to the environment (with substances measured in physical units). An example of such an extension is the National Accounting Matrix including Environmental Accounts (NAMEA), whose conceptual framework and empirical application originate from Keuning (2000).

The NAMEA is a statistical information system, whose representation typically includes a conventional national accounting matrix, extended by three accounts (sub-matrices) on the environment (represented in physical units): a substances account (pollutants – e.g., CO_2 and SO_2; and natural resources – e.g., oil); an account for global environmental effects (e.g., greenhouse effect, ozone layer depletion); and an account for national environmental effects (e.g., acidification, eutrophication, wastes). Perhaps one of NAMEA's most important strengths is that it is ready for use in analytical applications, allowing the scrutiny of the contribution of each sector not only to GDP but also to the major environmental problems (Sheng and Simon, 2000, p. 171).

3.4.2 Waste Flows Input-Output Analysis

The construction of I-O models of residuals flows to explore the impacts of waste issues has not been very common. Generally, the waste-environment-economy I-O models cover only a restricted set of residuals (e.g., Duchin and Lange (1998) use an environmental I-O model to explore the prospects for reducing plastic waste in the US). As emphasized by Nakamura and Kondo (2001) attempts to deal with one waste as a separate problem (the one problem – one solution approach) tends to be ineffectual and usually just shifts the problem from one place to another.

However, some exceptions do exist. A study by Førsund (1985) considering the national economy of Norway, provides a good illustration of an I-O system extended to consider the national aggregated waste flows. Examples of other modelling approaches addressing solid waste generation and management at a macro level include Nakamura (1999), Nakamura and Kondo (2000; 2001), Zeng et al. (2000) and Barata (2002).

3.4.3 Environmental Footprint Applications

A recent development in ecological economics has been the notion of the 'environmental footprint' (Wackernagel and Rees, 1996). In its original form, the 'footprint' of a country or region was considered to be the area of land effectively utilized to supply that country's economic consumption. For example, Japan draws upon timber resources in South East Asia, the USA on oil from the Middle East, etc. A related notion is that of 'environmental pressure', where the concern is not to represent environmental impact in terms of land area, but instead using a vector of effects (e.g., resource depletion, various pollutants, biodiversity loss, etc.)

Initial studies considered only the direct relationships between countries/regions, but it was soon pointed out that indirect effects could also be important. Proops and Atkinson (1998) and Proops et al. (1999) used an I-O model of trade between countries to calculate the total effects of trade on environmental damage, and to re-attribute this damage from the countries where it occurred to those countries which caused it, through their (direct and indirect) consumption activities. There have been similar applications by Eder and Narodslawsky (1999), Lenzen and Murray (2001), Machado et al. (2001) and Muradian et al. (2002)

3.5 INPUT-OUTPUT MODELS OF ENERGY USE

The importance of energy to economic systems became widely recognized in the 1970s, and became the primary concern of what has come to be known as 'Energy Analysis' (Costanza, 1980, p. 432). Brown and Herendeen (1996, p. 220) define energy analysis as 'the process of determining the energy required directly and indirectly to allow a system (usually an economic system) to produce a specified good or service'.

The studies mentioned in section 3.3 can be considered as benchmarks of an approach that would be further developed by some energy analysts during the 1970s and the 1980s, extending the use of I-O analysis to the energy field (Machado, 2000, p. 2). Such energy-based I-O analysis, which was pioneered by Herendeen and Hannon and their associates at the Energy Research Group at the University of Illinois (Gowdy and Miller, 1987, p. 1388), allows the interrelationships between various producing sectors of the economy to be detailed and examined, permitting a wide range of applications.

3.5.1 The Energy Balance Condition

The starting point for the treatment of the flow of energy involved in the flow of goods in an economy, using an I-O format, is the idea of the 'conservation of embodied energy'; i.e., that energy 'used' by a sector is considered as 'embodied' within the output of that sector. Of course, this is a strictly accounting procedure. Very little of the energy used in a good's manufacture is actually physically embodied in the good; most of it is simply dissipated. It should be stressed that this method of accounting balance of energy has only a tenuous relation to the First Law of Thermodynamics.

This assumption of energy balance allows one to write:

$$\sum_{i=1}^{n} \varepsilon_{ki} x_{ij} + e_{kj} = \varepsilon_{kj} X_{J} \qquad (3.20)$$

Here:

- x_{ij} is the transaction from sector i to sector j.
- X_j is the total output of sector j.
- ε_{kj} is the 'embodied energy intensity' of type k per unit of X_j (i.e., the (direct and indirect) energy required to produce a monetary unit of sector j's output).
- e_{kj} is the external direct energy input of type k to sector j (i.e., the energy taken from the nature by sector j, which is non-zero only for primary energy sectors).

Thus, this expression shows that the energy embodied in any sector's output equals the total amount of energy embodied in all that sector's inputs plus the primary energy input, which is non-zero only for primary energy sectors (Miller and Blair, 1985, p. 206).

The approach uses a 'hybrid' I-O table, meaning that the transactions table flows (x_{ij}), as well as the total outputs are expressed in physical units (e.g., toe, Joules, etc.) for energy sectors and in monetary units for non-energy sectors; accordingly, the units of ε_{kj} are toe/toe for energy sectors, and toe/monetary units for non-energy sectors (Bullard and Herendeen, 1975, p. 74).

Considering the above equation for each sector simultaneously, in matrix notation we can write:

$$\varepsilon X + E = \varepsilon \hat{x} \qquad (3.21)$$

Here: ε is the ($m \times n$) matrix of energy intensity coefficients; $\hat{x}$ is a ($n \times n$) diagonal matrix of the total outputs (X_j on the diagonal); X is the transactions matrix; E is the ($m \times n$) matrix of direct external energy inputs (this has elements that are zero, except for the primary energy sectors, which are placed along the principal diagonal (where $k = j$)).

Given the identity $X = A\hat{x}$, one can substitute for X in the above equation:

$$\varepsilon A\hat{x} + E = \varepsilon \hat{x} \qquad (3.22)$$

This reorganizes to give:

$$\varepsilon = E\hat{x}^{-1}(I - A)^{-1} \qquad (3.23)$$

Defining $\hat{e} \equiv E\hat{x}^{-1}$, the solution for the energy intensity coefficients may be written as:

$$\varepsilon = \hat{e}(I - A)^{-1} \qquad (3.24)$$

Here $\hat{e}$ is an ($m \times n$) matrix of zeros, except for the energy sectors (diagonal) location, whose values depend on the energy conversion efficiencies. If, as usually happens, one ignores the effect of energy conversion efficiencies then their value will be unity. This was noted by Miller and Blair (1985), who also examined the extension of the model to account for conversion efficiencies. Therefore, what this matrix $\hat{e}$ does is to 'select' the m energy rows from the Leontief inverse (Casler and Rose, 1998, p. 352).

It is notable that this equation is identical in form to the price I-O equation. This is because the same method of analysis has been used, imputing the value/embodied energy of inputs to the value/embodied energy of outputs.

3.5.2 Structural Decomposition Analysis

Another concern of energy analysis is the consideration of changes in patterns of energy use, which can be analysed through a technique that has become very popular and that is usually designated as 'Input-Output Structural Decomposition Analysis'.

Structural decomposition analysis is an analytical tool capable of computing the various 'sources' of change in an economy, and the majority of the early papers on structural decomposition analysis used a basic three-part decomposition. This results almost 'naturally' from the I-O formulation. For example, the equation for total industrial energy use is given by:

$$E = \hat{e}(I - A)^{-1}\hat{y}$$
(3.25)

The basic rationale for structural decomposition analysis is splitting this identity into its components. Thus, in this I-O formulation, productive energy use depends on three categories of factors; and, accordingly, changes in its patterns might have three kinds of sources (Proops, 1984):

- changes in direct energy intensities, reflecting changes in the technology within each sector (the $\hat{e}$ matrix);
- changes in the structure of inter-industry trading (the $(I-A)^{-1}$ matrix); and/or
- changes in the structure and level of final demand (the $\hat{y}$ diagonal matrix).

Now, over time these three factors can change independently, causing an overall change in productive use of energy in economies (E). If, over time, $\hat{e}$ changes by $\Delta\hat{e}$, $(I-A)^{-1}$ changes by $\Delta(I-A)^{-1}$, and $\hat{y}$ changes by $\Delta\hat{y}$, then the overall change ΔE is given by the central difference equation (Proops, 1988, p. 210):

$$\Delta E = \Delta\hat{e}(I - A)^{-1}\hat{y} + \hat{e}\,\Delta(I - A)^{-1}\hat{y} + \hat{e}(I - A)^{-1}\Delta\hat{y} + \frac{1}{4}\Delta\hat{e}\,\Delta(I - A)^{-1}\Delta\hat{y}$$
(3.26)

One of the strong points of this technique is that it allows the overcoming of many of the static characteristics of I-O models, since it allows, e.g., the analysis of changes over time in technological coefficients and sectoral mix. Further, to do this the technique requires only two I-O tables, one for the initial year and another (real or projected) for the terminal year of the analysis (Casler and Rose, 1998, p. 350). Another important merit of structural decomposition analysis is that it also allows the examination of responses to price changes; i.e., it can be applied to the I-O dual equation to examine the influence on prices of various sources of changes (Rose, 1999, p. 1172).

3.5.3 A Note on Method

In this discussion of energy I-O models there has been a rather different presentation form that for the more general environmental I-O models, in the preceding section, in that the models have been represented algebraically. In particular, the central role of the 'energy intensity' has been stressed. Also, the method of decomposition has been applied to energy use. However, these methods could equally be applied to other models of resource use and pollution, invoking 'waste intensities', or 'resource intensities', and decomposing them into their appropriate components. (For applications of these methods to the I-O modelling of carbon dioxide emissions, see e.g. Proops et al., 1993, and Cruz, 2002.)

3.6 DYNAMIC INPUT-OUTPUT MODELS

Static I-O theory derives the changes in the variables of a given economic system from the observed changes in the underlying structural relationships. Dynamic theory goes further, and shows how certain changes in the variables can be described 'on the basis of fixed, that is, invariant, structural characteristics of the system' (Leontief, 1951/1986, p. 53).

In summary, a dynamic model must allow for the:

> … structural relations between stocks (capital) and flows (output) and take explicit account of the fact that substantial increases in output will create additional capacity requirements so that projected changes in final demand will not only require more intermediate goods, but also investment goods from all appropriate sectors in the economy (Richardson, 1972, p. 184).

It should be noted that dynamic I-O models bear some similarity to neo-Austrian models, which are discussed in detail in Chapter 4.

3.6.1 Basic Dynamic Input-Output Models

Dynamic input-output analysis derives from the static approach, through the consideration of lags, or of rates of change over time of sectoral interdependencies. The attention focuses on structural relations between stocks of durable instruments of productions (fixed capital of the sectors) and flows of material inputs and flows of outputs.

In static input-output models, the final demand vector **y** comprises of consumption (**c**) and investment goods (**h**), that is, additions to the stocks of fixed capital items such as buildings, machinery, tools etc. So we can write:

$$\mathbf{y} = \mathbf{Dh} + \mathbf{c} \qquad\qquad (3.27)$$

Here, **D** is the matrix of the technological structure of investments. **D** has non-zero rows only for those sectors (which are basically two: machinery and construction), that provide investment goods into other sectors. (NB We use **h** for the investment vector, rather than the more usual **i**, to avoid confusion with the unit matrix, **I**.)

In dynamic input-output models, investment demand is explained within the model. The approach chosen is the following: the additions to the stocks of durable capital goods are technologically required, given the technique in use, in order to allow for an expansion of productive capacity that matches the expansion in the level of output effectively demanded. A simple dynamic Leontief model has the following form:

$$\mathbf{x}(t) = \mathbf{Ax}(t) + \mathbf{B}\{\mathbf{x}(t + 1) - \mathbf{x}(t)\} + \mathbf{c}(t) \qquad\qquad (3.28)$$

Here **B** is the square matrix of fixed capital coefficients, and b_{ij} defines the stock of products of industry j required per unit of capacity output of industry i, and is thus a stock–flow ratio. The time path of all the n components of final consumption $\mathbf{c}(t)$, $t = t_0,...,T$, as well as the levels of outputs at the initial point of time, $\mathbf{x}(t_0)$, are assumed to be given. Hence, we have a system of n difference equations.

From the perspective of statistical data availability, a more accurate way of introducing the time dimension into a static input-output model (i.e., $\mathbf{x} = \mathbf{Ax} + \mathbf{y}$) is by adding to it the explicit dynamics of the capital goods. Such a dynamic model assumes the fixed capital assets $K_i(t)$ of the sector i to grow as a result of investment $H_i(t)$, and to decrease due to physical wear and obsolescence. The capital changes are thus modelled by the following equations (Solow, 1956):

$$K_i(t + 1) = (1 - \mu_i)K_i(t) + \eta_i H_i(t), \quad i = 1, n, \quad t = t_0, T \qquad\qquad (3.29)$$

Here μ is the vector of depreciation coefficients for the fixed assets per annum; η is the vector of the ratios of the materialized investments to their present volume.

The output of each sector is described by the production function:

$$X_i(t) = F_i(t, K_i, L_i), \quad i = 1, n \qquad\qquad (3.30)$$

This equation characterizes the sector's maximal production capabilities with the given values of capital K and labour L. Time dependence is taken into account as an exogenous effect of technical change upon the production capability.

The model can be used in *simulation* modes, where a group of variables is initially set, and the others are calculated by solving the system of difference equations. Alternatively, the model can be formulated as an *optimal control problem* (see, for instance, Krotov, 1981, 1982), where a certain criterion (such as overall final consumption) is maximized.

An extension of this model, reflecting the joint development of economic and ecological systems within a region, is described below.

3.6.2 Dynamic Ecological-Economic Input-Output Model

This section provides an example of a comprehensive model, accounting for most important aspects of joint economy-environment impacts, which in one form or another can be found in numerous models available in the literature.

The model addresses dynamic interactions between n sectors of an economy and its main natural resources (such as water, air, soil, forests, mineral and bio-resources), described by m 'state of the environment' indicators (Gurman, 1981, 1990; Safonov, 1996a). Each natural resource is subject to economic use, self-restoration, artificial restoration, and internal impacts within the ecosystem itself.

The actual set of economic sectors and natural resources (state of the environment indicators) differs between particular regions (countries) under study.

We note that in the model below, variables and parameters which carry the superscript 'Z' (but not only those) relate to the ecological sub-system of the model.

The main components (blocks) of such a model are as follows:

1. *Block of generalized inter-industry balance*
$$\mathbf{x} = \mathbf{A}\mathbf{x} + \mathbf{D}\mathbf{h} + \mathbf{A}^Z\mathbf{z} + \mathbf{D}^Z\mathbf{h}^Z + \mathbf{c} + \mathbf{x}^{imp} + \mathbf{x}^{exp} \tag{3.31}$$

2. *Blocks of fixed assets dynamics for the economy and the nature restoration sectors*
$$K_i(t+1) = (1-\mu_i)K_i(t) + \eta_i H_i(t), \ i = 1, n \tag{3.32}$$
$$K_j^Z(t+1) = (1-\mu_j^Z)K_j^Z(t) + \eta_j^Z H_j^Z(t), \ j = 1, m \tag{3.33}$$

3. Block of natural resources (state of the environment) dynamics

$$\mathbf{r}(t+1) = \mathbf{Q}(\mathbf{r}(t) - \mathbf{r}^*(t)) - (\mathbf{Ex} - \mathbf{E}^H\mathbf{h} + \mathbf{E}^C\mathbf{c} + \mathbf{E}^Z\mathbf{h}^Z + \mathbf{e}^N N) + \mathbf{Jz}$$
$$+ \mathbf{m}^{imp} - \mathbf{m}^{exp} \tag{3.34}$$

4. Block of production functions

$$X_i(t) = F_i(t, K_i, L_i), \quad i = 1, n \tag{3.35}$$

$$Z_j(t) = F_j^Z(t, K_j^Z, L_j^Z), \quad j = 1, m \tag{3.36}$$

5. Block of structure matrices dynamics

$$\mathbf{A}(t) = \mathbf{F}_A\{t, \mathbf{A}(t-1), ..., \mathbf{A}(t-\tau_1), \mathbf{x}(t)\} \tag{3.37}$$

$$\mathbf{A}^Z(t) = \mathbf{F}_{A^Z}\{t, \mathbf{A}^Z(t-1), ..., \mathbf{A}^Z(t-\tau_2), \mathbf{z}(t)\} \tag{3.38}$$

$$\mathbf{D}(t) = \mathbf{F}_D\{t, \mathbf{D}(t-1), ..., \mathbf{D}(t-\tau_3), \mathbf{h}(t)\} \tag{3.39}$$

$$\mathbf{D}^Z(t) = \mathbf{F}_{D^Z}\{t, \mathbf{D}^Z(t-1), ..., \mathbf{D}^Z(t-\tau_4), \mathbf{z}(t)\} \tag{3.40}$$

Here:
- $\mathbf{x}$, $\mathbf{c}$ are respectively the vectors of outputs and net consumption of products;
- $\mathbf{x}^{imp}$, $\mathbf{x}^{exp}$ are respectively the vectors of imports and exports of products;
- $\mathbf{z}$ is the intensity vector of artificial (exogenous with respect to environment) restoration of resources;
- $\mathbf{k}$, $\mathbf{k}^Z$ are the fixed assets vectors for the economic sectors, and the sectors of nature restoration, respectively;
- $\mathbf{h}$, $\mathbf{h}^Z$ are gross investments vectors into capital assets of economic sectors, and sectors of nature restoration, respectively;
- μ, μ^Z and η, η^Z are the respective depreciation and investment lags coefficients vectors;
- $\mathbf{r}$ is the vector of the state of the environment (natural resources) variables;
- $\mathbf{r}^*$ is the undisturbed (or 'desired') state of the natural resources;
- $\mathbf{m}^{imp}$, $\mathbf{m}^{exp}$ are the migration of natural resources to/from the region;
- $\mathbf{A}$, $\mathbf{A}^Z$ are the matrices of direct expenses per unit of $\mathbf{X}$, and $\mathbf{z}$;
- $\mathbf{D}$, $\mathbf{D}^Z$ are the matrices of technological structure of investments;
- $\mathbf{Q}$ is the matrix of self-restoration coefficients (diagonal elements) and the mutual influence of natural resources (non-diagonal elements, e.g. impact of air or water pollution on the state of biological resources or forests);
- $\mathbf{E}$ is the matrix of resource expenditures (or pollution) in the production process (per the unit of $\mathbf{x}$);
- $\mathbf{E}^I$, $\mathbf{E}^Z$ are the matrices of expenditures of resources in the process of capital assets formation (per unit of $\mathbf{h}$, and $\mathbf{h}^Z$ respectively);

- $\mathbf{E}^C$ is the matrix of resource expenditures on net consumption of products (per unit of **c**);
- **J** is the diagonal matrix with elements equal +1 or -1, subject to whether the restoration of resource (flow of z) leads to growth or decrease of the variable **R** (the latter in the case of pollution);
- $\mathbf{e}^N$ is the vector of coefficients, which account for the anthropogenic non-industrial load on natural resources;
- N is the population of the region; and
- production functions **F**, $\mathbf{F}^Z$, respectively, for the economy and natural restoration sectors, can also depend on the state of the environment **r** (and in general, **F**, $\mathbf{F}^Z$ are non-linear).

The region can also be considered as a territory divided into several districts (sub-regions), connected by a transport network and by the possible migration of resources. In this case, every district (sub-region) is described by a standard sub-model of the above type.

The dynamics of the state of the environment variables (**r**) is assumed to be linear, to simplify the information requirements. These equations describe the region's environment in terms of deviation from some 'undisturbed' state ($\mathbf{r}^*$) of the ecosystem of the region. Assuming there is no anthropogenic impact on natural resources (neither exploitation nor restoration), the equations solution $\mathbf{r}(t)$, in the limit will tend to $\mathbf{r}^*$.

The change of technological production processes, consumption and life styles, and other factors which influence the specific expenditures of production and resources exploitation, are taken into account in the model by the introduction of the time-dependence of the matrices **A**, **D**, **E**, $\mathbf{E}^C$, $\mathbf{E}^N$, $\mathbf{A}^Z$, $\mathbf{D}^Z$.

In the general case, these matrices may also depend on **r**. In particular, the relationship $\mathbf{Q}(\mathbf{r})$ accounts for the fact that, in the case of a strong disturbance of the natural environment, the latter may lose the ability of self-restoration.

Due to the modular structure of the above model, one can readily change its configuration to adapt to information availability. Data requirements, though, as already mentioned above, remain the main issue in practical applications of such complex multi-dimensional dynamic models.

A simplified modification of the above ecological-economic I-O model was proposed in Safonov (1996b), for a German air pollution dynamics study. The economic sectors were classified according to their contribution to air pollution, and the most significant pollutants were selected for both production and consumption of the goods of each sector. Emission functions were built for each sector, as functions of capital assets in air-cleaning activities, technological change and time. Separately, the household emissions were evaluated, using statistical analysis.

The model thus enables analysis of dynamics of anthropogenic emissions and the comparison of the investment scenarios within different strategies of environmental-economic development.

3.7 CONCLUSIONS

In this chapter we have set out to demonstrate three major features of the input-output approach to modelling:

- The standard I-O model is well established, flexible and allows economies to be analysed through the consideration of many producing sectors, which are themselves interconnected through inter-industry purchasing. This multi-sectoral model can be represented with standard matrix algebra, allowing the 'solution' of the model for the vector of total outputs ($\mathbf{x}$) in terms of a given structure of final demand ($\mathbf{y}$) and a known matrix of technological coefficients ($\mathbf{A}$).
- The standard I-O model can be easily extended to include economy-environment interactions in a number of ways, but always with the advantage of remaining multi-sectoral and solvable with matrix algebra. Indeed, modern spreadsheet packages are easily powerful enough to perform the linear algebraic manipulations necessary, making the implementation of such I-O models very straightforward.
- The I-O model can be made dynamic, to allow the analysis of changing relations of demand and production, and/or changing economy-environment relations.

Overall, we believe the I-O method has much to recommend it for ecological economics, though, as for any method, it is not without its drawbacks. The three principal criticisms which can be levelled at this method, are:

- The need for a great deal of data to establish the model, especially if a large numbers of sectors are considered.
- The fact that the model is linear, so that complexities of interaction through non-linear relations are not easily treated.
- For dynamic models, not only is there an even greater data demand than for static I-O models, but also the long-run dynamics of the system can prove problematic, and even unstable in some circumstances.

Notwithstanding these drawbacks, we believe the I-O method is both powerful and easily applied to modelling economy-environment interactions, and belongs in the tool kit of all ecological economists.

REFERENCES

Amir, S. (1989), 'On the use of ecological prices and system-wide indicators derived therefrom to quantify man's impact on the ecosystem', *Ecological Economics*, **1**, 203–31.

Barata, E. (2002), *Solid Waste Policy in Portugal: An Environmental Input-Output Approach*, PhD thesis, SPIRE, Keele University, UK.

Brown, M. and R. Herendeen (1996), 'Embodied energy analysis and EMERGY analysis: a comparative view', *Ecological Economics*, **19**, 219–35.

Bullard, C. and R. Herendeen (1975), 'The energy cost of goods and services', *Energy Policy*, **3**, 268–78.

Casler, S. and A. Rose (1998), 'Carbon dioxide emissions in the U.S. economy: a structural decomposition analysis', *Environmental and Resources Economics*, **11**, 349–63.

Costanza, R. (1980), 'Embodied energy and economic valuation', in I. Sohn (ed.), *Readings in Input-Output Analysis: Theory and Applications*, New York: Oxford University Press, pp. 432–44.

Cruz, L. (2002), *A Portuguese Energy-Economy-Environment Input-Output Model: Policy Applications*, PhD Thesis, SPIRE, Keele University, UK.

Cumberland, J. (1966), 'A regional interindustry model for analysis of development objectives', *Papers of the Regional Science Association*, **17**, 65–94.

Daly, H. (1968), 'On economics as a life science', *The Journal of Political Economy*, **76**, 392–406.

Duchin, F. and G. Lange (1998) 'Prospects for the recycling of plastics in the United States', *Structural Change and Economic Dynamics*, **9**, 307–31.

Eder, P. and M. Narodoslawsky (1999), 'What environmental pressures are a region's industries responsible for? A method of analysis with descriptive indices and input-output models', *Ecological Economics*, **29**, 359–74.

Førsund, F. (1985), 'Input-output models, national economic models, and the environment', in A. Kneese and J. Sweeney (eds), *Handbook of Natural Resource and Energy Economics*, Vol. I, Amsterdam: Elsevier, pp. 325–41.

Gowdy, J. and J. Miller (1987), 'Technological and demand change in energy use: an input-output analysis', *Environment and Planning A*, **19**, 1387–98.

Gurman, V. (ed.) (1981), *The Interaction of Nature and the Economy of the Baikal Region*, Novosibirsk: Nauka Publishers (in Russian).

Gurman, V. (ed.) (1990), *The Ecological-Economic Strategy of the Regional Development*, Novosibirsk: Nauka Publishers (in Russian).

Hannon, B. (1973), 'The structure of ecosystems', *Journal of Theoretical Biology*, **41**, 535–46.

Hannon, B. (1998), 'How might nature value man?', *Ecological Economics*, **25**, 265–79.

Isard, W., C. Choguill, J. Kissin, R. Seyfarth, R. Tatlock, K. Basset, J. Furtado and R. Izumita (1972), *Ecologic-Economic Analysis for Regional Development: Some Initial Explorations with Particular Reference to Recreational Resource Use and Environmental Planning*, New York: The Free Press.

Keuning, S.J. (2000), 'Indicators and accounts of sustainable development: the NAMEA approach', in S. Simon and J. Proops (eds), *Greening the Accounts*, Cheltenham: Edward Elgar, pp. 71-98.

Koopmans, T. (1951), 'Analysis of production as an efficient combination of activities', in T. Koopmans (ed.), *Activity Analysis of Production and Allocation (Proceedings of a Conference)*, New York: Wiley, pp. 33–97.

Krotov, V. (1981, 1982), 'Investigation of nonlinear optimization models of the multisectoral economy development', *Automation and Remote Control*, **42** (10, 11), **43** (1).

Lenzen, M. and S. Murray (2001), 'A modified ecological footprint method and its application to Australia', *Ecological Economics*, **37**, 229–55.

Leontief, W. (1936), 'Quantitative input-output relations in the economic system of the United States', *Review of Economics and Statistics*, **18**, 105–25.

Leontief, W. (1951/1986), 'Input-output economics', in W. Leontief (ed.), *Input-Output Economics*, Oxford: Oxford University Press, 2nd edn, pp. 3–18.

Leontief, W. (1970), 'Environmental repercussions and the economic structure: an input-output approach', *Review of Economics and Statistics*, **52**, 262–71.

Leontief, W. (1973), 'National income, economic structure, and environmental externalities', in M. Moss (ed.), *Studies in Income and Wealth: The Measurement of Economic and Social Performance*, vol. 38, New York: National Bureau of Economic Research. Reprinted in W. Leontief (ed.), *Input-Output Economics*, Oxford: Oxford University Press, 2nd edn 1986, pp. 261–72.

Leontief, W. and D. Ford (1972), 'Air pollution and the economic structure: empirical results of input-output computations', in A. Brody and A. Carter (eds), *Input-Output Techniques*, Amsterdam: North-Holland. Reprinted in W. Leontief (ed.), *Input-Output Economics*, Oxford: Oxford University Press, 2nd edn 1986, pp. 273–93.

Machado, G. (2000), 'Energy use, CO_2 emissions and foreign trade: an I-O approach applied to the Brazilian case', 13th International Conference on Input-Output Techniques, Macerata, Italy.

Machado, G., R. Schaeffer and E. Worrell (2001), 'Energy and carbon embodied in the international trade of Brazil: an input-output approach', *Ecological Economics*, **39**, 409–24.

Miller, R. and P. Blair (1985), *Input-Output Analysis: Foundations and Extensions*, New Jersey: Prentice Hall.

Muradian, R., M. O'Connor and J. Martinez-Alier (2002), 'Embodied pollution in trade: the "environmental load displacement" of industrialized countries', *Ecological Economics*, **41**, 51–67.

Nakamura, S. (1999), 'An interindustry approach to analyzing economic and environmental effects of the recycling of waste', *Ecological Economics*, **28**, 133–45.

Nakamura, S. and Y. Kondo (2000), 'Recycling, landfill consumption, and CO_2 emissions: analysis by waste input-output models', Working Paper Series, No. 2007, Institute for Research and Contemporary Political and Economic Affairs, Waseda University, Tokyo.

Nakamura, S. and Y. Kondo (2001), 'Input-output analysis of waste management', Working Paper Series, No. 0102, School of Political Science and Economics, Waseda University, Tokyo.

Proops, J. (1984), 'Modelling the energy input-output ratio', *Energy Economics*, **6**, 47–51.

Proops, J. (1988), 'Energy intensities, input-output analysis and economic development', in M. Ciaschini (ed.), *Input-output Analysis: Current Developments*, London: Chapman and Hall, pp. 201–15.

Proops, J. and G. Atkinson (1998), 'A practical sustainability criterian when there is international trade', in S. Faucheux, M. O'Connor and J. van der Straaten, *Sustainable Development: Concepts, Rationalities and Strategies*, Amsterdam: Kluwer, pp. 169–94.

Proops, J., M. Faber and G. Wagenhals (1993), *Reducing CO_2 Emissions: A Comparative Input-Output Study for Germany and the UK*, Heidelberg: Springer-Verlag.

Proops, J., G. Atkinson, G. von Schlotheim and S. Simon (1999),'International trade and the sustainability footprint: a practical criterion for its assessment', *Ecological Economics*, **28**, 75–97.

Richardson, H. (1972), *Input-Output and Regional Economics*, London: Weidenfeld and Nicholson.

Rose, A. (1999), 'Input-output structural decomposition analysis of energy and the environment', in J. van den Bergh (ed.), *Handbook of Environmental and Resource Economics*, Cheltenham: Edward Elgar, pp. 1164–79.

Safonov, P. (1996a), 'A system of dynamic models for ecological-economic regional development', in S. Faucheux, D. Pearce and J. Proops (eds), *Models of Sustainable Development*, Cheltenham: Edward Elgar, pp. 302–20.

Safonov, P. (1996b), 'Dynamic ecology-economy interactions modeling: some experience and perspectives of application in Russian and German Context', *Proceedings of the ESEE Inaugural Conference*, University of Versailles (UVSQ), France, May 1996.

Sheng, F. and S. Simon (2000), 'Alternative green accounting methodologies', in S. Simon and J. Proops (eds), *Greening the Accounts*, Cheltenham: Edward Elgar, pp. 155–80.

Solow, R. (1956), 'A contribution to the theory of economic growth', *Quarterly Journal of Economics*, **70**, 65–94.

Stone, R. (1970), 'Demographic input-output: an extension of social accounting', in A. Brody and A. Carter (eds), *Contributions to Input-Output Analysis*, Amsterdam: North-Holland, pp. 293–319.

Stone, R. (1986), 'Social accounting: the state of the art', *Scandinavian Journal of Economics*, **88**, 453–72.

Victor, P. (1972), *Pollution: Economics and Environment*, London: George Allen and Unwin.

Wackernagel, M. and W. Rees (1996), *Our Ecological Footprint: Reducing Human Impact on the Earth*, Gabriola Island, BC: New Society.

Zeng, G., X. Yuan, P. Zhang, H. Guo, G. Huang and L. Hemelaar (2000), 'Environmental input-output model with a focus on the solid waste sectors', *Journal of Environmental Sciences*, **12**, 178–83.

4.   Neo-Austrian Models

Malte Faber and John Proops[1]

4.1 INTRODUCTION

Neo-Austrian modelling is still a relatively unfamiliar technique to many ecological economists, although there is now a significant body of published work on the method and its applications. (Here we draw mainly on Faber and Proops, 1998; Faber et al., 1999.)

In this chapter we aim to introduce the method, offering a rather brief sketch of its history, indicating how neo-Austrian models are constructed and can be applied to environmental issues, and giving a hint on some of its wider applications. In more detail our aims are:

- To demonstrate the techniques of neo-Austrian modelling, to show how one can introduce various new techniques of production in a straightforward and intuitive way. (It is the 'construction kit' of modelling techniques; Hicks, 1970, p. 257.) This allows one to model innovation and technical progress. As well as having a simple and additive structure, one can drive the dynamics in various ways from full intertemporal optimization, through rolling myopic plans, to simple savings ratios.
- To show the richness of its application to environmental matters, including its usefulness in modelling human-nature interactions. For example, the Laws of Thermodynamics show us that joint production of waste materials is inevitable; this joint production is simply embodied in the neo-Austrian framework.
- To demonstrate the usefulness of the model in two epistemologically distinct situations. Concerning historical understandings (i.e., *ex post* analysis), we know already what new techniques have emerged, using new factors of production and producing new goods. So we can seek to explain the corresponding evolution using the concept of time preference, neo-Austrian ideas such as superiority of roundaboutness, time horizon of decision making, and the thermodynamically necessary relations to nature deriving from production and consumption. Concerning forecasting future

developments (i.e., *ex ante* analysis), the very structure of the neo-Austrian model, and its openness to extensions through the invention and innovation of new techniques, always reminds us that forecasting economic evolution is more of an art than a science. The scenario analysis that neo-Austrian analysis allows is, however, very well suited to exploring policy options based on alternative notions of future states of the world.

The remainder of the chapter has the following structure. Section 4.2 discusses approaches to modelling, and offers a brief description of the historical roots of this approach. Section 4.3 introduces the simplest neo-Austrian model, with three sectors. This simple model is extended in Section 4.4, to include the environmental issues of natural resource use, pollution emissions, and recycling. Section 4.5 outlines some other areas of application of the neo-Austrian model, while Sector 4.6 offers some conclusions.

4.2 APPROACHES TO MODELLING

One can identify two polar approaches to economic modelling.

- To begin with the preconception of human behaviour and human motivations, and to construct models consistent with this preconception.
- To construct models which are empirically oriented, so the prime aim is to represent the activities observed.

We would see neoclassical economics as being of the former type, with its stress on marginal changes on both the consumption and production sides. Concerning production, the neo-Austrian approach is more in the second category, stressing the distinctiveness of methods of production. Thus the neo-Austrian approach, because of its empirical orientation, easily allows considerations of such issues as the introduction of new techniques, decision making time-horizons, structural change and, of course, the temporal thermodynamic necessities of resource use and waste production (as discussed in Section 4.4).

4.2.1 The History of Neo-Austrian Modelling

Neo-Austrian capital theory is a revival of Austrian capital theory, which started in the late-nineteenth century. The characteristic adjective 'Austrian' stems from the nationality of the founder of the Austrian School, Carl Menger (1840–1921). At the end of the nineteenth century this School was, with the Neoclassical School, whose most original member was Leon Walras (1834–1910), the most important approach in economics.

The Austrian approach emphasizes the 'vertical' time structure of an economy; i.e., the fact that production takes time: raw materials have first to be extracted and then intermediate goods have to be manufactured, before the consumption good can be produced. In contrast to the Austrian view, the neoclassical (Walrasian) approach stresses the 'horizontal' time structure of an economy. That is, the interdependencies between its markets during one period of time are at the forefront of the analysis (cf. Faber, 1986, p. 12). The second great Austrian economist, Eugen von Böhm-Bawerk (1851–1914), who at the end of the nineteenth century was perhaps the most influential and well-known economist in the world, was the founder of Austrian capital theory. As Schumpeter (1954, p. 847) wrote: 'A few of the best minds in our field ... have in fact considered him ... [as] ... one of the great architects of economic science'.

The insight of the Austrian School, that production takes time, led Böhm-Bawerk to his concept of the 'roundaboutness' of the production process, and this in turn led to the concept of 'superiority'. Taken together, these two concepts led to his famous notion of the 'superiority of roundboutness' (discussed further in Section 4.3). For various reasons (Faber et al., 1999, pp. 24–6) the Austrian theory of capital fell into oblivion in the 1930s. However, the unsatisfactory way in which neoclassical capital theory treated time led to a revival of Austrian capital theory in the 1970s (Bernholz, 1971; Hicks, 1973), which was the beginnings of neo-Austrian capital theory (see Faber et al., 1999, pp. 30–34, for further details).

4.2.2 Motivation for the Approach

The essence of neo-Austrian capital theory is that it takes an historical approach to economies. It seeks to model how economies evolve, through the invention of new techniques of production, and the accumulation of corresponding stocks of new capital goods specific to those techniques. For example, if one imagines early humans as being comparable to other species, the only means they have to satisfy their wants is through the use of their bodies (e.g., as a bear may hunt live animals, scavenge on dead ones, and forage for plants). Clearly, such behaviour limits the possibilities for the growth of the bear (or early human) population, and indeed we normally observe a stationary set of relationships between species, at least over time horizons of hundreds or thousands of years.

However, an essential characteristic of humans is that they use tools (or capital goods). Indeed, while humans are classified as *homo sapiens* (wise men), they might better be described as *homo faber* (tool-using men). What is the outcome of this propensity of humans to use tools, and how might we model it? One outcome is that the ability of humans to access the resources out of nature is improved; indeed, this must be exactly the motivation for using tools/capital goods. However, such tool-using on nature will tend to be self-limiting, as the use of tools will make the aspects of nature they exploit scarcer and therefore more difficult to access. For example, there is very good evidence that when humans first entered Australia (about 40 thousand years ago) and then North America (about 20 thousand years ago), both continents contained megafauna (e.g., in Australia giant kangaroos, and in North America, giant bison, giant armadillos, etc.). Very shortly after humans entered these ecosystems, these megafauna disappeared, almost certainly because their hunting tools allowed the humans to predate on them so successfully (Crosby, 1986). So the easy hunting of the early years after human entry to these continents gave way to hunting which was more difficult (on the remaining smaller and less rewarding fauna). That is, the use of capital goods produced constraints on its long-run success.

The consequence was an incentive to search for new techniques of hunting, using new hunting tools (i.e., new sorts of capital). So, historically, we believe that the order of the evolution of hunting tools was: the spear, the spear with throwing stick, the net, the bow and arrow, the gun.

Now, the use of tools requires that first they be produced. Of course, this production involves time and effort that could be spent in other activities, such as hunting (without these tools). Under what circumstances would it be considered worthwhile to produce tools? The first obvious necessary condition is that humans have sufficient foresight to envisage the future benefits of present foregone consumption possibilities. So humans need to be able to consider and envisage future events as being in some way comparable with present experiences. For example, fishing with a net is much more effective than fishing with a spear, and fishing with a boat and a net is better still. The benefits of present foregone consumption are clear in this case. We see also from these examples that different time horizons are involved: producing a spear takes less time than producing a boat.

The next necessary condition is that the human needs to be reasonably assured that the benefits from the foregone consumption actually accrue to that individual (or social group). Thus the notion of property rights also flows from the use of capital goods. Of course, to maintain these property rights, some sort of rule of law is also necessary. Therefore, the introduction of capital goods begins to structure the basic requirements for human society; i.e., foresight, property rights, and the rule of law.

So one essential aim of neo-Austrian capital theory is to seek to model the historical development of societies, through the invention and bringing into use of new techniques and new types of capital, over the course of time.

Other aims are to analyse the present structure of the economy and to develop scenarios for future developments.

We now move to a more technical introduction to neo-Austrian capital theory, using the simplest possible model. At this stage it is worth noting that the representation of the neo-Austrian approach we use draws on Koopmans (1951) 'activity analysis' method.

4.3 THE THREE-SECTOR MODEL

We begin with a simple model of production for consumption. This model is initially rather unrealistic, as we do not include either the use of natural resources, or the production of polluting wastes. However, the model will be extended to include these aspects of human-nature interactions in the next section. This discussion serves to introduce the main structure and concepts of the approach.

Let us therefore consider a society where the only non-produced scarce factor of production is labour, which is used directly to produce the consumption good. (For fuller discussion of this model, see Faber and Proops, 1998, Chapters 10, 11; Faber et al., 1999, Chapters 3, 4). We can represent this quite simply if we make the reasonable assumption that the output of the consumption good is proportional to the input of labour. So we can write this (Process 1) as:

$L_1 \rightarrow X_1$; i.e., labour L_1 is transformed into the consumption good X_1.

The proportionality assumption gives:

$$\frac{L_1}{l_1} = X_1 ; \qquad\qquad (4.1)$$

Here, l_1 characterizes the production process 1 (Process 1). It is the amount of labour needed to generate one unit of the consumption good.

In the course of time, people will find that it is more productive to manufacture the consumption good by using capital goods. So let us assume that the consumption good can be produced not only with labour alone, but also by labour *combined with* (⊕) a capital good. We represent this (Process 2) as:

$$L_2 \oplus K_2 \rightarrow X_2 ; \qquad\qquad (4.2)$$

i.e., labour is combined with capital to produce the consumption good.

We again assume proportionality of inputs, and that the production factors are complementary, with l_2 units of labour, combined with the *use* of k_2 units of capital, needed to manufacture 1 unit of the consumption good, i.e.:

$$\frac{L_2}{l_2} = \frac{K_2}{k_2} = X_2 . \tag{4.3}$$

However, before it can be employed in this production process, the capital good must first be produced. We assume labour alone can be used to manufacture new, extra capital good, (in Process 3), i.e.:

$$L_3 \rightarrow \Delta K . \tag{4.4}$$

We again assume proportionality of input to output, giving:

$$\frac{L_3}{l_3} = \Delta K . \tag{4.5}$$

The quantity of new capital good (produced in period t) is added to any already available capital good $K(t)$ in period t, to be available in period $t+1$; i.e.:

$$K(t+1) = K(t) + \Delta K(t) . \tag{4.6}$$

One would usually represent this capital as having the property that, over time, it would *deteriorate* (in line with the Laws of Thermodynamics). This deterioration would be at a characteristic rate c. It is straightforward to extend this model to include such capital deterioration (Faber and Proops, 1998, pp. 205–7; Faber et al., 1999, pp. 58–60), giving:

$$K(t+1) = (1-c)K(t) + \Delta K(t) . \tag{4.7}$$

For the sake of simplicity we assume that the total amount of labour available, L, each period is exogeneously given, hence the labour restriction in each period is given by:

$$L_1 + L_2 + L_3 \leq L. \tag{4.8}$$

In summary, this model:

- Involves two scarce factors of production, (non-produced) labour and a (produced) capital good.
- Produces two outputs, the consumption good and new capital good (i.e., investment).
- Uses three production processes. Processes 1 and 2 manufacture the same physical consumptions good. Process 1 uses only labour to produce the consumption good. Process 2 uses labour and the capital good, to produce the consumption good. Process 3 uses only labour to produce the capital good.
- The capital good must be produced before it is used, accumulates over time with new investment, and may deteriorate with use.
- In each period there exists a labour constraint.

4.3.1 Techniques of Production

If we initially focus attention on two production periods, we can represent the time structure of production in this model as in Figure 4.1.

Time Period	Technique 1 Process 1	Technique 2 Process 2	Process 3
1	Labour ↓ Consumption good	- -	Labour ↓ Capital good
2	Labour ↓ Consumption good	Labour ⊕ Capital good ↓ Consumption good	

Figure 4.1 Time structure of production

We can speak of production of the consumption good as being possible by two *Techniques*. Here, a technique of production is defined to be the minimal combination of production processes to produce the consumption good from the non-produced input; so:

Technique T_1 = {Process 1},
Technique T_2 = {Process 2, Process 3}.

(For a fuller discussion of the notion of a technique, see Faber and Proops, 1998, p. 180; Faber et al., 1999, p. 111.)

- Technique 1 consists of only Process 1, and takes only one period to manufacture the consumption good, with labour alone.
- Technique 2 consists of first, Process 3, to manufacture the capital good in one period, and then, in the next period, Process 2 to use the capital good with labour, to produce the consumption good.

Because of its more complex temporal structure, we can speak of Technique 2 as being more *roundabout* than Technique 1 (Faber et al., 1999, pp. 46–50).

We now must address the issue of when Technique 2 would be regarded as superior to Technique 1. If we assume that the capital good is long-lasting, and can be used for several periods once it has been produced, the decision of whether the capital good will be manufactured at all will obviously depend on how far-sighted is the decision maker; i.e. it will depend on the time horizon. (For a fuller discussion of the role of the time horizon in the investment decision, see Faber and Proops, 1991a; Faber et al., 1999, Chapter 5.)

If there is only a two-period horizon, and if we measure the benefit of each technique as simply the sum of consumption over the two periods, we can show that Technique 2 has 'two-period superiority of roundaboutness' over Technique 1 if:

$$S(2) \equiv \frac{l_1 - l_2}{l_3 k_2} > 1. \tag{4.9}$$

If we extend the time horizon to n periods we find the condition for superiority becomes:

$$S(n) \equiv \frac{l_1 - l_2}{l_3 k_2} - \frac{c}{1 - (1-c)^{n-1}} + 1 > 1. \tag{4.10}$$

For an infinite time horizon it is:

$$S(\infty) \equiv \frac{l_1 - l_2}{l_3 k_2} + (1-c) = S(2) + (1-c) > 1. \tag{4.11}$$

(Full derivations of these relations are in Faber et al., 1999, Chapters 3 and 5.)

We can show that $S(n)$ is a strictly increasing function of n (Faber et al. 1999, pp. 114–16); i.e., the longer is the time horizon, the more likely are we to find that Technique 2 is superior to Technique 1, and therefore likely to be brought into use. We note in passing that a necessary decision to bring a technique into use depends on the degree of superiority; i.e., that the degree of superiority is greater than one. Whether this is the case or not depends on two kinds of factors:

- On technical factors (coefficients of production and the rate of deterioration).
- On a subjective factor (the length of the time horizon, for as we have seen: the longer the time horizon, the higher the degree of superiority).

4.3.2 The Investment Decision

From the above outline, it is clear that the dynamics of neo-Austrian models are determined by the decision to accumulate new capital; i.e., to invest. To give a detailed description of how this decision is taken, there are two obvious approaches.

- Optimization of an intertemporal welfare function.
- The use of a savings ratio (as in simple macroeconomic models; see Faber and Proops, 1993; Faber et al., 1999, Chapter 8).

The intertemporal optimization approach can itself be of two types (Faber and Proops, 1998, pp. 222–40):

- Full intertemporal optimization, with an indefinite time horizon.
- Rolling-myopic optimization, where only a limited number of time periods are considered, and only the first few time periods of this plan are considered binding, before a new myopic optimization occurs.

Regarding these two optimization approaches, which is selected will obviously depend on the attitude towards the future, and in particular the degree to which it can be predicted (see Faber and Proops, 1998, Chapters 7, 8). If it is felt that the relevant properties of world are stable and known, then a full intertemporal approach will be most efficient. However, in the face of uncertainty about future conditions in the world (e.g., relating to technical change or environmental damage), then a rolling myopic approach is more likely to be appropriate.

4.3.3 The Traverse

An important notion in neo-Austrian modelling is that of the 'traverse' (Hicks, 1965). This term is taken from rock climbing, and in that context means the movement across a rock face from one point of firm attachment to another. In its neo-Austrian sense, it means the movement of an economy from one steady state to another, through the process of capital accumulation.

The essence of the notion is that the important and interesting parts of economic activity occur while the economy is *not* at a steady state (or equilibrium) but rather is somehow 'unbalanced' (like a rock climber on an exposed rock face).

Perhaps a society is initially in a steady state, having a certain technology of production available to it. If a new technique of production is invented, and is found to be worth bringing into use (because it has enough 'superiority of roundaboutness' over the appropriate time horizon), then it will be innovated, with consequent effects on the economic structure, the wage and interest rates, the distribution of income, environmental resource use and damage, and the level of output per capita. Eventually, in the absence of any further changes to technology (or the environment), the economy will achieve a new equilibrium steady-state (perhaps steady state growth, if the population is increasing).

While neo-Austrian capital theory can specify the nature of the beginning and final steady-states, its greatest strength is that it allows one to explore, in a disaggregated and detailed way, the time structure of economic activities between these steady-states, during the traverse (Faber, 1979, pp. 164–6).

4.3.4 The Input-Output Representation of the Neo-Austrian Model

As has been outlined in Chapter 3 of this volume, input-output (I-O) analysis is an extremely widely used tool in ecological economics. As neo-Austrian models are necessarily multi-sectoral, these too can be represented in I-O format. This allows not only the simple representation of the production relations (for each time period) in a familiar format, but also the calculation of the prices that such a production technology support. (For a fuller discussion, see Faber et al., 1999, pp. 61–6.)

If we use the simple three process model (for the sake of simplicity, without deterioration of capital) outlined above, we see that there are two sorts of output, the consumption good and the new capital good (i.e., new investment). Similarly, there are two factors of production, labour and (produced) capital. We can represent these inputs and outputs to the three processes as in Table 4.1, where each I-O sector corresponds to the similarly numbered production process.

We see this is a very simple I-O table, with *no* intermediate demand (though below there will be environmental neo-Austrian models where there are intermediate demand elements).

Table 4.1   Input-output representation of the simple neo-Austrian model

Sectors	1	2	3	Output
1	-	-	-	X_1
2	-	-	-	X_2
3	-	-	-	ΔK
Labour	L_1	L_2	L_3	
Capital	-	K_2	-	

However, the strength of this table is that we can now introduce prices for labour (L), capital use (K), the consumption output (X), and new capital (ΔK). It is important to note the distinction between the two prices of capital: the price for its production (the price of ΔK), and the rental rate for its use (the price of K). Using self-evident price nomenclature, we can rewrite the I-O table to represent the values of the various inputs and outputs, as in Table 4.2.

Table 4.2   Value input-output representation of the simple neo-Austrian model

Sectors	1	2	3	Output
1	-	-	-	$p_X X_1$
2	-	-	-	$p_X X_2$
3	-	-	-	$p_{\Delta K}\Delta K$
Labour	$p_L L_1$	$p_L L_2$	$p_L L_3$	
Capital	-	$p_K K_2$	-	

In the usual I-O way, for each sector the values of inputs and outputs can be equated, to give three price equations:

$$p_L L_1 = p_X X_1 ; \qquad p_L L_2 + p_K K_2 = p_X X_2 ; \qquad p_L L_3 = p_{\Delta K}\Delta K . \qquad (4.12)$$

Combining these equations with the above relationships between the inputs, outputs and technical coefficients for each sector, allows one to solve for the prices, if one takes one of the prices as a *numéraire* (usually this the price of labour, i.e., $p_L=1$). This gives:

$$p_X = l_1 ; \qquad p_{\Delta K} = l_3 ; \qquad p_K = \frac{l_1 - l_2}{k_2} . \qquad (4.13)$$

Of course, an alternative method of identifying the prices for the system is to set up a full dynamic optimization system, solving with the method of Lagrange, where the Lagrange multipliers are the shadow prices of the constraints (see Faber and Proops, 1998, 214–19; Faber et al., 1999, pp 67–71). This method has the advantage of finding the (different) prices for each commodity in each period. However, our experience is that for the purposes of most modelling, the I-O method of finding prices is to be much preferred, for its extreme simplicity.

4.4 INTRODUCING RESOURCES AND THE ENVIRONMENT

The method so far presented, has an obvious flaw for ecological economists: it takes no explicit account of nature! Fortunately the above representation of the production process is simple to extend, to include such important items as: the use of natural resources as an input to production; the corresponding emission of polluting wastes from production; and we can even include a waste treatment sector if we wish. Indeed, a great strength of the neo-Austrian approach is flexibility and ease of extension (cf. Faber et al., 1999, Chapters 8, 9).

Another strength of the neo-Austrian approach is that its emphasis on the time structure of production, as well as its historical orientation, leads naturally to a consideration of irreversibility conditions. As has been shown elsewhere, this can be appropriately considered by including thermodynamic relationships (Faber et al., 1995). Indeed, the laws of physics can be simply used to give structure to neo-Austrian models of human-nature interactions. The Laws of Conservation of Mass and Energy can be used to constrain the physical input and output coefficients for the processes, to ensure that the assumed production processes are firmly based on physical reality. At a more fundamental level, the Second Law of Thermodynamics tells us that any real production process must involve the production of entropy, which leaves the production process in some form, perhaps as polluting waste materials. The production of the desired goods necessarily causes the production of wastes; i.e., 'all production is joint production' (Faber et al., 1998; Baumgärtner et al., 2001). This necessary joint production is something that the neo-Austrian approach to modelling handles very comfortably within its straightforward and disaggregated production structure.

4.4.1 Resource Extraction

In the first environmental example, we turn to the extraction of a non-renewable natural resource. In particular, this allows the natural resource rent to be included in the intertemporal price system of the neo-Austrian model.

(This section draws on Faber and Proops, 1993; Faber et al., 1999, Chapter 8.)

   A simple model might include the natural resource as an input to the construction of new capital (i.e., an input to Process/Sector 3). Of course, the natural resource must first be extracted, which we assume takes place in a new Process/Sector 4. The natural resource, as it occurs in the ground, constitutes a basic factor of production (along with labour and capital). We can specify the production technology for Process/Sector 4 in the terminology presented earlier. In Process 4, labour is combined with the non-extracted natural resource, to give the extracted natural resource:

$$M \oplus L_4 \rightarrow M \; ; \; \text{i.e.:} \qquad \frac{L_4}{l_4} = M \; . \tag{4.14}$$

We also need to modify the technology for Process 3, to take account of the input of the natural resource. We get:

$$M \oplus L_3 \rightarrow \Delta K \; ; \; \text{i.e.:} \qquad \frac{M}{r_3} = \frac{L_3}{l_3} = \Delta K \; . \tag{4.15}$$

Here, r_3 is the natural resource required to produce one unit of the new capital good.

   We can extend Table 4.1 to include the extraction and use of the natural resource (M), as shown in Table 4.3.

Table 4.3   Input-output representation of the neo-Austrian model with resource extraction

Sectors	1	2	3	4	Output
1	-	-	-	-	X_1
2	-	-	-	-	X_2
3	-	-	-	-	ΔK
4	-	-	M	-	-
Labour	L_1	L_2	L_3	L_4	
Capital	-	K_2	-	-	
Resource	-	-	-	M	

We see that the resource term, M, appears twice. First, as a factor of production, with labour and capital, and second as an (intermediate) input of production, from Sector 4 to Sector 3.

We can now further extend the model by introducing prices, though here we need two more prices than appeared in Table 4.2. First, there is the resource rent, applicable to the natural resource as a factor of production (i.e., its pre-extraction 'price in the ground'). We call this p_R. The new second price corresponds to the (market) price at which the extracted resource is sold by Sector 4 to Sector 3. We call this p_M. Using these prices, we can construct Table 4.4.

Table 4.4   Value input-output representation of the neo-Austrian model with resource extraction

Sectors	1	2	3	4	Output
1	-	-	-	-	$p_X X_1$
2	-	-	-	-	$p_X X_2$
3	-	-	-	-	$p_{\Delta K} \Delta K$
4	-	-	$p_M M$	-	-
Labour	$p_L L_1$	$p_L L_2$	$p_L L_3$	$p_L L_4$	
Capital	-	$p_K K_2$	-	-	
Resource	-	-	-	$p_R M$	

We can now find four price equations from Table 4.4, following the procedure described above, by equating the values of inputs and outputs for the four sectors; i.e.:

$$p_L L_1 = p_X X_1 ; \qquad (4.16)$$

$$p_M M + p_L L_3 = p_{\Delta K} \Delta K ; \qquad (4.18)$$

$$p_L L_2 + p_K K_2 = p_X X_2 ; \qquad (4.17)$$

$$p_R M + p_L L_4 = p_M M . \qquad (4.19)$$

Substituting these relationships (and those for Processes 1 and 2) into the price equations (again taking labour as the *numéraire*, i.e., p_L=1) gives:

$$p_X = l_1 ; \qquad p_{\Delta K} = l_3 + p_M r_3 ; \qquad p_K = \frac{l_1 - l_2}{k_2} ; \qquad p_M = l_4 + p_R . \qquad (4.20)$$

We note that the first and third equations are identical to those in Section 4.3.4. The second equation tells us that the price of new capital (in labour value units) now depends on the amount of labour used, and on the amount and price of the natural resource required. The final equation above has the very straightforward interpretation:

Natural Resource Price = Extraction Cost + Resource Rent.

The above model, with its I-O representation, is necessarily static. However, we can add dynamics simply by introducing a rule for the choice of new capital accumulation in each period (i.e.; $\Delta K(t)$).

As mentioned above, one method of specifying ΔK is to use a savings rule, from gross domestic product (GDP – Y). For this model, that is simply the sum of the value of final outputs or the sum of the value of basic factor inputs; i.e.:

$$Y = p_L(L_1+L_2+L_3+L_4) + p_K K + p_r M = p_X(X_1+X_2) + p_{\Delta K}\Delta K. \qquad (4.21)$$

One can then define new investment in each period to be given by:

$$\Delta K(t) = sY(t); \quad \text{i.e.} \quad K(t+1) = K(t) + \Delta K(t) = K(t) + sY(t). \qquad (4.22)$$

This would give a dynamic model, where the capital accumulation over time would generate a time-path of output (of the various types), as well as altering the balance of the distribution of labour between the sectors (the total quantity of labour can be assumed to be growing over time, at a positive, zero or even negative rate). Also, and most importantly for our purposes, it would define a time-path of resource extraction. (For a fuller discussion, see Faber et al., 1999, Chapter 8.)

This very simple model can be made more realistic by allowing the resource rent itself to vary over time. Two obvious approaches here would be either to follow standard resource economics theory, or to use empirical evidence on resource prices. In the first case, we could specify that the resource rent follow the Hotelling Rule; i.e., p_R increases at the interest rate (which here could be taken to be the rental rate of capital, p_K) (see Dasgupta and Heal, 1979, p. 156). In this case would write:

$$\frac{p_R(t) - p_R(t-1)}{p_R(t-1)} = p_K; \quad \text{i.e:} \quad p_R(t) = p_R(t-1)(1 + p_K). \qquad (4.23)$$

In the second case, we could specify the rental rate of the resource to be falling over time (as has been the common experience for almost all natural resources over the past century; cf. Barnett and Morse, 1963; Proops, 2004). We note in passing that the determination of the resource rent has important implications to the distribution of income between developed and developing countries (cf. Jöst, 1994; Proops, 2004).

4.4.2 Pollution

The second application of the neo-Austrian approach to the environment relates to pollution production and abatement (cf. Speck, 1997; Faber et al., 1999, Chapter 10). For example we could specify a model where each production process may produce wastes, which are polluting; e.g., for Process 2, where Z_2 represents polluting waste output:

$$L_2 \oplus K_2 \rightarrow X_2 \oplus Z_2; \qquad \text{i.e.:} \quad \frac{L_2}{l_2} = \frac{K_2}{k_2} = \frac{Z_2}{z_2} = X_2. \qquad (4.24)$$

We can specify two ways in which this waste may be dealt with. First, we could use pollution abatement techniques, which used economic resources (e.g., labour). Second, we could introduce natural processes of pollution degradation, which would require no use of economic resources.

Using our original production technology, as represented in Table 4.1, we could add two more sectors: Sector 4 is pollution abatement, and Sector 5 is natural pollution degradation. In Sector 4 labour L_4 is used to neutralize pollution. This gives us the production/pollution system shown in Table 4.5.

Table 4.5   Input-output representation of the neo-Austrian model with pollution

Sectors	1	2	3	4	5	Output	Pollution
1	-	-	-	-	-	X_1	-
2	-	-	-	-	-	X_2	Z_2
3	-	-	-	-	-	ΔK	Z_3
4	-	-	-	-	-	-	$-A$
5	-	-	-	-	-	-	$-D$
Labour	L_1	L_2	L_3	L_4	-		
Capital	-	K_2	-	-	-		
Polln Degr	-	-	-	-	$-D$		

Here, the pollution produced in Sectors 2 and 3 is denoted by Z_i. The pollution abatement (Sector 4) is indicated by A, and the natural pollution degradation (Sector 5) is indicated by D. (These are shown with negative signs to indicate *reduction* of pollution.) If the stock of pollution at time t is given by $Q(t)$, then we can write:

$$Q(t+1) = Q(t) + Z_1(t) + Z_2(t) - D(t) - A(t). \qquad (4.25)$$

We could also make the amount of natural pollution degradation that occurs in each period dependent on, e.g., the stock of pollution: $D(t) = f(Q)$.

We could then introduce prices into the model, as above, to calculate the costs of pollution abatement, and the value to society of natural pollution degradation. Finally, we could give the model a dynamics, through establishing the rate of capital accumulation, by one of the techniques discussed above. Also, there would need to be established a rule to determine the amount of pollution abatement in each period. This could be either dependent on the level of net emission, or the pollution stock, or some other rule. This would then give the dynamics of the model, showing capital accumulation, labour use, and most importantly for us, pollution emissions, natural degradation and abatement, plus the full set of corresponding prices for the system.

4.4.3 Recycling

An alternative way of reducing the emission of polluting waste is to recycle this material (cf. Faber et al., 1999, Chapter 11). This may be done by a specific Process/Sector; e.g., processed waste from Processes 2 and 3 may be used as a substitute for extracted raw material. Using the natural resource model outlined above, we might add a further Process/Sector 6, which uses labour and waste material from Sector 3, and produces recycled material (M), for use in place of raw material. We can represent this recycling as producing -R units of pollution, as in Table 4.6. (Again, the negative sign indicates a reduction in pollution.)

Table 4.6   Input-output representation of the neo-Austrian model with recycling

Sectors	1	2	3	4	5	6	Output	Pollution
1	-	-	-	-	-	-	X_1	-
2	-	-	-	-	-	-	X_2	Z_2
3	-	-	-	-	-	-	ΔK	Z_3
4	-	-	-	-	-	-	-	-A
5	-	-	-	-	-	-	-	-D
6	-	-	M	-	-	-	-	-R
Labour	L_1	L_2	L_3	L_4	-	L_6		
Capital	-	K_2	-	-	-	-		
Polln Red'n	-	-	-	-	-D	-R		

Again, we could assume that Process 6 uses labour in fixed proportion to the amount of material recycled. In this model, pollution reduction now comes in two forms: natural pollution degradation (-D) and recycling (-R). The relationship for the pollution emission is now:

$$Q(t+1) = Q(t) + Z_1(t) + Z_2(t) - D(t) - A(t) - R(t). \tag{4.26}$$

We could go one step further towards reality, and combine the resource, pollution and recycling models. Using insights from the Second Law of Thermodynamics and the Mass Balance Principle, discussed above, would also give constraints on the various environmental and production coefficients in the model (see Faber et al., 1999, Chapter 11). We could also easily add prices to this extended model. Finally, as discussed above, the model could be given an internal dynamics by including a choice of investment path, together with a pollution abatement/recycling policy, and a changing natural resource rent also. As noted in the introduction, the neo-Austrian approach is very like a construction kit, and it is extremely simple to add new Processes/Sectors, to capture further aspects of reality that need modelling.

4.5 OTHER APPLICATIONS

Other areas to which the neo-Austrian approach has been applied include the following.[2]

4.5.1 Growth Theory

It has been shown that if one takes the approach of neoclassical growth theory, and focuses on the steady state rather than the traverse, then the properties of the neo-Austrian model are almost identical to those of the neoclassical (i.e., Swan/Solow) model, even to the extent of having almost identical properties with regard to optimal consumption paths. This suggests that the neo-Austrian approach contains the neoclassical model as a special case, at least in respect of most of its properties. (Stephan, 1995, Chapters 6–8; Proops and Speck, 1996; Faber et al., 1999, Chapter 6.)

4.5.2 Long-Run Interactions between Economies and Nature

The very nature of neo-Austrian modelling naturally lends itself to long-run considerations. In particular, it is excellent for exploring how the introduction of new techniques of production (because of superiority of roundaboutness) impacts on nature, and how this in turn rebounds on economic activity (Faber et al., 1990; Faber and Proops, 1993; Faber and Proops, 1998, Chapter 12).

4.5.3 National Accounting and the Environment

As has been demonstrated above, the neo-Austrian approach lends itself to representation in an input-output framework, which is also the basis of national accounts. Using the neo-Austrian dynamics of capital accumulation, resource depletion and pollution emissions, which have been sketched above, the issue of how national accounts should be modified to account for environmental issues can be easily assessed. In particular, the Samuelson/Weitzmann argument for considering the consumption stream, rather than GDP, occurs as a natural conclusion (Faber and Proops, 1991b; Faber et al., 1999, Chapter 7).

4.5.4 International Trade and the Environment

Using its 'construction kit' properties, it is relatively simple to extend the neo-Austrian model to encompass international trade, by constructing extra production processes, and representing these as a multi-country I-O model. In particular, models considering trade and environment relations between 'rich' and 'poor' countries have produced some stimulating results, on the distributional effects of climate change taxes (Jöst, 1994; Faber et al., 1999, Chapter 9) and the trade impact of falling resource rents (Proops, 2004).

4.5.5 Empirical Studies

It is relatively straightforward to use the neo-Austrian model for empirical work, as long as reasonable predictions for the various technological coefficients can be estimated (or 'guesstimated'). Examples of such work include studies of water quality (Faber et al., 1983), resource depletion (Faber and Wagenhals, 1988), and the history of production processes in the iron and steel industry (Faber et al., 1999, Chapter 12).

4.6 CONCLUSIONS

In this necessarily brief sketch of the method, we have tried to show the strengths of neo-Austrian modelling, which we would summarize as follows:

• The approach focuses on changes over real (historical) time. In particular, the concept of the 'superiority of roundaboutness' shows why capital accumulation and economic change occur, through the introduction of new techniques of production.

- The method is very straightforward to implement, using easily constructed, estimated and understood production processes.
- The models can be easily represented in terms of I-O models, allowing the simple calculation of the corresponding price system.
- There is a range of methods of giving the model dynamics, from intertemporal optimization through to the use of savings ratios.
- Environmental issues can be introduced simply, either through joint production (for pollution), or the introduction of new production processes (for resource extraction, pollution abatement, recycling, etc.).
- Finally, the simple structure of the models means that simulations are easy to perform; spreadsheets are sufficient for most purposes.

The considerable strengths of the neo-Austrian approach do have a cost, though. In particular, we should advise the reader of the following difficulties involved in the method.

- In analytical terms, in contrast to neoclassical production-environment models, the neo-Austrian models generate a lot of mathematical formalism on the page. For example, the simple neoclassical production function, $f(K,L)$, is replaced by a number of processes. In particular, if the neo-Austrian approach is used for analytical rather than simulation work, variables and equations soon accumulate.
- For simulation purposes, the approach is rather 'data hungry'. There are many coefficients that need numerical form, and establishing these can be demanding.

However, we feel the benefits of the method far outweigh its costs, and see it as a useful and intuitively appealing approach to modelling human-nature interactions.

NOTES

1. We are grateful to Ralph Winkler for critical comments.
2. We confine ourselves in the following to areas that are directly relevant to ecological economics. For relationships to dynamic games with macroeconomic investment, see Böge et al. (1982) and Faber (1986, Chapters 13–16).

REFERENCES

Barnett, H. and C. Morse (1963), *Scarcity and Growth: The Economics of Resource Scarcity*, Baltimore MD: Johns Hopkins University Press.

Baumgärtner, S., H. Dyckhoff, M. Faber, J. Proops and J. Schiller, (2001), 'The concept of joint production and ecological economics', *Ecological Economics*, **36**, 365–72.

Bernholz, P. (1971), 'Superiority of roundabout processes and positive rate of interest: a simple model of capital and growth', *Kyklos*, **24**, 687–721.

Böge, W., M. Faber and W. Güth (1982), 'A dynamic game with macroeconomic investment decisions under alternative market structures', in M. Deistler, E. Fürst and G. Schwödiauer (eds), *Games, Economic Dynamics, and Time Series Analysis*, Vienna: Physica-Verlag, pp. 227–50.

Crosby, A. (1986), *Ecological Imperialism*, Cambridge: Cambridge University Press.

Dasgupta, P.G. and G.M. Heal (1979), *Economic Theory and Exhaustible Resources*, Cambridge: Cambridge University Press.

Faber, M. (1979), *Introduction to Modern Austrian Capital Theory*, Heidelberg: Springer-Verlag.

Faber, M. (ed.) (1986), *Studies in Austrian Capital Theory*, Heidelberg: Springer-Verlag.

Faber, M. and G. Wagenhals (1988), 'Towards a long-run balance between economic and environmental protection', in W. Salomons and U. Förstner (eds), *Environmental Impact and Management of Mine Tailings and Dredged Materials*, Heidelberg: Springer-Verlag.

Faber, M. and J. Proops (1991a), 'The innovation of techniques and the time-horizon: a neo-Austrian approach', *Structural Change and Economic Dynamics*, **2**, 143–58.

Faber, M. and J. Proops (1991b), 'National accounting, time and the environment', in R. Costanza (ed.), *Ecological Economics: The Science and Management of Sustainability*, New York: Columbia University Press, pp. 215–33.

Faber, M. and J. Proops (1993), 'Natural resource rents, economic dynamics and structural change: a capital theoretic approach', *Ecological Economics*, **8**, 17–44.

Faber, M. and J. Proops (with R. Manstetten) (1998), *Evolution, Time, Production and the Environment*, 3rd edn, Heidelberg: Springer-Verlag.

Faber, M., H. Niemes and G. Stephan (1983), *Umweltschutz und Input-Output-Analyse. Mit zwei Fallstudien aus der Wassergütewirtschaft*, Tübingen: Mohr (Paul Siebeck).

Faber, M., J. Proops, M. Ruth and P. Michaelis (1990), 'Economy-environment interactions in the long-run: a neo-Austrian approach', *Ecological Economics*, **2**, 27–55.

Faber, M., H. Niemes and G. Stephan (1995), *Entropy, Environment and Resources: An Essay in Physico-Economics*, 2nd edn, Heidelberg: Springer-Verlag.

Faber, M., J. Proops and S. Baumgärtner (1998), 'All production is joint production: a thermodynamic analysis', in S. Faucheux, J. Gowdy and I. Nicolaï (eds), *Sustainability and Firms: Technological Change and the Changing Regulatory Environment*, Cheltenham: Edward Elgar, pp. 131–58.

Faber, M., J. Proops and S. Speck (with F. Jöst) (1999), *Capital and Time in Ecological Economics: Neo-Austrian Modelling*, Cheltenham: Edward Elgar.

Hicks, J. (1965), *Capital and Growth*, Oxford: Oxford University Press.

Hicks, J. (1970), 'A neo-Austrian growth theory', *Economic Journal*, **80**, 257–81.

Hicks, J. (1973), *Capital and Time: A Neo-Austrian Theory*, Oxford: Oxford University Press.

Jöst, F. (1994), *Klimaänderungen, Rohstoffknappheit und wirtschaftliche Entwicklung. Ein neo-Östereichisches Zwei-Regionen Modell*, Heidelberg: Physica-Verlag.

Koopmans, T. (1951), 'Analysis of production as an efficient combination of activities', in T. Koopmans, (ed.), *Activity Analysis of Production and Allocation*, New York: Wiley, pp. 33–97.

Proops, J. (2004), 'The growth and distributional consequences of international trade in natural resources and capital goods: a neo-Austrian analysis', *Ecological Economics*, **48**, 83–91.

Proops, J. and S. Speck (1996), A comparison of neoclassical and neo-Austrian growth models, *Structural Change and Economic Dynamics*, 7, 172–92.

Schumpeter, J. (1954), *History of Economic Analysis*, London: George, Allen and Unwin.

Speck, S. (1997), 'A neo-Austrian five process model with resource extraction and pollution abatement', *Ecological Economics*, **21**, 91–103.

Stephan, G. (1995), *Introduction into Capital Theory*, Heidelberg: Springer-Verlag.

5.   Entropy in Ecological Economics

Kozo Mayumi and Mario Giampietro

5.1 INTRODUCTION

The concept of entropy can often be found in scientific discussions about the sustainability of human progress and this explains its popularity in the literature of ecological economics. The concept of entropy entails acknowledging the unavoidable existence of limits on both what can be achieved by technology and what can be known by scientific inquiry due to 'entropic indeterminacy'. Having said that, however, it should be noted that there is a dialectical penumbra concerning the interpretation of how such a concept can be used in practical applications. This chapter offers a critical appraisal of the usefulness of the entropy concept for better structuring the discussion of the sustainability of human development.

The remainder of this chapter is structured as follows. Section 5.2 gives an historical overview and interpretation of the entropy concept, while Section 5.3 reviews some applications of the entropy concept in ecological economics and ecosystem analysis. Section 5.4 extends the entropy concept to embrace Prigogine's scheme, involving nested hierarchical systems, and Section 5.5 offers some conclusions.

5.2 AN HISTORICAL OVERVIEW OF THE INTERPRETATION OF 'ENTROPY'

Originally the concept of entropy occurred, even if in implicit form, when dealing with qualitative aspects of energy transformations within thermal engines. Sadi Carnot (in *Reflections on the Motive Power of Fire*, 1824) proposed the existence of a set of predictable relations between the work produced by a steam engine and the characteristics of the heat transfer associated with its operation. Émile Clapeyron, in 1834, restated Carnot's principle in analytical form (Mendoza, 1960).

In 1854, in his fourth memoir, Clausius almost reached the entropy law: he stated (Clausius, 1867, p. 129):

... the equation $[\oint dQ/T = 0]$ is the analytical representation, for all *reversible cyclical processes*, of the second fundamental theorem in the mechanical theory of heat.

In 1862, in his sixth memoir, Clausius explained the physical meaning of the magnitude 'S'. However, it was in 1865, in his ninth memoir, that he proposed to call this magnitude 'entropy'. Details on this historical birth process of the term entropy are important, since they show that the concept of entropy was alien to the prevailing mechanistic epistemology at that time. Clausius restated both the First Law of Thermodynamics ('the energy of the universe is constant') and the Second Law ('the entropy of the universe tends to a maximum'), assuming 'the universe' to be an isolated system (Clausius, 1867, p. 365).

At this point, it is useful to note a general misunderstanding of William Thomson's (later Lord Kelvin) idea of the 'heat death' of the universe. This idea was not based on a 'deep' interpretation of the second law of thermodynamics, i.e., the entropy law. Rather, Thomson (1882), by perusing several of his own papers, mistakenly concluded that the sun was created due to the collision and fusion of small objects, such as meteorites and that, therefore, the source of energy in the universe (which was all coming from solar energy) was essentially gravitational potential energy. Thus, in Thomson's mistaken view, heat death merely reflects the dissipation of solar energy in the universe using this gravitational potential energy. But this was equivalent to assuming that the sum of these two energy forms was a constant. In the final analysis, his interpretation more reflects the implications of the First Law of thermodynamics, rather than the Second Law.

Utilizing the development of the kinetic theory of gases (in particular, Maxwell's theory of transport) Boltzmann discovered a quantity called H, which can be identified with the negative of the entropy, based on molecular chaos and probability (Boltzmann, 1964). However, due to an apparent contradiction between the law of increasing entropy and the principles of Newtonian mechanics (a problem raised at that time by several eminent theorists such as Loschmidt (1876) and Zermelo (1896)), Boltzmann tried to search for a new interpretation of his H-theorem. During this process, Boltzmann finally equated the increase in entropy with the statement that the probability of the state of the system of particles must constantly increase. He formulated the equation as:

$$S = k \log W = -kH \tag{5.1}$$

where S is entropy, k is now called the Boltzmann constant, and W represents the number of ways particles can be arranged in a given state, while keeping the total energy constant. Boltzmann himself acknowledged that the H-theorem and the entropy law are 'only theorems of probability [that] can never be proved mathematically by means of the equations of dynamics alone' (Boltzmann, 1895). In fact, when adopting Boltzmann's ideas, the distinction between ontology and epistemology is blurred. That is, this additional interpretation of the concept opened an unfortunate door that could be used to relate the concept of entropy to that of 'information' and 'ignorance'. Shannon was, in part, responsible for this additional confusion, when he introduced yet another definition of entropy, related to the characterization of communication channels with noise (Shannon and Weaver, 1964, originally published in 1948 by Shannon). He proposed the name 'entropy of an information source'. For this purpose, Shannon considered two different concepts:

a. the number of messages to be transmitted; and
b. the capacity of a communication channel, as if they were equivalent.

Then he called the resulting generalization of these two concepts 'information'.

Even though thermal engines with friction and communication channels with noise have very little in common, the confusion about the concept of 'thermo-entropy' and the concept of 'information-entropy' was reinforced by the fact that the index of uncertainty proposed by Shannon is formally isomorphic with the equation provided by Boltzmann. Since then, the unfortunate and misleading 'isomorphism' between negative entropy in information science and the statistical interpretation of thermodynamics entropy by Boltzmann was further reinforced by the work of Szilard (1929), Jaynes (1957), and Brilllouin (1951a, 1951b, 1953, 1962). For more on this alleged equivalence, see Mayumi (1997).

In conclusion, in the first century of its life various meanings were attached to the concept of entropy by different 'users'. Perhaps due to the predominant addiction to formalism, and because of the obvious ambiguity of the term, the label entropy became associated with non-equivalent concepts such as 'irreversibility', 'arrow of time', 'expected trends toward disorder', 'expected directional changes in the quality of energy forms' and 'quantitative assessments of information flows among communicating systems'. All of these concepts were associated with sometimes misleading and confusing formal definitions of entropy (for details, see Proops, 1987). However, there has been a common connotation associated with the label entropy until the first half of the twentieth century. The concept of entropy (no matter how defined) was always associated with a clear 'prophet-of-doom' flavour. The universe is condemned to heat-death, disorder will prevail, irreversibility and friction are the unavoidable bad guys that are here to disturb the beautiful order of our universe and the work of scientists.

The innate ambiguity about the concept of entropy, however, is so pervasive that it even made it possible to overcome this negative connotation. A dramatic change in the perception of the role of entropy in the evolution of life arrived, in fact, in the second half of the twentieth century. This turn was initiated by the ideas of surplus entropy disposal by Schrödinger (1967, in an added note to Chapter 6 of *What is Life* in 1945) and then by the work of the Prigogine school of non-equilibrium thermodynamics (Prigogine, 1961; Glansdorf and Prigogine, 1971; Nicolis and Prigogine, 1977; Prigogine, 1978; Prigogine and Stengers, 1984). With the introduction of the class of dissipative systems, the concept of entropy finally emerged from the original role of the 'villain'. Self-organization and emergence are both strictly associated with the ability to export surplus entropy generated within the system into the environment. Schneider and Kay (1994) reformulated the Second Law and suggested that 'as systems are moved away from equilibrium they will take advantage of all available means to resist externally applied gradients'. Actually, looking at the evolution of biological systems, Brooks and Wiley (1988) came to see *Evolution as Entropy* (as stated in the title of their famous book). For an expert in thermodynamics, such a title can appear as an insult, because entropy is a state function in classical thermodynamics! But this is the 'magic' of entropy, as it were. First of all, in their book, Brooks and Wiley used a definition of entropy derived from information theory; secondly, they explored new frontiers (looking for new meanings) associated with the paradigm shift about how to perceive evolution. In this task, the ambiguity of the term might have been a blessing for them. In fact, after having accepted that irreversibility and friction are no longer the bad guys, the information entropy concept within their framework became the essential element which sustains and drives the evolution of the complex organization of dissipative systems.

All of this confusion about the possible proper use of the notion of entropy generated a bifurcation in the use of this concept to discuss the future of human progress. Those working within a thermodynamic framework, using an analytical tool kit developed for the analysis of isolated thermodynamic systems, tend to focus on death and decay. Those working within information theory, and in relation to open adaptive systems, tend to point to a forced process of emergence and renewal. Reflecting this deep polarization, some scientists suggest that potential improvements in the ability to handle information (more knowledge) will make humans able to reduce the requirement of energy and other environmental services for societal metabolism (i.e., the myth of dematerialization of developed society). This is the position of neoclassical economists and technological optimists – the so called 'cornucopians'. However, other scientists, such as Georgescu-Roegen, challenged these ideas by using the concept of entropy in the traditional way. That is, to say that the perpetual motion preached by the neoclassical gospel (e.g., full substitutability of limiting production factors) is a myth.

At this point we must be reminded that the entropy concept in classical thermodynamics 'applies only to an isolated system as a whole' (Georgescu-Roegen, 1971). For example, the famous formulation of maximum work done by a system in an external medium (Landau and Lifshitz, 1980) could not have been successful if the system as a whole (the medium together with the system) were not considered to be an isolated one. In fact, Prigogine himself admits the Gibbs formula extended to non-equilibrium thermodynamics has not been validated (Prigogine, 1961). This implies that nobody thus far has proved that entropy in an isolated system is identical to 'entropy' in non-equilibrium thermodynamics. So, without a proper insulated boundary, even the concept of entropy in classical thermodynamics might not be applicable to any real situations, let alone to other domains including social and ecosystem phenomena.

The point we want to make in this chapter is that in all of the discussions about sustainability of human progress, the concept of entropy has always been used in a metaphorical way. We use here the definition of metaphor suggested by Rosen (1985, Section 3.6). According to his idea, in a modelling relation, two models are metaphorically related if there is a functional 'dictionary' (a kind of semantic homomorphism), through which the properties of one of the two models can be translated into corresponding properties of the other in general terms. This implies that the validity of the analogy between the two models has to be checked in semantic terms. Such a validity check cannot be performed in syntactic (e.g., using a formal system of inference or algorithms) terms.

For example, open systems are considered to be a useful metaphor for studying and representing biological development processes. That is, the metaphor of metabolic systems entails that a known pattern of dissipation can be associated with a given identity for the dissipative system. In turn, this identity can be associated with a mechanism of self-organization and an expected set of favourable boundary conditions. General principles can be applied to the behaviour of dissipative systems. When a metaphor is valid, then it becomes possible to extrapolate the validity of a given principle or a perceived relation of causality (proved with direct measurement within a given context in relation to a modelling relation), referring to a given typology of dissipative system to different typologies of dissipative systems (operating in a different context and requiring a different formal model and about which it is not possible to perform 'a direct experimental check'). For example, we can say that a dissipative system that is operating at the maximum of its dissipation rate (be it a worker providing maximum effort or a car running at maximum speed) will consume its typical energy input at a rate higher than the average. (The validation obtained with a model based on food consumption, will make it possible to make inferences about a model based on gasoline consumption.)

To make things more difficult, nobody seems to be concerned with the epistemological foundations associated with an operationalization of the concept of entropy, and this generates an additional complication. The discussion over the metaphorical message implied by such a concept is often based on contrasting applications derived from:

a. assessments of quality of energy exchanges among dissipative systems (a thermodynamic interpretation of entropy); and/or
b. assessments based on an analysis of evolutionary trends of systems processing and exchanging information (an interpretation of entropy related to information theory).

In this situation, it is impossible to reach an agreement on what the 'entropic metaphor' means, without carefully checking whether or not the two non-equivalent ways of representing reality using the same label 'entropy' are reducible to each other.

The rest of this chapter provides an overview of works based on the concept of entropy in the literature of ecological economics and discusses the impossibility of applying, in formal terms, Prigogine's scheme to a nested hierarchical system, due to the epistemological predicament of complexity.

5.3 THE USE OF THE CONCEPT OF ENTROPY IN ECOLOGICAL ECONOMICS AND ECOSYSTEM ANALYSIS

It is natural to start this section with the two pioneers in the field of ecological economics: Nicholas Georgescu-Roegen and Kenneth Boulding. Georgescu-Roegen's bioeconomics paid special attention to the human mode of exosomatic evolution and its consequence of human addiction to growing levels of consumption of energy and mineral resources (Georgescu-Roegen, 1971, 1976). According to his vision, scarcity of mineral resources, as well as energy shortage in view of entropy law, ultimately sets a limit on the survival of the human species on this planet. Due to the fact that the earth is closed with respect to matter and that there are present technological limitations of the direct use of solar energy, he emphasized the importance of mineral resources in production processes, leading him to propose a 'Fourth Law of Thermodynamics': complete recycling is impossible.

In general, Georgescu-Roegen put more emphasis on the 'input side', as it were. On the other hand, it should be noted that Boulding was the first economist to predict the importance of waste material management (i.e., high entropy waste management) in view of joint production: 'Oddly enough, it seems to be in pollution rather than in exhaustion that the problem is first becoming salient' (Boulding, 1975, p. 12). Concerning the importance of mineral resources, Boulding (1975, p. 7) once stated that there 'is, fortunately, no law of increasing material entropy'. However, Boulding finally recognized the importance of mineral resources and stated: '[the] exhaustion of concentrated materials in the form of ores may turn out in the long run to be a more intractable problem than that of energy' (Boulding, 1978, p. 295). These two giants' works stimulated further research into several different but related directions.

5.3.1   Entropy Law and its Relevance to Scarcity of Exhaustible Natural Resources in Economic Modelling

As Amir (1994, p. 126) aptly remarked, 'the question of whether or not it is necessary to include explicitly the laws of thermodynamics in economic theory in general, and the theory of natural resource use in particular, has not been yet resolved'. Within this debate (Burness et al., 1980; van Gool and Bruggink, 1985; Daly, 1986; Khalil, 1990; Giampietro and Pimentel, 1991; Lozada, 1991; Young, 1991; Daly, 1992; Townsend, 1992; Rebane, 1995; Lawn, 1999; see also Daly, 1997) there are many issues raised among researchers:

a. whether or not technological progress will succeed in replacing fossil fuels by direct use of solar energy;
b. whether or not entropy imposes a long-run, absolute scarcity which technological change, resource substitution, and exploration cannot reverse;
c. whether or not the entropy law helps us to understand the nature and necessity of the constraint on economic scale and growth;
d. whether or not the entropy law offers an alternative principle of evaluation that substitute for markets;
e. whether or not technology is subject to the entropy law; and
f. considering the inevitable loss of matter and energy due to the entropy law, what would be the final goal of technological development?

5.3.2 The Debate on Georgescu-Roegen's Fourth Law of Thermodynamics

Georgescu-Roegen defines perpetual motion of the 'third kind' as a closed thermodynamic system that can perform work at a constant rate *forever*, or that can perform *forever* work between its subsystems. He then claims that perpetual motion of the 'third kind' is impossible. This claim has generated an intense debate in the field of ecological economics (Bianciardi et al., 1993; Kümmel, 1994; Månsson, 1994; Bianciardi et al., 1996; Converse, 1996, 1997; Ayres, 1999; Craig, 2001; Kåberger and Månsson, 2001). In fact, if the theoretical framework of thermodynamics is strictly followed, it is relatively easy to reach the following result: it is *possible* to construct a *closed* engine which will work in a complete cycle, and produce no effect except the raising of a weight, the cooling of a heat-reservoir at a higher temperature, and the warming of a heat-reservoir at a lower temperature (Mayumi, 1993). In short, this closed system is nothing but a Carnot engine.

The Carnot engine with its fluid is indeed a closed system, because heat can be exchanged during two isothermal processes (expansion and compression) through the base of the cylinder. However, the Carnot engine is a ideal type of engine. In reality, any working engine is an individual realization of such a type, which will have 'special' differences from the general template used for its construction. These differences are due to specific characteristics of lower level components (the material structure) and stochastic events associated with the history of such an organized structure. This is why 'material entropy' is critically important for our ecological salvation, even though we share the view of critics of the 'Fourth Law' that it is impossible to write a general 'material entropy formula' proving the impossibility of full recycling. Again, this is a statement that for now can be validated by a semantic check, but not proved by a formal theorem.

The main point of Georgescu-Roegen is that energy is represented in models as a homogeneous substance and, according to these models, energy conversions from one form into another can be easily accomplished, according to the laws included in the model. On the other hand, when looking at the same transformations in terms of matter, we always find that material elements are highly heterogeneous and every element has some unique physicochemical properties. This feature of matter explains the reason that the practical procedures for unmixing liquids or solids differ from case to case and consist of many complicated steps. Seemingly, the only possible way of reaching a quantitative measure of material entropy is to calculate indirectly the amounts of matter and energy for returning to the initial state of matter in bulk in question given the available technology. The proper initial state of matter in bulk is deeply related to our multi-dimensional value system: to what state should the degraded matter should be transformed? Further, Georgescu-Roegen states:

a. because matter in bulk and energy are not convertible into each other, without considering the overall availability of energy and mineral resources; and
b. because of the unavoidable uncertainty about future technological coefficients and critical ecological thresholds,

it is impossible to judge which equivalent recovering technology (e.g., one with more energy and less matter, or the one with less energy and more matter) is ecologically preferable.

Bridgman (1961) seems to support Georgescu-Roegen's view: 'the energy concept has no meaning apart from a corresponding process. One cannot speak of the equivalence of the energy of mass and radiation unless there is some process (not necessarily reversible) by which one can get from mass to radiation' (Bridgman, 1961, p. 94). Although dissipation of matter is included in the second law, dissipation of matter 'in principle, can be avoided at the cost of increased energy input and heat production. This is in turn may become forbiddingly high, if one would try to recollect even the last atom' (Kümmel, 1994, p. 195). Kümmel's argument would suggest a possible use of the entropy concept as a pollution indicator, due to the nature of joint production required by thermodynamic principles (Boulding, 1978; Faber et al., 1983; Kümmel, 1989; Baumgärtner et al., 2001).

5.3.3 Can We Define Sustainability of Ecological Systems Using Physically Measurable Evidence?

This question was formulated in these terms by Hannon et al. (1993). For this issue, the Japanese physicist Tsuchida gave a convincing argument in the 1970s (e.g., Tsuchida and Murota, 1987). There are two categories of open steady-state systems (an analytical definition of the second category is yet to be made). Heat flow, electric current and water flow are examples of systems belonging to the first category. These systems are not in equilibrium as a whole. Nevertheless, it is possible to study these systems as if they were at a type of equilibrium (i.e., local equilibrium). The open steady-state systems of the first category have been investigated extensively by the Prigogine school. If the steady-state of a system occurs sufficiently close to an equilibrium state, it may be characterized by the principle of minimum entropy production: the entropy production has local minimum value at steady state. However, this principle is subject to severe restrictions, because it is valid in the range of linear thermodynamics of irreversible processes and because the phenomenological coefficients may be considered as constants satisfying the Onsager relations (e.g., Prigogine, 1961).

However, it is not sure whether or not the principle of minimum entropy production can be applied to the study of the entire domain of biological systems. On the contrary, a living thing is really a big entropy production factory, as it were. At room temperature, glucose is very stable and is not oxidized easily but, in a living thing, glucose is oxidized very easily. It turns out that the idea of a steady-state system of the first category and the principle of minimum entropy production are not powerful tools for studies in biology.

Another clue to the study of life concerns cycles in a living system. After a complete cyclic process, it is necessary to dispose of the entropy generated within the system into a larger system that contains the original system as a part. Without the ability of entropy disposal, a living system cannot maintain a steady state. Therefore, there must be harmonious connections among subsystems in order to dispose of entropy which ultimately belongs outside those subsystems. An open steady-state system with these characteristics can be termed as of the second category (Mayumi, 2001, p. 50).

Now, it is possible to see how the earth disposes of thermal entropy generated within its system and the essential role played by land in thermal entropy disposal. Air convection and the water cycle constitute an atmospheric heat engine, which guarantees the existence of life on earth by continually discarding entropy into outer space. Within this heat engine, water and air circulate between the surface area of the earth (15C on average) and the air at high altitudes (–18C). Roughly, thermal entropy generated after various activities on the earth is discarded annually at a rate of 34.6 cal/deg C/cm^2.

The low temperature of the upper atmosphere (–18C), created by the adiabatic expansion of the air, is also important. It is possible to dispose of more of the thermal entropy of radiation of the same quantity of heat at a lower temperature than at a higher temperature. In addition, at about –18C, the vapour pressure is sufficiently low, and the air is so dry, that sunlight can pass easily through the atmosphere. Water cycles emerge due to the asymmetry of the atmosphere. This asymmetry is created by the fact that the molecular weight of water vapour is 18, while the average molecular weight of air is 29. This difference in molecular weight creates an air pump, as it were, to lift water vapour to the upper atmosphere against gravity. If the earth's primitive atmosphere had consisted mainly of methane CH_4 (molecular weight 16) instead of carbon dioxide, neither asymmetry nor life would have been possible. Through the operation of water cycles created by the earth's primitive atmosphere, living things on the earth can dispose of heat entropy. A nested hierarchical structural model of an open steady-state system of the second category can be used to illustrate how, on earth, entropy is effectively disposed of.

In conclusion, to maintain the steady state, an open steady-state system of the second category must be contained in a larger open steady-state system also of the second category. Plants use sunlight to produce glucose. Entropy generated in a plant is discarded mainly by the evaporation of water from leaves. Activities of animals are accompanied by the production of waste heat and matter. This heat entropy is disposed of ultimately by water cycles and air convection. When organic wastes, excreta and dead matter from the grazing food chain are decomposed, water again plays a vital role in the disposal of thermal entropy generated during the related process of decomposition.

Water cycles are both outside and inside the food chain. There is a heat radiation system outside of water cycles. In this way, entropy produced at each stage in the system of the earth is passed to a larger system, which contains the original system. Soil and sea are contact points, so to speak, with the water cycle and the food chain. Soil is composed of inorganic minerals as well as humus. Humus transforms ultimately 'material entropy' (detritus) into 'heat entropy'. Without sufficient moisture, soil cannot dispose of entropy, as there is no humus in the soil; this is a typical situation in the desert. As far as matter is concerned, the earth is virtually a closed system in the sense of classical thermodynamics. Because the earth is a closed system, special types of matter (i.e., air and water) are not dispersed and lost to outer space due to gravity, so that air and water keep the earth in a quasi-steady state by continual thermal entropy disposal. Therefore, matter (air and water) matters, too, in this special sense. While Georgescu-Roegen emphasizes the importance of matter *in general*, he may not sufficiently have appreciated the significance of special substances, such as air and water, and the key role of the gravitational field for maintaining the quasi-steady state.

5.3.4 Possible Use of Innovative Concepts Developed in Non-Equilibrium Thermodynamics

The work begun by Prigogine's school of non-equilibrium thermodynamics and self-organization can be used to enrich our understanding of the self-organization of human society, especially in relation to the issue of compatibility with natural resources and environmental constraints (O'Connor, 1991; Binswanger, 1993), or to the analysis of the self-organization of ecosystem development (Kay and Schneider, 1992; Kay, 2000).

In relation to the former issue, non-equilibrium thermodynamics perspectives furnish a rich impetus for a co-evolutionary vision in ecological economics (cf. Chapter 2). It focuses on critical issues, such as the fuzzy boundary between the economic process and the environment, and the time-indeterminacies associated with the forecasting of the evolutionary trajectories of the complex economy-environment. The use of the concept of entropy in this framework, however, does not do away with the need for a complementary analysis of institutional and ethical dimensions of human action in their own right.

In relation to the second direction of research, there are several interesting works in ecosystem development and ecosystem health. Schneider and Kay (1994) introduced 'the restated Second Law' as: 'ecosystems will develop structures and functions selected to most effectively dissipate the gradients imposed on them while allowing for the continued existence of the ecosystem' (Schneider and Kay, 1994, p. 26.). They were forced to admit the difficulty in defining entropy and entropy production in non-equilibrium systems, a difficulty which is reflected in an unavoidable ambiguity in the meaning of the expression 'gradients'. Schneider and Kay aptly remarked that the Second Law – as restated by them – is a necessary but not a sufficient condition for life. They stated that 'ecosystems develop in a way which systematically increase their ability to degrade the incoming solar energy' (Schneider and Kay, 1994, p. 38).

A similar view of the direction of ecosystem evolution had already been presented under a different guise, by the energetic analysis of Lotka and its re-interpretation by Odum. We refer to Lotka's maximum energy flux (Lotka, 1922) and Odum's maximum power principle (Odum and Pinkerton, 1955, elaborated further in Odum, 1996). There is another important line of research by R. Ulanowicz, concerning the growth and development of natural communities (Ulanowicz, 1980, 1997), based on the application of thermodynamics to networks. According to Ulanowicz, 'a knowledge of the flow structure within a natural community is assumed to be sufficient to describe the behavior of far-from-equilibrium, self-organizing systems' (Ulanowicz, 1980, p.223). Using information theoretic considerations of network structures, he introduces an index of ecosystem growth and development and terms it *ascendency*. In this way he tries to quantify those factors that help constraints flows along certain preferred pathways within an ecosystem. Ascendency can be interpreted as 'the average degree of unambiguity with which an arbitrary compartment communicates with any other compartment in the system' (Ulanowicz, 1980).

5.3.5 Additional Stretching of the Concept of Entropy to the Issue of Sustainable Development

It is possible to find a considerable number of papers in the literature, which try to relate the concept of entropy to the discussion of sustainability and issues such as information, knowledge, and evolution (e.g., Wicken, 1980; Wiley and Brooks, 1982; Brooks and Wiley, 1988; Bailey, 1990; Ayres, 1994; Ruth, 1995). Obviously, it is possible to find in this category a few attempts stretching the concept of entropy far beyond the permissible range of applications to a proper use of non-equilibrium thermodynamics. Interesting examples of such a search for metaphors are provided by the mentioned book of Brooks and Wiley (1988) and the book of the sociologist Bailey, where he presents his 'social entropy theory' (Bailey, 1990).

5.4 PRIGOGINE'S SCHEME AND NESTED HIERARCHICAL SYSTEMS

In this section we investigate the epistemological impasse related to the parallel representation of entropy changes, which are perceived as occurring simultaneously on various hierarchical levels (and therefore perceived and represented in parallel on different space-time scales), using the well known scheme of Prigogine. This epistemological impasse is deeply related to the impossibility of handling the complex nature of time in a formal way (Rosen, 1985).

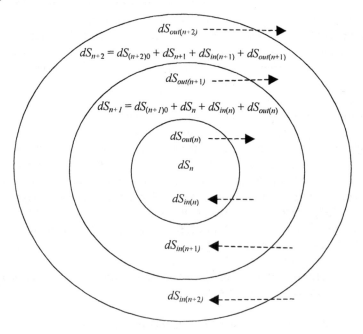

Figure 5.1   Prigogine's scheme applied to a nested hierarchical system

Suppose there are three open steady-state systems, which are nested and hierarchically organized, and that system i is contained in system $(i+1)$. This is shown in Figure 5.1. Both, the process of entropy production and the process of entropy exchange, operate simultaneously in the nested system. However, for the sake of simplicity, assume that entropy exchange with its larger nested level occurs first, and entropy production follows. Since the steady state is characterized by no net change in entropy, introducing the amount of entropy production dS_i within system i gives:

$$dS_{out(i)} = dS_i + dS_{in(i)}. \tag{5.2}$$

$dS_{(i+1)}$ includes dS_i, $dS_{in(i)}$, $dS_{out(i)}$, and entropy production $dS_{(i+1)0}$ generated within system $(i+1)$, but does not include entropy production in system i. Thus:

$$dS_{i+1} = dS_{(i+1)0} + dS_i + dS_{in(i)} + dS_{out(i)}. \tag{5.3}$$

From (5.2) and (5.3):

$$dS_{out(i+1)} - dS_{in(i+1)} = dS_{(i+1)0} + dS_i + dS_{in(i)} + dS_{out(i)}, \tag{5.4}$$

and

$$dS_{out(n)} - dS_{in(n)} = dS_n. \tag{5.5}$$

Here, equation (5.5) is the ordinary relationship characterizing a steady state for system n: the sum of entropy production and entropy exchange is zero. Equation (5.4) is characteristic of the nested hierarchical system. System $(i+1)$ has to dispose of entropy production $dS_{(i+1)0}$ and entropy exchange $dS_{in(i+1)} - dS_{out(i+1)}$. In addition, system $(i+1)$ has to have an *ability* to dispose of entropy production dS_i and entropy exchange $dS_{in(i)} + dS_{out(i)}$.

After having proceeded in a formal way to apply Prigogine's scheme to a nested hierarchical system, several evident problems can be immediately detected even by a cursory look at Figure 5.1.

Figure 5.1 must have (at least) two parallel non-equivalent mappings of entropy production and entropy exchange on different interfaces belonging to different hierarchical levels. One mapping is a view from within system n, which is a black box, as it were, unknown to us unless we would draw another interface (or boundary) within system n. The other mapping is from the outside of system n, related to the compatibility of the behaviour within system n (a black box) with its environment, including system $(n+1)$ and system $(n+2)$. According to Georgescu-Roegen (1971, p. 214):

> ... by deciding to identify a process by its boundary we have implicitly given up any thought of [analytically] describing what happens within that boundary, that is, inside the process. Should we wish to learn something about what happens inside, we must draw *another* boundary across the process and thus divide it into *two* processes to be studied separately. These processes could not have been part of our analytical picture before the new boundary was drawn because of the simple principle 'no boundary, no process'.

It is important to observer that by 'boundary' Georgescu-Roegen meant two elements:

a. the frontier of the process; and
b. the duration of the process.

The concept of duration has to do with the definition of the relation between a time differential (the smallest time duration that makes it possible, for the experimental setting, to detect a 'before' and an 'after'), and a time horizon for which the model makes sense (the larger time duration that makes possible to hold the hypothesis of quasi-steady state, that is ignoring the unavoidable process of 'becoming' of dissipative systems). Thus, every time we draw a boundary to investigate what happens within a black box, we have to deal with at least two processes separately, implying that we have to deal with two durations of each process:

a. the dynamics of processes occurring inside parts of the black box; and
b. the dynamics of processes occurring between the black box and its context.

Models referring to these two durations are not necessarily compatible with each other. In fact, the perception, representation and the measurement scheme related to each process will entail the definition of a specific time differential and time horizon. When dealing with the simultaneous analysis of processes across levels and scales, the definition of a time differential $(dt)_n$ at one level will become incompatible with the definition of a time differential $(dt)_{n+1}$ at an adjacent level. It is now obvious that the idea of being able to keep coherence in such a chain of formalizations across levels and scales is ludicrous.

To illuminate the difficulty in investigating what happens within a black box, let us consider an example from the thermodynamics of irreversibility. The entropy change within a thermodynamic system must be the same for the following two cases:

a. the system receives amount of heat Q irreversibly from a heat reservoir having higher temperature T_1; and
b. the system receives the same amount of heat Q reversibly from a heat reservoir having the same temperature T_2 ($T_2 < T_1$) as the system.

With this information, we can infer indirectly the amount of entropy production associated with the irreversible process; that is, the difference between entropy change in the system (Q/T_2) and entropy change in heat reservoir ($-Q/T_1$). So, to identify entropy production within the system is operationally difficult unless we have other information associated with entropy exchange occurring at the interface. However, to obtain information on entropy exchange occurring at interfaces poses another impasse when we try to apply Prigogine's scheme to any actual processes. For a relatively simple thermodynamic system, it is possible to control only those pathways through which we allow any entropy exchange with a larger system. However, in any real situations (e.g., that encountered in ecological systems), it is virtually impossible to identify entropy exchange, let alone entropy production.

This issue is related to the identification problem associated with a nested hierarchical system. That is, the identification of a given direction of causality in a nested hierarchical system is impossible, because this system operates on multiple scales and levels. For example, metaphorically speaking, the concept of 'consumer democracy' assumes that consumers determine what types of goods are to be produced in the future when choosing goods in the market. They provide an explanation to the question of *why* certain goods remain and others disappear. On the other hand, when looking at technical aspects of the production process, that is, *how* goods are produced, the selection of goods in the market can only be done *after* these goods are produced.

Coming back to Figure 5.1, as soon as we look for the simultaneous validity of all the formalizations of entropy entities in the figure, referring to non-equivalent sets of representation of events perceived on different hierarchical levels, it becomes clear that this task would require the simultaneous adoption of assumptions – associated with identities of elements and definition of space-time scales – which will result in inconsistencies.

In the situation represented in Figure 5.1, it is meaningless to look for a formal and substantive mechanism of accounting based on the concept of entropy (or exergy), or whatever other new thermodynamic function we want to introduce to address qualitative differences in energy flows. Qualitative differences of energy assessments are not 'substantive', as they always depend on the preliminary decision about how to perceive and characterize an autocatalytic loop across levels and scales. The behaviour of a loop within a thermodynamic system is said to be autocatalytic, a term borrowed from the field of chemistry that is equivalent to self-enhancing (Ulanowicz, 1997, p. 42). If we insist on looking to thermodynamic analysis to provide substantive quality assessment to energy forms, we simply keep trying to answer questions that cannot be answered.

For example, what do we mean, when we refer to the various triplets of 'entropies' shown in the nested chain in Figure 5.1, with internal entropy production? What 'entropic assessment' related characterization of the system do we have in mind (e.g., rate of change of entropy, rate of generation of entropy, rate of disposal of entropy)? Moreover, such an assessment should be related to which substantive definition of 'system'? So, what is 'the system' when dealing with a nested hierarchy of elements necessarily open on the top? How do we deal with the representation of the energy dissipation of individual elements in the middle? Should we be using a descriptive domain reflecting the perception and representation of events from within the black box, or a descriptive domain reflecting the perception and representation of events from its context? Moreover, the representation from the outside will be different for different contexts. As noted earlier, both non-equivalent representations are needed and relevant, but they are not reducible to each other, since they are based on different definitions of time and space. Finally, how should we decide about what are the relevant forms of energy to be included in, or neglected from, the accounting of interactions at different levels? Should we account for gravitational energy when accounting for the energy consumption of households living in coastal areas? Very few include such an input (except the Odum school), even though tides can represent relevant agents determining the characteristics of the admissible environment of these households.

5.5 CONCLUSION

It should be noted that the main message of the new paradigm entailed by complexity, is about the unavoidable existence of inherent incommensurability in the definition of terms and the set of identities assigned to nested hierarchical systems, operating across scales. In fact, these systems are 'becoming' in time, their identity being updated on different levels and scales, at different rates. This means that wholes, parts and their contexts, require for their analysis the parallel use of non-equivalent descriptive domains (representations of patterns on different scales and different selections of relevant attributes), which become obsolete at different paces (Giampietro, 2003).

This new paradigm of complexity is the child of the major revolution started with classical thermodynamics and continued by non-equilibrium thermodynamics. Both revolutions used the concept of entropy as a banner. In particular, the non-equilibrium paradigm represents a final departure from reductionist epistemology, since it implies accepting working with system-dependent and context-dependent definitions. For example, the concept of 'negative entropy' is not a substantive concept. Rather, this is a 'construction' (an artifact) entailed by the identity of a dissipative system operating at a given point in space and time. Negative entropy, in fact, reflects the perception and representation of 'quality', referring to both energy inputs and energy transformations, which are associated with a particular pattern of dissipation (or typology of metabolism) of a specific dissipative system, which is operating within a given context (an admissible environment). To put it in another way, food is an energy input for humans but not for cars. The definition of what should be considered 'useful energy' in ultimate analysis depends on the goals of the system operating within a given context. Fish are expected to operate and reproduce inside the water, whereas birds cannot fly below the ground. These can seem trivial observations, but it is not possible to define a 'substantive formalism' able to define qualitative aspects of energy forms applicable to all conceivable dissipative systems operating in reality, when considering all of the conceivable scales (from sub-atomic particles to galaxies) and the conceivable attributes that could result relevant for the analyst (observable qualities linked to relevant characteristics). Dissipative systems are:

a. open (they are what they eat) – and this blurs the distinction between system and environment across scales; and
b. becoming in time (they are all special because of their history) – and this requires a continuous updating of the set of types used to characterize them.

Classical thermodynamics first, and non-equilibrium thermodynamics later on, gave a fatal blow to the mechanistic Newtonian epistemology. However, we cannot replace the hole left by the collapse of Newtonian mechanistic epistemology just by using a set of new terms derived from non-equilibrium thermodynamics (e.g., disorder, information, entropy, negentropy) as if they were 'substantive' concepts (i.e., definable in a strictly physical sense as context-independent). We should always recall the caveat noted by Bridgman (1961, pp. 166–8):

> It is not easy to give a logically satisfying definition of what one would like to cover by 'disorder' ... Thermodynamics itself, I believe, must presuppose and can have meaning only in the context of a specified 'universe of operations', and any of the special concepts of thermodynamics, such as entropy, must also presuppose the same universe of operations.

This cannot be done in a universe in which not only the observed system is becoming in time, but also the observer is becoming something else. An observer with different goals, experience, fears and knowledge will never perceive and represent energy forms, energy transformations and associated quality indices in the same way as a previous observer. Entropy can be used as a very powerful metaphor, but like all metaphors, it always requires the implementation of semantic checks. That is, the entropy concept can be very useful when discussing how to share meaning about a problem structuring of sustainability issues, but should not be used to write optimizing protocols.

REFERENCES

Amir, S. (1994), 'The role of thermodynamics in the study of economics and ecological systems', *Ecological Economics*, **10** (2), 125–42.

Ayres, R.U. (1994), *Information, Entropy and Progress*, Woodbury NY: AIP Press.

Ayres, R.U. (1999), 'The second law, the fourth law, recycling and limits to growth', *Ecological Economics*, **29** (3), 473–83.

Bailey, K.D. (1990), *Social Entropy Theory*, Albany NY: State University of New York Press.

Baumgärtner, S., H. Dyckhoff, M. Faber, J. Proops and J. Schiller (2001), 'The concept of joint production and ecological economics', *Ecological Economics*, **36** (3), 365–72.

Bianciardi, C., E. Tiezzi and S. Ulgiati (1993), 'Complete recycling of matter in the frameworks of physics, biology and ecological economics', *Ecological Economics*, **8** (1), 1–5.

Bianciardi, C., E. Tiezzi and S. Ulgiati (1996), 'Response: The "recycle of matter" debate: physical principles versus practical impossibility', *Ecological Economics*, **19** (3), 195–6.

Binswanger, M. (1993), 'From microscopic to macroscopic theories: entropic aspects of ecological and economic processes', *Ecological Economics*, **8** (3), 209–34.

Boltzmann, L. (1895), 'On certain questions of the theory of gases', *Nature*, **51**, 413–15.

Boltzmann, L. (1964), *Lectures on Gas Theory*, Berkeley CA: University of California Press.

Boulding, K.E. (1975), 'The economics of the coming Spaceship Earth', in H. Jarrett (ed.), *Environmental Quality in a Growing Economy*, Baltimore MD: Johns Hopkins University Press, pp. 3–14.

Boulding, K.E. (1978), *Ecodynamics: A New Theory of Societal Evolution*, Beverly Hills CA: Sage Publications.

Bridgman, P. (1961), *The Nature of Thermodynamics*, New York: Harper.

Brillouin, L. (1951a), 'Maxwell's demon cannot operate: information and entropy I', *Journal of Applied Physics*, **22**, 334–7.

Brillouin, L. (1951b), 'Physical entropy and information theory II', *Journal of Applied Physics*, **22**, 338–43.

Brillouin, L. (1953), 'The negentropy principle of information', *Journal of Applied Physics*, **24**, 1152–63.

Brillouin, L. (1962), *Science and Information Theory* (Second edition), New York: Academic Press.

Brooks, D.R. and E.O. Wiley (1988), *Evolution as Entropy: Toward a Unified Theory of Biology*, 2nd edn, Chicago: University of Chicago Press.

Burness, S., R. Cummings, G. Morris and I. Paik (1980), 'Thermodynamic and economic concepts as related to resource-use policies', *Land Economics*, **56** (1), 1–9.

Clausius, R. (1867), *Mechanical Theory of Heat, with its Applications to the Steam-Engine and to the Physical Properties of Bodies* (ed. T.A. Hirst), London: John van Voorst.

Converse, A.O. (1996), 'On complete recycling', *Ecological Economics*, **19** (3), 193–4.

Converse, A.O. (1997), 'On complete recycling, 2', *Ecological Economics*, **20** (1), 1–2.

Craig, P.P. (2001), 'Energy limits on recycling', *Ecological Economics*, **36** (3), 373–84.

Daly, H. (1986), 'Thermodynamic and economic concepts as related to resource-use policies: comment', *Land Economics*, **63** (3), 319–28.

Daly, H. (1992), 'Is the entropy law relevant to the economics of natural resource scarcity? Yes, of course it is', *Journal of Environmental Economics and Management*, **23**, 91–5.

Daly, H. (ed.), (1997), *Ecological Economics*, Special Issue: The Contribution of Nicholas Georgescu-Roegen, **22** (3).

Faber, M., H. Niemes and G. Stephan (1983), *Entropy, Environment and Resources*, Berlin: Springer-Verlag.

Georgescu-Roegen, N. (1971), *The Entropy Law and the Economic Process*, Cambridge MA: Harvard University Press.

Georgescu-Roegen, N. (1976), *Energy and Economic Myths: Institutional and Analytical Economic Essays*, New York: Pergamon.

Giampietro, M. (2003), *Multi-Scale Integrated Analysis of Agroecosystems*, Boca Raton: CRC Press.

Giampietro, M. and D. Pimentel (1991), 'Energy efficiency: assessing the interaction between humans and their environment', *Ecological Economics*, **4** (2), 117–44.

Glansdorf, P. and I. Prigogine (1971), *Thermodynamics Theory of Structure, Stability and Fluctuations*, New York: Wiley.

Hannon, B., M. Ruth and E. Delucia (1993), 'A physical view of sustainability', *Ecological Economic*, **8** (3), 253–68.

Jaynes, E.T. (1957), 'Information theory and statistical mechanics', *Physical Review*, **106**, 620–30.

Kåberger, T. and B. Månsson (2001), 'Entropy and economic processes: physics perspective', *Ecological Economics*, **36** (1), 165–79.

Kay, J. (2000), 'Ecosystems as self-organizing holarchic open systems: narratives and the second law of thermodynamics', in S.E. Jorgensen and F. Muller (eds), *Handbook of Ecosystems Theories and Management*, London: Lewis Publishers, pp. 135–60.

Kay, J.J. and E.D. Schneider (1992), 'Thermodynamics and measures of ecosystem integrity', in *Ecological Indicators*, Volume 1, D.H. McKenzie, D.E. Hyatt and V.J. Mc Donald (eds), *Proceedings of the International Symposium on Ecological Indicators*, Fort Lauderdale FL: Elsevier, pp. 159–82.

Khalil, E. (1990), 'Entropy law and exhaustion of natural resources: is Nicholas Georgescu-Roegen's paradigm defensible?', *Ecological Economics*, **2** (2), 163–78.

Kümmel, R. (1989), 'Energy as a factor of production and entropy as a pollution indicator in macroeconomic modelling', *Ecological Economics*, **1** (2), 161–80.

Kümmel, R. (1994), 'Energy, entropy – economy, ecology', *Ecological Economics*, **9** (3), 194–6.

Landau, L.D. and E. Lifshitz (1980), *Statistical Physics* Volume 1, Oxford: Pergamon.

Lawn, P.A. (1999), 'On Georgescu-Roegen's contribution to ecological economics', *Ecological Economics*, **29** (1), 5–8.

Loschmidt, J. (1876), 'Über den Zustand des Wärmegleichgewichtes eines Systems von Körpern mit Rücksicht auf die Schwerkraft', *Sitzungberichte der K. Wiener Akademie*, **73**, 128–42.

Lotka, A.J. (1922), 'Contribution to the energetics of evolution', *Proceedings of the National Academy of Sciences*, **8**, 37–48.

Lozada, G.A. (1991), 'A defense of Nicholas Georgescu-Roegen's paradigm', *Ecological Economics*, **3** (2), 157–60.

Månsson, B. (1994), 'Recycling of matter', *Ecological Economics*, **9** (3), 191–2.

Mayumi, K. (1993), 'Georgescu-Roegen's "fourth law of thermodynamics", the modern energetic dogma, and ecological salvation', in L. Bonati, U. Cosentino, M. Lasagni, G. Moro, D. Pitea and A. Schiraldi (eds), *Trends in Ecological Physical Chemistry*, Amsterdam: Elsevier, pp. 351–64.

Mayumi, K. (1997), 'Information, pseudo measures and entropy: an elaboration on Nicholas Georgescu-Roegen's critique', *Ecological Economics*, **22** (3), 249–59.

Mayumi, K. (2001), *The Origins of Ecological Economics: The Bioeconomics of Georgescu-Roegen*, London: Routledge.

Mendoza, E. (ed.), (1960), *Reflections on the Motive Power of Fire by Sadi Carnot and Other Papers on the Second Law of Thermodynamics by É. Clapeyron and R. Clausius*, New York: Dover Publications.

Nicolis, G. and I. Prigogine (1977), *Self-Organization in Non-Equilibrium Systems*, New York: Wiley.

O'Connor, M. (1991), 'Entropy, structure, and organizational change', *Ecological Economics*, **3** (2), 95–122.

Odum, H.T. (1996), *Environmental Accounting. EMergy and Environmental Decision Making*, New York: Wiley.

Odum, H.T. and R.C. Pinkerton (1955), 'Time's speed regulator: the optimum efficiency for maximum power output in physical and biological systems', *American Scientist*, **43**, 321–43.

Prigogine, I. (1961), *Introduction to Thermodynamics of Irreversible Processes*, 2nd edn, New York: Wiley.

Prigogine, I. (1978), *From Being to Becoming*, San Francisco: W.H. Freeman.

Prigogine, I. and I. Stengers (1984), *Order Out of Chaos*, New York: Bantam Books.

Proops, J.L.R. (1987), 'Entropy, information and confusion in the social sciences', *The Journal of Interdisciplinary Economics*, **1**, 225–42.

Rebane, K.K. (1995), 'Energy, entropy, environment: why is protection of the environment objectively difficult?', *Ecological Economics*, **13** (2), 89–92.

Rosen, R. (1985), *Anticipatory Systems: Philosophical, Mathematical and Methodological Foundations*, New York: Pergamon.

Ruth, M. (1995), 'Information, order and knowledge in economic and ecological systems: implications for material and energy use', *Ecological Economics*, **13** (2), 99–114.

Schneider, E.D. and J.J. Kay (1994), 'Life as a manifestation of the second law of thermodynamics', *Mathematical and Computer Modelling*, **19**, 25–48.

Schrödinger, E. (1967), *What is Life, and Mind and Matter*, London: Cambridge University Press.

Shannon, C.E. and W. Weaver (1964), *The Mathematical Theory of Communication*, Urbana ILL: University of Illinois Press.

Szilard, L. (1929), 'Über die Entropieverminderung in einem thermodynamischen System bei Eingriffen intelligenter Wesen', *Zeitschrift für Physik*, **53**, 840–56.

Thomson, W. [Lord Kelvin] (1882), *Mathematical and Physical Papers of W. Thomson*, Volume 1, Cambridge: Cambridge University Press.

Townsend, K.N. (1992), 'Is the entropy law relevant to the economics of natural resource scarcity? Comment', *Journal of Environmental Economics and Management*, **23**, 96–100.

Tsuchida, A. and T. Murota (1987), 'Fundamentals in the entropy theory of ecocycle and human economy', in G. Pillet and T. Murota (eds), *Environmental Economics*, Geneva: R. Leimgruber, pp. 11–35.

Ulanowicz, R.E. (1980), 'An hypothesis on the development of natural communities'. *Journal of Theoretical Biology*, **85**, 223–45.

Ulanowicz, R.E. (1997), *Ecology, the Ascendent Perspective*, New York: Columbia University Press.

van Gool, W. and J.J.C. Bruggink (eds), (1985), *Energy and Time in the Economic and Physical Sciences*, Amsterdam: Elsevier.

Wicken, J.S. (1980), 'Thermodynamic theory of evolution', *Journal of Theoretical Biology*, **87**, 9–23.

Wiley, E.O. and D.R. Brooks (1982), 'Victims of history: a non-equilibrium approach to evolution', *Systemic Zoology*, **31** (1), 1–24.

Young, J.T. (1991), 'Is the entropy law relevant to the economics of natural resource scarcity?', *Journal of Environmental Economics and Management*, **21**, 169–79.

Zermelo, E. (1896), 'Über einen Satz der Dynamik und die mechanische Wärmetheorie', *Annalen der Physik und der Chemie*, **57**, 485–93.

6.   Thermodynamic Models

Stefan Baumgärtner

6.1 INTRODUCTION

Integrating methods and models from thermodynamics and from economics promises to yield encompassing insights into the nature of economy-environment interactions. The division of labour between thermodynamics and economics seems to be obvious. Thermodynamics should provide a description of human societies' physical environment, while economics should provide an analysis of optimal individual and social choice under environmental scarcities.

But the task is difficult. Being a branch of physics, thermodynamics is a natural science. It explains the world in a descriptive and causal, allegedly value-free manner. On the other hand, economics is a social science. While it pursues to a large extent descriptive and causal (so-called 'positive') explanations of social systems, it also has a considerable normative dimension. Valuation is one of its basic premises and purposes. Bringing together thermodynamics and economics in a common analytical framework therefore raises all kinds of questions, difficulties and pitfalls.

This chapter lays out the rationale, concepts, and caveats for developing and using thermodynamic models in ecological economics. Section 6.2 sketches the historical origins of this endeavour. Section 6.3 develops the fundamental rationale of employing thermodynamic concepts and models in ecological economics. Section 6.4 briefly introduces the elementary concepts and laws of thermodynamics. Section 6.5 gives an overview of different approaches to incorporating thermodynamic concepts into economic analysis, and assesses their respective potential for ecological economics. Section 6.6 surveys various implications and insights from thermodynamic models in ecological economics. Section 6.7 concludes by assessing the role of thermodynamics for ecological economics, and for the discussion of sustainability.

6.2 HISTORICAL ORIGINS

The origins of thermodynamics are in the nineteenth century when practitioners, engineers and scientists like James Watt (1736–1819), Sadi Carnot (1796–1832), James Prescott Joule (1818–1889), Rudolph Clausius (1822–1888) and William Thomson (the later Lord Kelvin, 1824–1907) wanted to understand and increase the efficiency at which steam engines perform useful mechanical work. From the very beginning, this endeavour has combined the study of natural systems and the study of engineered systems – created and managed by purposeful human action – in a very particular way, which is rather unusual for a traditional natural science such as physics.

Not surprisingly then, the laws of thermodynamics were found by economists to be concepts with considerable implications for economics.[1] For instance, economists such as Kenneth Boulding (1966), Robert Ayres and Allen Kneese (1969), and Nicolas Georgescu-Roegen (1971) turned to thermodynamics when they wanted to analyse economy-environment interactions in an encompassing way, and analytically root the economy in its biogeophysical basis.

In a first step, the Materials Balance Principle was formulated based on the thermodynamic Law of Conservation of Mass (Boulding, 1966; Ayres and Kneese, 1969; Kneese et al., 1972). In view of this principle, all resource inputs that enter a production process eventually become waste. By now, this is an accepted and undisputed piece of resource, environmental and ecological economics.

At the same time, Georgescu-Roegen (1971) developed an elaborate and extensive critique of economics based on the laws of thermodynamics, and in particular the Entropy Law, which he considered to be 'the most economic of all physical laws' (Georgescu-Roegen, 1971, p. 280).[2] His contribution initiated a heated debate on the question of whether the Entropy Law – and thermodynamics in general – is relevant to economics (Burness et al., 1980; Daly, 1992; Kåberger and Månsson, 2001; Khalil, 1990; Lozada, 1991; 1995; Norgaard, 1986; Townsend, 1992; Williamson, 1993; Young, 1991; 1994).[3] While Georgescu-Roegen had, among many other points, formulated an essentially correct insight into the irreversible nature of transformations of energy and matter in economies, his analysis is to some extent flawed by wrongly positing what he calls a 'Fourth Law of Thermodynamics' (Ayres, 1999).[4] It may be for this reason that the Second Law and the entropy concept have not yet acquired the same undisputed and foundational status for resource, environmental and ecological economics as have the First Law and the Materials Balance Principle.

But as Georgescu-Roegen's work and the many studies following his lead have shown, the Entropy Law, properly applied, yields insights into the irreversible nature of economy-environment interactions that are not available otherwise (Baumgärtner et al., 1996). Both the First and the Second Laws of Thermodynamics therefore need to be combined in the study of how natural resources are extracted, used in production, and give rise to emissions and waste, thus leading to integrated models of ecological-economic systems (e.g. Baumgärtner, 2000a; Faber et al., 1995; Perrings, 1987; Ruth, 1993; 1999).

6.3 FUNDAMENTAL RATIONALE

6.3.1 Different Perspectives on Economy-Environment Interactions

When economists started to analyse the flow of resources, goods, services and money in an economy, the picture was rather simple: there are two groups of economic agents, consumers and producers; producers deliver goods and services to consumers, and consumers give the resources with which they are endowed, labour in particular, to producers. Thus, there is a circular flow of commodities in an economy. There is an equivalent circular flow of money counter to that primary flow, as consumers pay money to producers for the goods they consume, and producers remunerate the labour force they receive from the consumers/labourers.[5]

Since the two corresponding flows, the primal flow of real commodities and the dual flow of monetary compensation, are exactly equivalent, it seems superfluous to always study both of them when analysing economic transactions and allocations. Hence, the convention was established in economics exclusively to consider the monetary flow. The current system of national economic accounts, which is meant to be a full representation of economic activity in an economy over one time period, therefore captures all transactions in monetary units; e.g., the provision of labour and capital, the trading of intermediate goods and services between different sectors of the economy, and final demand for consumer goods.

Of course, this picture is too simple, as it neglects the use of natural resources and the emission of pollutants and wastes. Both activities are a necessary aspect of economic action. In the early nineteenth century, the subdiscipline of environmental and resource economics emerged to deal with the question of how to take into economic account the use of natural resources on the one hand and the emission of pollutants and wastes on the other (Gray, 1913, 1914; Pigou, 1912, 1920; Hotelling, 1931). The picture now appeared as follows: there is a circular flow – actually: two equivalent circular flows – between consumers and producers which form the core of economic activity. In addition, there is an inflow of natural resource and an outflow of emissions and wastes. Thus, a linear throughflow of energy and matter drives the circular flow of economic exchange.

One conceptual problem from the very beginning of environmental and resource economics is the following. While the description of economic activity is generally in monetary terms, the inflow of natural resources as well as the outflow of emissions and wastes does not have an obvious value dimension. Although an obvious fact in real terms, it is very difficult to capture in monetary terms, as there are normally no markets for these flows, such that they do not carry an obvious price tag. But taking these flows into economic account – based on the understanding that economics analyses transactions in monetary terms – requires monetarization of these flows. As a consequence, valuation of environmental goods, services and damages became a major challenge. The aim was to complement the real dimension of these flows with the corresponding (dual) value dimension.

A further step in the development of ecological-economic thinking was the insight that the inflow of natural resources (resource economics) and the outflow of emissions and wastes (environmental economics) are not independent. Obviously, these two flows are linked by economic activity; i.e., economic activity transforms natural resources into emissions and wastes. But these two flows are also linked because they originate and terminate in the natural geobiophysical environment. For example, environmental pollutants released into natural ecosystems may impair the ecosystems' ability to produce the ecosystem goods and services, e.g., timber or fish, which are then used as a natural resource by the economy. This means, the extraction of natural resources, the production of goods and services within the economy, as well as the emission of pollutants and wastes, all happen within the system of the natural geobiophysical environment.

This is the 'vision' (in the sense of Schumpeter)[6] of ecological economics: ecological economics views the human economy as an open subsystem of the larger, but finite, closed, and non-growing system of non-human nature (Boulding, 1966; Georgescu-Roegen, 1971; Daly, 1977; Ayres, 1978; Faber and Proops, 1990; and many more). In this view, the human economy is a part of nature. In contrast, in the view of traditional environmental and resource economics, Nature is treated as a part of the human economy. Both 'Resources' and 'Environment' are treated as additional economic sectors in the system of national economic accounts, and flows to and from these sectors are accounted for in monetary units.

The change of perspective from 'nature as part of the economy' to 'the economy as part of nature' amounts to a scientific revolution not unlike the transition from the heliocentric to the geocentric world view in the Copernicanean revolution (Brown, 2001).

6.3.2 Duality Between the Real and Monetary Descriptions and the Role of Thermodynamics

As we have seen, economic analysis, including environmental and resource economics, is based on the idea of duality between the flow of real commodities and services (measured in physical units) and an equivalent value flow (measured in monetary units), and consequently focuses solely on the value dimension. But as far as the throughflow of energy and matter through the economy is concerned, the value of this flow is far from obvious. Markets cannot give the values we are looking for, as markets typically do not exist in this domain. And where they exist, the resulting values are distorted due to ubiquitous externalities and public goods.

As a consequence, the valuation of natural goods and services has to be set up explicitly as a non-market process, and elaborate theories and techniques have been proposed for this purpose.[7] All of these techniques require, to a greater or lesser extent, an adequate, prior description in real terms of the particular commodity or service to be valued. In other words, before individuals or society can value something, they have to have a rather good idea of what exactly that something is. This holds, in particular, for the energy and material resources used in production as well as for the emissions and wastes generated as by-products of desired goods.

Here lies the relevance of thermodynamics. Being the branch of physics that deals with transformations of energy and matter, thermodynamics is an appropriate natural science foundation for providing a description in real terms of what goes on when human societies interact with the non-human environment. In particular, thermodynamics captures the energy/matter dimension of economy-environment interactions. Thus, it is a necessary complement and prerequisite for economic valuation.

6.4 CONCEPTS AND LAWS OF THERMODYNAMICS

Thermodynamics is the branch of physics that deals with macroscopic transformations of energy and matter. Briefly summarized, the fundamental concepts and laws of phenomenological thermodynamics can be stated as follows.[8]

6.4.1 Systems and Transformations

With respect to the potential exchange of energy and matter between the inside and the outside of the system under study, one distinguishes between the following types of thermodynamic system:

- *Isolated* systems exchange neither energy nor matter with their surrounding environment.
- *Closed* systems exchange energy, but not matter, with their surrounding environment.
- *Open* systems exchange both energy and matter with their surrounding environment.

A system is said to be in *thermodynamic equilibrium* when there is complete absence of driving forces for change in the system. Technically, the various potentials of the system are at their minimum, such that there are no spatial variations of any of the intensive variables within the system. *Intensive* variables are quantities which do not change when two separate but identical systems are coupled. In contrast, *extensive* variables are quantities whose value for the total system is simply the sum of the values of this quantity in both systems. For example, temperature and pressure are intensive variables while mass and volume are extensive ones. As long as there are spatial variations in, say, temperature within a system, it is not yet in thermodynamic equilibrium, but there exists a potential for change. The equilibrium state is characterized by a uniform temperature throughout the system.

Consider an isolated system which undergoes a transformation over time between some initial equilibrium state and some final equilibrium state, either by interaction with its environment or by interaction between different constituents within the system. If the final state is such that no imposition or relaxation of constraints upon the isolated system can restore the initial state, then this process is called *irreversible*. Otherwise the process is called *reversible*. For example, at some initial time a gas is enclosed in the left part of an isolated box; the right part is separated from the left part by a wall and is empty. Now, the separating wall is removed. The molecules of the gas will then evenly distribute themselves over the entire volume of the box. The thermodynamic equilibrium of the final state is characterized by a uniform density of molecules throughout the entire volume. Reintroducing the wall into the isolated system separating the left part from the right half would not restore the initial state of the system. Nor would any other imposition or relaxation of constraints on the isolated system be able to restore the initial state. Therefore, the transformation given by the removal of the wall is an irreversible transformation of the isolated system.[9] Generally, a process of transformation can only be reversible if it does not involve any dissipation of energy, such as through, e.g., friction, viscosity, inelasticity, electrical resistance or magnetic hysteresis.

6.4.2 The Fundamental Laws of Thermodynamics

The *First Law of Thermodynamics* states that in an isolated system (which may or may not be in equilibrium) the total internal energy is conserved. This means that energy can be neither created nor destroyed. However, it can appear in different forms, such as heat, chemical energy, electrical energy, potential energy, kinetic energy, work, etc. For example, when burning a piece of wood or coal the chemical energy stored in the fuel is converted into heat. In an isolated system the total internal energy, i.e. the sum of energies in their particular forms, does not change over time. In any process of transformation only the forms in which energy appears change, while its total amount is conserved.

Similarly, in an isolated system the total mass is conserved (*Law of Conservation of Mass*). Obviously, if matter cannot enter or leave an isolated system, the number of atoms of any chemical element within the system must remain constant. In an open system which may exchange matter with its surrounding, a simple *Materials Balance Principle* holds: the mass content of a system at some time is given by its initial mass content plus inflows of mass minus outflows of mass up to that point in time. The law of mass conservation, while often regarded as an independent conservation law besides the law of energy conservation, is actually an implication of the First Law of Thermodynamics. According to Einstein's famous relation $E=mc^2$ mass is a form of energy, but mass can only be transformed into non-material energy, and vice versa, in nuclear reactions. Therefore, neglecting nuclear reactions it follows from the First Law of Thermodynamics that mass and non-material energy are conserved separately.

In any process transforming energy or matter, a certain amount of energy is irrevocably transformed into heat. The variable *entropy* has been defined by Rudolph Clausius (1854; 1865) such as to capture this irrevocable transformation of energy: if a certain amount of heat dQ is reversibly transferred to or from a system at temperature T, then dS = dQ/T defines the change in entropy S. Clausius showed that S is a state variable of the system; i.e., it remains constant in any reversible cyclic process and increases otherwise. The *Second Law of Thermodynamics*, the so-called Entropy Law, states the unidirectional character of transformations of energy and matter: With any transformation between an initial equilibrium state and a final equilibrium state of an isolated system, the entropy of this system increases over time or remains constant. It strictly increases in irreversible transformations, and it remains constant in reversible transformations, but it cannot decrease.

Entropy, in this view, can be interpreted as an indicator for the system's capacity to perform useful work. The higher the value of entropy, the higher the amount of energy already irreversibly transformed into heat, the lower the amount of free energy of the system and the lower the system's capacity to perform work. Expressed the other way round, the lower the value of entropy, the higher the amount of free energy in the system and the higher the system's capacity to perform work. Hence, the statement of the Second Law of Thermodynamics amounts to saying that, for any process of transformation, the proportion of energy in the form of heat to total energy irreversibly increases or remains constant, but certainly never decreases. In other words, with any transformation of energy or matter, an isolated system loses part of its ability to perform useful mechanical work and some of its available free energy is irreversibly transformed into heat. For that reason, the Second Law is said to express an irreversible degradation of energy in isolated systems over time. At the same time, the economic relevance of the Second Law becomes obvious.

While the notion of entropy introduced to phenomenological thermodynamics by Clausius is based on heat, Ludwig Boltzmann (1877) introduced a formally equivalent notion of entropy that is based on statistical mechanics and likelihood. His notion reveals a different interpretation of entropy and helps to show why it irreversibly increases over time. Statistical mechanics views gases as assemblies of molecules, described by distribution functions depending on position and velocity. This view allows the establishment of connections between the thermodynamic variables, i.e., the macroscopic properties such as temperature or pressure, and the microscopic behaviour of the individual molecules of the system, which is described by statistical means.[10] The crucial step is to distinguish between microstates and macrostates of a system. The *microstate* is an exact specification of the positions and velocities of all individual particles; the *macrostate* is a specification of the thermodynamic variables of the whole system.

Boltzmann assumed that all microstates have equal *a priori* probability, provided that there is no physical condition which would favour one configuration over the other. He posited that every macrostate would always pass to one of higher probability, where the probability of a macrostate is determined by the number of different microstates realizing this macrostate. The macroscopic thermal equilibrium state is then the most probable state, in the sense that it is the macrostate which can be realized by the largest number of different microstates. Boltzmann defined the quantity Ω, counting the number of possible microstates realizing one macrostate, and related this to the thermodynamic entropy S of that macrostate. He used $S = k \log \Omega$, with k as a factor of proportionality called Boltzmann's constant. Entropy can thus be taken as a measure of likelihood: highly probable macrostates, that is macrostates which can be realized by a large number of microstates, also have high entropy. At the same time, entropy may be interpreted as a measure of how orderly or mixed-up a system is. High entropy, according to the Boltz-

mann interpretation, characterizes a system in which the individual constituents are arranged in a spatially even and homogeneous way ('mixed-up
systems'), whereas low entropy characterizes a system in which the individual constituents are arranged in an uneven and heterogeneous way ('orderly
systems'). The irreversibility stated by the Second Law in its phenomenological formulation (in any isolated system entropy always increases or
remains constant) now appears as the statement that any isolated macroscopic
system always evolves from a less probable (more orderly) to a more probable (more mixed-up) state, where Ω and S are larger.

Whereas the Second Law in its Clausius or Boltzmann formulation makes
a statement about isolated systems in thermodynamic equilibrium only, the
study of closed and open systems far from equilibrium has shown (Prigogine,
1962; 1967) that entropy is also a meaningful and useful variable in closed
and open systems. Any open system is a subsystem of a larger and isolated
system. According to the conventional formulation of the Second Law the
entropy of the larger and isolated system has to increase over time, but the
entropy of any open subsystem can, of course, decrease. Viewing open
systems as subsystems of larger and isolated systems reveals, however, that
an entropy decrease in an open subsystem necessarily has to be accompanied
by an entropy increase in the system's environment, that is the rest of the
larger, isolated system, such that the entropy of the total system increases.

A generalization of the Second Law is possible such that it refers not only
to isolated systems. Irrespective of the type of thermodynamic system under
study, and irrespective of whether the system is in thermodynamic equilibrium or not, it is true that entropy cannot be annihilated; it can only be
created (Falk and Ruppel, 1976, p. 353). This more general, system independent formulation of the Second Law implies the usual formulations for
isolated systems. The relevance of the system independent formulation of the
Second Law lies in the fact that most real systems of interest are not isolated
but closed or open. Hence, the latter formulation is the form in which the
Second Law is apparent in everyday life.

6.4.3 Quantification and Application

The entropy concept is essential for understanding how resource and energy
scarcity, as well as the irreversibility of transformation processes, constrain
economic action (Georgescu-Roegen, 1971; Baumgärtner, 2003a). However,
it is a very abstract concept and it is notoriously difficult to apply in specific
contexts. One of the complications is due to the fact that a system's capacity
to perform work depends not only on the state of the system, but also on the
state of the system's environment. Therefore, for applications of the fundamental thermodynamic insights in the areas of mechanical and chemical

engineering, as well as in economics, it is useful to relate the system's ability to perform work to a certain standardized reference state of its environment. *Exergy* is defined to be the maximum amount of work obtainable from a system as it approaches thermodynamic equilibrium with its environment in a reversible way (Szargut et al., 1988, p. 7). Exergy is also commonly called *available energy* or *available work* and corresponds to the 'useful' part of energy, thus combining the insights from both the First and Second Laws of Thermodynamics. Hence, exergy is what most people mean when they use the term 'energy' carelessly, e.g., when saying that 'energy is used' to carry out a certain process.

The relationship between the concepts of entropy and exergy is simple, as $W_{lost} = T_0 S_{gen}$ (*Law of Gouy and Stodola*), where W_{lost} denotes the potential work or exergy lost by the system in a transformation process, T_0 denotes the temperature of the system's environment, and S_{gen} denotes the entropy generated in the transformation. This means, as the system's entropy increases as a consequence of irreversible transformations according to the Second Law, the system loses exergy or some of its potential to perform work. Exergy, unlike energy, is thus not a conserved quantity. While the entropy concept stresses that with every transformation of the system something useless is created, the exergy concept stresses that something useful is diminished. These developments are two aspects of the same irreversible character of transformations of energy and matter.

As the system might consist simply of a bulk of matter, exergy is also a measure for the potential work embodied in a material, whether it is a fuel, food or other substance (Ayres, 1998; Ayres et al., 1998). The exergy content of different materials can be calculated for standard values specifying the natural environment, by considering how that material eventually reaches thermodynamic equilibrium with its environment with respect to temperature, pressure, chemical potential and all the other intensive variables.[11] Taking a particular state of the system's environment as a reference point for the definition and calculation of exergy may be considered as a loss of generality as compared to the entropy concept. However, this referencing seems to be permissible since all processes of transformation – be it in nature or in the economy – are such that:

- all of the materials involved eventually do reach thermodynamic equilibrium with the natural environment; and
- the environment is so large that its equilibrium will not be affected by the particular transformation processes under study.

While both the entropy and the exergy concept yield the same qualitative insights into the fundamentally irreversible character of transformations of energy and matter, the exergy concept is more tangible, as it is directly related to the very compelling idea of 'available work' and it can be more easily quantified than entropy.

6.5 DIFFERENT APPROACHES

How can thermodynamic concepts, laws and results be incorporated in a fruitful manner into economic analysis? This has been attempted in basically four ways,[12] which are very different in the intellectual approach they take. In the following, I shall describe each of them in detail and assess their potential for ecological economics.

6.5.1 Isomorphism of Formal Structure

Both thermodynamics and economics can formally be set up as problems of optimization under constraints. For example, equilibrium allocations in an economy can be viewed as a result of the simultaneous utility maximization under budget constraints of many households and profit maximization under technological constraints of many firms. Likewise, equilibrium micro- or macrostates of a thermodynamic system can be derived from the minimization of a thermodynamic potential, such as, e.g., Helmholtz or Gibbs free energy, under the constraints of constant pressure, volume, chemical potential etc. The mathematical structure of both economic and thermodynamic problems is, thus, formally equivalent. There is an isomorphism between the two types of problems and their respective solutions.

As a consequence, one may exploit this formal isomorphism to obtain insights into the structure of economic equilibrium allocations from studying the structural properties of thermodynamic equilibria. To be sure, these insights pertain to the formal structure of equilibrium solutions only, and they do not in themselves contain any substantive content about thermodynamics or economics. For instance, based on what is known as the *Le Chatelier Principle* in thermodynamics (Kondepudi and Prigogine, 1998, pp. 239–40), Samuelson (1947) established the method of *comparative statics* in economics. This method explains the changes in the equilibrium solution of a constrained maximization problem (economic or thermodynamic) when one of the constraints is marginally tightened or relaxed. This has proved to be a very powerful tool and has found widespread use in modern economics.

Yet, it seems that the potential for exploiting the isomorphism of formal structures in thermodynamic and economic equilibria was fairly limited and is, by now, largely exhausted.

6.5.2 Analogies and Metaphors

A second approach takes thermodynamic concepts and transfers them into economic thinking as analogies and metaphors (Faber and Proops, 1985; Proops, 1985, 1987). For example, under this approach, 'order' and 'disorder' in an economy are interpreted as expressions of 'social entropy', or the economy is seen as a 'self-organizing dissipative system far from thermodynamic equilibrium'. Typically, no attempt is made under this approach to clearly define the various terms, such as 'order', 'entropy' or 'equilibrium', in either thermodynamic or economic terms. Instead, these terms are used to evoke certain associations with the reader.

To a reader who is well trained in both thermodynamics and economics, it remains unclear whether a term such as, e.g., 'equilibrium' refers to thermodynamic equilibrium (in the sense of a thermodynamic system being in a state of minimal thermodynamic potential, e.g., Helmholtz free energy) or to economic equilibrium (in the sense of an economy of households and firms being in a state of market equilibrium where demand equals supply). Certainly, using these terms in such a loose manner cannot have the status of making exact and deductive scientific statements about economic systems.

Despite these large difficulties, the analogies and metaphors approach has merit as a heuristic, as it allows one to see economic phenomena in a new light. Thus, it generates new and potentially fruitful questions, rather than answering existing ones. In that sense, it is more a 'vision' in the sense of Schumpeter, than a rigorous analytical approach.

6.5.3 Energy, Entropy and Exergy Theories of Value

Some people argue that economic values based on subjective individual preferences are to some extent arbitrary and might be misleading in achieving sustainable solutions for environmental problems. In contrast, these people argue, sustainability requires the identification of the 'true' and 'objective' value of nature's goods and services, and of damages to these. Often, thermodynamic quantities are proposed to give such an 'objective' value rod, e.g., energy (Costanza, 1981; Hannon, 1973, 1979; Hannon et al., 1986; Odum, 1971), (low) entropy[13] or exergy (Bejan et al., 1996, p. 407).[14] In all of these cases, the argument is as follows. Energy (or alternatively exergy, low entropy) is the only really scarce factor here on Planet Earth. It measures the ultimate scarcity that we face in dealing with nature. Therefore, the amount of energy (exergy, low entropy) contained in every good or service measures its 'true' scarcity, and therefore should be taken as its value. Decisions concerning sustainability, so goes the argument, must be based on such energy/entropy/exergy-values, as they represent the ultimate scarcities.

From the economic point of view, this argument is untenable. It is untenable for the very same reasons that, for example, a labour theory of value as advocated by David Ricardo or Karl Marx is untenable, and any other single-factor theory of value would be untenable, be that factor energy, labour, oxygen, or whatever. 'Value', as it is understood in economics, results from the interplay of human goals and ends on the one hand (e.g., profit maximization, utility maximization or sustainability), and scarcity of means to achieve these ends on the other hand (e.g. natural resources, capital, labour, or time). The higher the goals and the scarcer the resources necessary to achieve them, the more valuable are these resources. There is an economic theorem which states that under very limiting assumptions the value of a good or service is given by the total amount of a factor of production (e.g., energy or labour) which has been used, directly or indirectly, in producing it. This is the so-called non-substitution theorem, and it has been proven in 1951 independently by four real masterminds of economics: Arrow (1951), Koopmans (1951), Georgescu-Roegen (1951) and Samuelson (1951).[15] This theorem identifies the conditions, under which a single-factor theory of value holds:

(A1)   There is only one primary, i.e., non-producible, factor of production.
(A2)   This factor is directly used in the production of every intermediate or final good or service.
(A3)   All production processes are characterized by constant returns to scale; i.e., scaling the amounts of all inputs by a factor of $\lambda > 0$ also scales the amount of output produced by the same factor λ.
(A4)   There is no joint production; i.e., every process of production yields exactly one output.

These are very restrictive assumptions. Only if (A1) − (A4) are fulfilled does a single-factor theory of value fully explain the value of goods and services. If one of them does not hold, a single-factor theory of value cannot provide a satisfactory explanation of value.

As for energy/entropy/exergy as a factor of production, one may safely assume that (A2) is fulfilled, and one may concede that (A1) can be taken to be fulfilled as well.[16] But in general, (A3) is not fulfilled, as many technologies are characterized by either increasing or decreasing returns to scale. Also, thermodynamic considerations, to which we shall turn in detail later, imply that every process of production is joint production, such that (A4) is violated. This means, while energy, entropy or exergy theories of value are conceivable in very restricted models (characterized by conditions A1 − A4) they must be rejected for real ecological-economic systems. To be sure, while energy, entropy or exergy are important factors in explaining value, value is a complex and encompassing phenomenon, and thermodynamic quantities alone cannot provide a satisfactory explanation of value.

6.5.4 Thermodynamic Constraints on Economic Action

Another approach to integrating insights from thermodynamics into economics starts from the observation that the laws of thermodynamics constrain economic action. Thermodynamic laws specify what is possible and what is not possible in the transformation of energy and matter. Such transformations play an important role in any economy, for example in:

- The extraction of natural resources from the geo-bio-chemical-physical environment.
- The use of these resources in the production of goods and services.
- The generation and emission of wastes and environmental pollutants as by-products of desired goods.
- The recycling of wastes into secondary resources.

All of these transformations of energy and matter are at the centre of interest in the field of ecological, environmental and resource economics. Hence, the laws of thermodynamics play an important role in describing relevant constraints and scarcities for the economic analysis of economy-environment interactions (Cleveland and Ruth, 1997).

This approach builds on a clear division of labour between the disciplines of thermodynamics and economics. The laws of thermodynamics are being used to capture the constraints on transformations of energy and matter. Their role is limited to this particular task. Based on this conceptualization of constraints, methods and concepts from economics are then being used to study allocations in an economy which result from the optimizing behaviour of firms and households; e.g., profit-maximizing resource extraction and production firms as well as utility-maximizing households purchasing the consumer goods so produced.

This approach can directly be operationalized, and it is empirically meaningful for ecological economics. It lends itself quite naturally to modelling. One can distinguish between different model types for integrated thermodynamic-economic analysis, according to which thermodynamic concepts and laws they incorporate:

- Models incorporating mass and the conservation of mass (First Law), either for one particular material (say, copper) or for a number of materials.

- Models incorporating energy and the conservation of energy (First Law), sometimes in variants such as emergy ('embodied energy').
- Models incorporating entropy and entropy generation (Second Law).
- Models incorporating energy and entropy, sometimes in the form of exergy (First and Second Law).
- Models incorporating mass, energy and entropy (First and Second Law).

Models based on the First Law are useful to study the economic implications from the scarcities due to physical conservation of mass and energy in the throughflow of materials and energy through the economy. Models based on the Second Law are useful to study the economic implications from the scarcities, due to the temporal directedness of this throughflow and its qualitative degradation by dissipation of energy and dispersal of matter.

6.6 IMPLICATIONS OF AND INSIGHTS FROM THERMODYNAMIC MODELS

The use of thermodynamic concepts, laws and models in ecological economics is an ongoing endeavour. So far, it has revealed a number of relevant implications and insights about different aspects of economy-environment interactions.[17]

6.6.1 Materials Balance: The 'Planet Earth' Perspective

The Materials Balance Principle is based on the Law of Conservation of Mass, as implied by the First Law of Thermodynamics (Boulding, 1966; Ayres and Kneese, 1969; Kneese et al., 1972, Ayres 1978).[18] Since mass cannot be created, but is conserved in all transformations, all material resource inputs that enter a production process (i) diminish the corresponding resource reservoir, and (ii) eventually become waste.

This principle has led to viewing the Earth, including the human society, as a 'spaceship' (Boulding, 1966), which is completely closed to the surrounding space in material terms. Thus, all material transformations on Earth should be managed in a self-reliant and sustainable way.

6.6.2 Irreversibility of (Micro- and Macro-) Economic Processes

All processes of macroscopic change are irreversible. Examples include natural processes, such as the growing and blooming of a flower, as well as technical processes, such as the burning of fossil fuels in combustion engines. The entropy concept and the Second Law of Thermodynamics have been coined such as to capture this fact of nature (Kondepudi and Prigogine, 1998; Zeh, 2001).

The relevance of thermodynamic irreversibility for economics lies in the fact that it precludes the existence of perpetual motion machines; i.e., devices which use a limited reservoir of available energy to perform work forever. It is an everyday experience that there exists no such thing as a perpetual motion machine. This holds for the micro-level, i.e., individual production processes, as well as for the macro-level, i.e., the economy at large (Georgescu-Roegen, 1971).

In order to make this insight accessible to economic analysis, it is necessary to adequately represent thermodynamic irreversibility as a constraint for economic action. Modern economic theory has devoted some effort to incorporating irreversibility into production theory. However, the standard irrversibility concept of economics, which is due to Arrow and Debreu (1954) and Debreu (1959), does not encompass thermodynamic irreversibility; it only establishes temporal irreversibility – a weaker form of irreversibility (Baumgärtner, 2000b).

6.6.3 Resource Extraction and Waste Generation

The insights described in Sections 6.6.1 and 6.6.2 have been applied, in particular, to the analysis of mineral resource extraction (e.g., Ruth 1995a, 1995b, 1995c), the generation of wastes and pollution (Kümmel, 1989; Kümmel and Schüssler, 1991), and the relation between the two (Faber, 1985; Faber et al., [1983] 1995). At a very abstract level, high entropy (or exergy lost) is the ultimate form of waste (Kümmel, 1989; Kümmel and Schüssler, 1991; Ayres and Martinás, 1995; Ayres et al., 1998).

6.6.4 Representation of the Production Process

Every process of production is, at root, a transformation of energy and matter (Ayres and Kneese, 1969). Hence, the laws of thermodynamics provide a suitable analytical framework for rigorously deducing insights into the physical aspects of production (Baumgärtner, 2000a). In particular, any representation of production in economic models should be in accordance with the laws of thermodynamics. Therefore, the neoclassical production function, which is the standard way of representing the production process in economic models, has been critically discussed against the background of thermodynamics. It has become apparent that this concept is incompatible with the laws of thermodynamics for a number of reasons:

(i)   Georgescu-Roegen (1971) claims that the neoclassical production function is incompatible with the laws of thermodynamics, basically because it does not properly reflect the irreversible nature of transformations of energy and matter, and because it confounds flow and fund quantities (Daly, 1997b; Kurz and Salvadori, 2003).

(ii)   One essential factor of production, which is very often omitted from the explicit representation, is energy (actually exergy) (Kümmel, 1989; Ayres, 1998).[19] Its exact role for the production process, and its interplay with other production factors, such as capital or material resources, is studied in engineering thermodynamics (e.g., Bejan, 1996, 1997; Bejan et al., 1996; see also Sec. 6.6.5 below).

(iii) The conservation laws for energy and matter imply that there are limits to substitution between energy-matter inputs, which are subject to the laws of thermodynamics, and other inputs such as labour or capital, which lie outside the domain of thermodynamics (Berry and Andresen, 1982; Berry et al., 1978; Dasgupta and Heal, 1979, Chap. 7).

(iv)   From the First and Second Laws of Thermodynamics it becomes obvious that '[g]iven the entropic nature of the economic process, waste is an output just as unavoidable as the input of natural resources' (Georgescu-Roegen 1975, p. 357). This holds not only for the economy at large, but for every individual process of production at the micro-level (Faber et al., 1998; Baumgärtner 2000a, Chapter 5; 2002; Baumgärtner and de Swaan Arons, 2003). As a consequence, there is no such thing as 'single production'; i.e., the production of just one single output as modelled by the neoclassical production function. Rather, all production is joint production; i.e., there is necessarily more than one output (Faber et al., 1998; Baumgärtner et al., 2001).

All of these apparent inconsistencies between the laws of thermodynamics and the standard assumptions about the neoclassical production function have led to more general descriptions of the production process, which blend the traditional theory of production with thermodynamic principles (Anderson, 1987; Baumgärtner, 2000a, Chap. 4; Pethig, 2003, Sec. 3.3).

6.6.5 Finite-Time/Finite-Size Thermodynamics: Exergy Engineering

Recent research in the applied field of engineering thermodynamics has addressed the circumstance that chemical and physical processes in industry never happen in a completely reversible way between one equilibrium state and another equilibrium state. Rather, these processes are enforced by the operator of the process and they are constrained in space and time. This has led to an extension of ideal equilibrium thermodynamics, known under the name of *finite-time/finite-size thermodynamics* (e.g., Andresen et al., 1984; Bejan, 1996, 1997; Bejan et al., 1996).

From the point of view of finite-time/finite-size thermodynamics, it becomes obvious that the minimum exergy requirement and minimum waste production in chemical or physical processes is considerably higher than that suggested by ideal equilibrium thermodynamics. The reason for the increased exergy requirement (which entails an increased amount of waste at the end of the process) lies in the fact that chemical and physical transformations are forced to happen over a finite time by the operator of the production plant, which necessarily causes some dissipation of energy.

The finite-time/finite-size consideration is a very relevant consideration for many production processes, in particular in the chemical industry. Finite-time/finite-size thermodynamics allows one to identify exactly, trace down and quantify exergetic inefficiencies at the individual steps of a production processes (Bejan, 1996, 1997; Bejan et al., 1996; Brodyansky et al., 1994; Creyts, 2000; Szargut et al., 1988), along the entire chain of a production process (Ayres et al., 1998; Cornelissen and Hirs, 1999; Cornelissen et al., 2000), for whole industries (Dewulf et al., 2000; Hinderink et al., 1999; Ozdogan and Arikol, 1981), and for entire national economies (Nakićenović et al., 1996; Schaeffer and Wirtshafter, 1992; Wall, 1987, 1990; Wall et al., 1994). Thus, it yields valuable insights into the origins of exergy losses and forms a tool for designing industrial production systems in an efficient and sustainable manner (Connelly and Koshland, 2001; de Swaan Arons and van der Kooi, 2001).

Furthermore, it becomes apparent that energy/exergy and time are sub- stitutes as factors of production in many production processes (Andresen et al., 1984; Berry and Andresen, 1982; Spreng, 1993). A production process may be speeded up at the expense of employing more energy/exergy, and the use of energy/exergy may be reduced by allowing the production process to just take longer. Prominent examples for such a trade-off relationship are transport services or chemical reaction processes.

6.6.6 Thermodynamic and Economic Efficiency

Both thermodynamics and economics analyse systems in terms of their 'efficiency'. Both concepts may be applied to the very same system; e.g., a production plant or a whole national economy. Yet, the thermodynamic and the economic notions of efficiency fundamentally differ, as they refer to very different variables of the system. In fact, the two notions are completely independent (Berry et al., 1978; Dasgupta and Heal, 1979, Chap. 7; Baum-gärtner, 2001). As a consequence, thermodynamic efficiency is neither necessary nor sufficient for economic efficiency, even when economic efficiency includes concerns for energy, resources and environmental quality.

6.6.7 Sustainability: Limits to Economic Growth

From the very beginning, the recourse to thermodynamic arguments in ecological economics was motivated by a long-term and global concern for the sustainable existence of humans on 'Planet Earth' (Boulding, 1966; Georgescu-Roegen, 1971; Daly 1973, [1977] 1991). The pre-analytic vision behind this concern was that of the human economy as an open subsystem of the larger, but finite, closed, and non-growing system of the biogeophysical environment.

In that view, thermodynamic analysis has helped to sketch the potential and limits of economic growth. It has turned out that there exist limits to the growth of energy-matter throughput through the economy, which may ultimately set limits to economic growth. This claim is vindicated by the following arguments:[20]

(i) Conservation of mass implies that the marginal product as well as the average product of a material resource input may be bounded from above (Baumgärtner, 2003b). This means that the usual Inada conditions (Inada, 1963) do not hold for material resource inputs. This is important since the Inada conditions are usually held to be crucial for establishing steady state growth under scarce exhaustible resources (e.g. Dasgupta and Heal, 1974; Solow, 1974; Stiglitz, 1974).

(ii) As described in Section 6.6.4 above, the conservation laws for energy and matter imply that there are limits to substitution between energy-matter inputs, which are subject to the laws of thermodynamics, and other inputs such as labour or capital, which lie outside the domain of thermodynamics (Berry and Andresen, 1982; Berry et al., 1978; Dasgupta and Heal, 1979, Chap. 7). This is important since substitutability among essential and scarce production factors (with an elasticity of substitution not smaller than one) is usually held to be crucial for establishing steady state growth (e.g., Dasgupta and Heal, 1974; Solow, 1974; Stiglitz, 1974).

(iii) Some have posited that resource scarcity can be overcome by recycling. However, thermodynamic analysis clearly shows that there are limits to recycling as well (Ayres, 1999; Craig, 2001).

(iv) Others have posited that technical progress is an important driver of economic growth, and that technical progress will continue. However, thermodynamic analysis clearly shows that there are limits to technical progress (Ruth, 1995a, 1995b, 1995c).

6.7 CONCLUSION AND CAVEAT: THERMODYNAMICS AND SUSTAINABILITY

Taken together, thermodynamic concepts, laws and models are relevant for ecological economics in various ways and on different levels of abstraction.

(i) As all processes of change are, at bottom, processes of energy and material transformation, the concepts and laws of thermodynamics apply to all of them. The framework of thermodynamics thus creates a unifying perspective on ecology, the physical environment, and the economy. This unifying framework, combined with economic and ecological analysis, allows questions that would not have been asked from the perspective of one scientific discipline alone.

(ii) On a more specific level, thermodynamic concepts allow the incorporation of physical driving forces and constraints into models of economy-environment interactions, both microeconomic and macroeconomic. They are essential for understanding to what extent resource and energy scarcity, nature's capacity to assimilate human wastes and pollutants, as well as the irreversibility of transformation processes, constrain economic action. Thermodynamic concepts thus allow economics to relate to its biogeophysical basis, and yield insights about that relationship which are not available otherwise.

(iii) On an even more applied level, thermodynamic concepts provide tools of quantitative analysis of energetic and material transformations for engineers and managers. They may be used to design industrial production plants or individual components of those such as to maximize their energetic efficiency, and to minimize their environmental impact.

With its rigorous but multifarious character as a method of analysis, its rich set of fruitful applications, and its obvious potential to establish relations between the natural world and purposeful human action, thermodynamics is one of the cornerstones of the conceptual foundations of ecological economics.

However, one important caveat seems to be in place. Thermodynamics is a purely descriptive science. That means, it only allows one to make statements of the kind 'If A, then B'. In particular, it is not a normative science. By itself, it neither includes nor allows value statements (Baumgärtner, 2000a, pp. 65–6) or statements of the kind 'C is a good, and therefore desirable, state of the world, but D is not'.[21] In contrast, sustainability is essentially a normative issue (Faber et al., 1995; Faber et al., 1996, Chap. 5). Sustainability is about the question 'In what kind of world do we want to live today and in the future?', thus, inherently including a dimension of desirability. A purely descriptive science alone, such as thermodynamics, cannot give an answer to that question.

Thermodynamics, however, is necessary to identify clearly the feasible options of development and their various properties, before a choice is then made about which option to choose based on some normative criteria. That choice requires a valuation or, more generally, a normative judgment of the different options at hand. It is therefore necessary not only to know the energetic and material basis of society's metabolism – both current and feasible alternatives – but also to link these thermodynamic aspects to the human perception and valuation of natural resources, commodity products and waste joint products, and the state of the natural environment.

The role of thermodynamics for conceiving sustainable modes of societal metabolism, therefore, is relative but essential. Thermodynamics is necessary to identify which options and scenarios of resource use, economic production, and waste generation are feasible and which are not. It, thereby, contributes to making informed choices about the future.

NOTES

1. In particular, in the late 1960s and early 1970s economists discovered the relevance of thermodynamics for environmental and resource economics. Pethig (2003), Spash (1999, p. 418) and Turner (1999, Section 2) describe this development in detail.
2. The works of Georgescu-Roegen are surveyed in a number of recent volumes (e.g. Beard and Lozada, 1999; Mayumi, 2001; Mayumi and Gowdy, 1999) and a special edition of the journal *Ecological Economics* (Vol. 22, No. 3, 1997).
3. See Baumgärtner et al. (1996) for a summary of that discussion.
4. Georgescu-Roegen posited that in a closed system, matter is distributed in a more and more disordered way. He called this claim the 'Fourth Law', in extension of the well established three laws of classical thermodynamics (see Section 6.4).
5. Later, this system was extended to include also savings and investment, as well as imports and exports.
6. Schumpeter (1954, p. 42) defines a *vision* as the 'preanalytic cognitive act that necessarily precedes any scientific analysis'.
7. For an overview see, e.g., Freeman (1993) or Hanley and Spash (1993).
8. Section 6.3 is taken from Baumgärtner (2002, Sec. 2.3). For a comprehensive introduction to (phenomenological) thermodynamics see Callen (1985), Kondepudi and Prigogine

(1998) or Zemansky and Dittman (1997).

9. Note that this does not mean that the initial state of the system can never be restored. However, in order to restore the system's initial state, the initially isolated system has to be opened to the influx of energy. For instance, the initial state could be restored by removing the system's insulation and performing work on the system from the outside, e.g., by pressing all of the molecules into the left part with a mobile wall that is initially at the right hand end of the system and from there on moves left.

10. Balian (1991), Huang (1987) and Landau and Lifshitz (1980) give an introduction to statistical mechanics.

11. Exergy values for many materials are typically calculated for an environmental temperature of 298.15 K and pressure of 101.325 kPa and can be found in tables, such as, e.g., in Szargut et al. (1988, Appendix).

12. Söllner (1997) distinguishes between three approaches. He does not take into account the formal isomorphism approach.

13. Burness et al. (1980, p. 7) and Patterson (1998) claim that Georgescu-Roegen (1971, Chap. 5) proposes a (low) entropy theory of value. This claim is wrong. On the contrary, Georgescu-Roegen (1971, p. 282) explicitly warns against such an interpretation. Note that Georgescu-Roegen (1979) also gives an explicit rebuttal of energy theories of value. See Baumgärtner et al. (1996, pp. 123–5) for details.

14. Patterson (1998) surveys different theories of value in ecological economics.

15. Note that three of these – Arrow, Koopmans, and Samuelson – were later awarded the Nobel Prize in Economics later on. (Some claim that the fourth – Georgescu-Roegen – also deserved it.)

16. One may as well consider space and time as primary production factors, as they surely enter every process of production in some sense. But then, energy is not the only primary factor any more.

17. Surveys of this area of research include Baumgärtner et al. (1996), Beard and Lozada (1999), Burley and Foster (1994), Daly (1997a), Mayumi and Gowdy (1999), Pethig (2003) and Ruth (1999).

18. Pethig (2003) surveys the Materials-Balance-Principle's origin and impact for environmental and resource economics.

19. Eonometric studies show that the production factor energy (exergy) explains an unexpectedly large share of economic growth observed over the twentieth century in the US, German or Japanese economies (Kümmel et al., 1985, 2000; Ayres et al., 2003).

20. Cleveland and Ruth (1997) present these arguments in more detail and review the relevant literature.

21. This holds even for the notion of *thermodynamic efficiency*, which is a purely technical notion (see the discussion in Section 6.6.6 above).

REFERENCES

Anderson, C.L. (1987), 'The production process: inputs and wastes', *Journal of Environmental Economics and Management*, **14**, 1–12.

Andresen, B., P. Salomon and R.S. Berry (1984), 'Thermodynamics in finite time', *Physics Today*, **37** (9), 62–70.

Arrow, K.J. (1951), 'Alternative proof of the substitution theorem for Leontief models in the general case', in T.C. Koopmans (ed.), *Activity Analysis of Production and Allocation*, New York: Wiley, pp. 155–64.

Arrow, K.H. and G. Debreu (1954), 'Existence of an equilibrium for a competitive economy', *Econometrica*, **22**, 265–90.

Ayres, R.U. (1978), *Resources, Environment and Economics: Applications of the Materials/Energy Balance Principle*, New York: Wiley.

Ayres, R.U. (1998), 'Eco-thermodynamics: economics and the second law', *Ecological Economics*, **26**, 189–209.

Ayres, R.U. (1999), 'The second law, the fourth law, recycling, and limits to growth', *Ecological Economics*, **29**, 473–83.

Ayres, R.U., L.W. Ayres and K. Martinás (1998), 'Exergy, waste accounting, and life-cycle analysis', *Energy*, **23**, 355–63.

Ayres, R.U., L.W. Ayres and B. Warr (2003), 'Exergy, power and work in the US economy 1900–1998', *Energy*, **28**, 219–73.

Ayres, R.U. and A.V. Kneese (1969), 'Production, consumption, and externalities', *American Economic Review*, **59**, 282–97.

Ayres, R.U. and K. Martinás (1995), 'Waste potential entropy: the ultimate eco-toxic?', *Economie Appliquée*, **48**, 95–120.

Balian, R. (1991), *From Microphysics to Macrophysics, Vol. I*, Heidelberg: Springer.

Baumgärtner, S. (2000a), *Ambivalent Joint Production and the Natural Environment. An Economic and Thermodynamic Analysis*, Heidelberg: Physica Verlag.

Baumgärtner, S. (2000b), 'Different notions of irreversibility in production', *Discussion Paper No. 337*, Department of Economics, University of Heidelberg, November 2000.

Baumgärtner, S. (2001), 'Thermodynamic and economic notions of efficiency', Contribution to the Symposium *Sustainable Processes and Products*, 30 May 2001, Delft University of Technology, Department of ChemTech.

Baumgärtner, S. (2002), 'Thermodynamics of waste generation', in K. Bisson and J. Proops (eds), *Waste in Ecological Economics*, Cheltenham: Edward Elgar, pp. 13–37.

Baumgärtner, S. (2003a), 'Entropy', in International Society for Ecological Economics (ed.), *Online Encyclopedia of Ecological Economics* (http://www.ecoeco.org/publica/encyc.htm).

Baumgärtner, S. (2003b), 'The Inada conditions for material resource inputs reconsidered', *Discussion Paper No. 396*, Department of Economics, University of Heidelberg.

Baumgärtner, S., H. Dyckhoff, M. Faber, J. Proops and J. Schiller (2001), 'The concept of joint production and ecological economics', *Ecological Economics*, **36**, 365–72.

Baumgärtner, S., M. Faber and J. Proops (1996), 'The use of the entropy concept in ecological economics', in Faber, M., R. Manstetten and J. Proops (1996), *Ecological Economics: Concepts and Methods*, Cheltenham: Edward Elgar., pp. 115–35.

Baumgärtner, S. and J. de Swaan Arons (2003), 'Necessity and inefficiency in the generation of waste: a thermodynamic analysis', *Journal of Industrial Ecology*, **7**, 113–24.

Beard, T.R. and G.A. Lozada (1999), *Economics, Entropy and the Environment: The Extraordinary Economics of Nicholas Georgescu-Roegen*, Cheltenham: Edward Elgar.

Bejan, A. (1996), *Entropy Generation Minimization*, Boca Raton: CRC Press.

Bejan, A. (1997), *Advanced Engineering Thermodynamics*, 2nd edn, New York: Wiley.

Bejan, A., G. Tsatsaronis and M. Moran (1996), *Thermal Design and Optimization*, New York: Wiley.

Berry, R.S. and B. Andresen (1982), 'Thermodynamic constraints in economic analysis', in W.C. Schieve and P. Allen (eds), *Self-Organization and Dissipative Structures: Applications in the Physical and Social Sciences*, Austin: University of Texas Press, pp. 323–38.

Berry, R.S., P. Salamon and G.M. Heal (1978), 'On a relation between economic and thermodynamic optima', *Resources and Energy*, 1, 125–37.

Boltzmann, L. (1877), 'Über die Beziehung eines allgemeinen mechanischen Satzes zum zweiten Hauptsatz der Wärmetheorie', *Sitzungsberichte der Kaiserlichen Akademie der Wissenschaften in Wien, Abt. 2*, **75**, 67–73.

Boulding, K.E. (1966), 'The economics of the coming spaceship Earth', in H. Jarrett (ed.), *Environmental Quality in a Growing Economy*, Baltimore: Johns Hopkins University Press, pp. 3–14.

Brodyansky, V.M., M.V. Sorin and P. Le Goff (eds) (1994), *The Efficiency of Industrial Processes: Exergy Analysis and Optimization*, Amsterdam: Elsevier.

Brown, L.R. (2001), *Eco-Economy. Building an Economy for the Earth*, New York: W.W. Norton.

Burley, P. and J. Foster (eds) (1994), *Economics and Thermodynamics: New Perspectives on Economic Analysis*, Dordrecht: Kluwer.

Burness, H.S., R.G. Cummings, G. Morris and I. Paik (1980), 'Thermodynamic and economic concepts as related to resource-use policies', *Land Economics*, **56**, 1–9.

Callen, H.B. (1985), *Thermodynamics and an Introduction to Thermostatics*, 2nd edn, New York: Wiley.

Clausius, R. (1854), *Fortschritte der Physik*, **10**.

Clausius, R. (1865), 'Über verschiedene für die Anwendung bequeme Formen der Hauptgleichungen der mechanischen Wärmetheorie', *Annalen der Physik*, **125**, 353–400.

Cleveland, C.J. and M. Ruth (1997), 'When, where and by how much does thermodynamics constrain economic processes? A survey of Nicholas Georgescu-Roegen's contribution to ecological economics', *Ecological Economics*, **22**, 203–23.

Connelly, L. and K.P. Koshland (2001), 'Exergy and industrial ecology', *Exergy*, 1, 146–65, 234–55.

Cornelissen, R.L. and G.G. Hirs (1999), 'Exergy analysis in the process industry', in A. Bejan and E. Mamut (eds), *Thermodynamic Optimization of Complex Energy Systems*, Dordrecht: Kluwer Academic Publishers.

Cornelissen, R.L., P.A. Nimwegen and G.G. Hirs (2000), 'Exergetic life-cycle analysis', in *Proceedings of ECOS 2000*, Enschede.

Costanza, R. (1981), 'Embodied energy, energy analysis, and economics', in H.E. Daly (ed.), *Energy, Economics, and the Environment*, Boulder: Westview Press.

Craig, P.P. (2001), 'Energy limits to recycling', *Ecological Economics*, **36**, 373–84.

Creyts, J.C. (2000), *Use of extended exergy analysis as a tool to optimize the environmental performance of industrial processes*, Ph.D. Thesis, Berkeley: University of California, Department of Mechanical Engineering.

Daly, H.E. (1973), *Toward a Steady-State Economy*, San Francisco: W.H. Freeman.

Daly, H.E. ([1977] 1991), *Steady State Economics. The Economics of Biophysical Equilibrium and Moral Growth*, 2nd edn, San Francisco: W.H. Freeman.

Daly, H.E. (1992), 'Is the entropy law relevant to the economics of natural resources? Yes, of course it is!', *Journal of Environmental Economics and Management*, **23**, 91–5.

Daly, H.E. (ed.) (1997a), *The Contribution of Nicholas Georgescu Roegen*, Special issue of *Ecological Economics*, **22** (3).

Daly, H.E. (1997b), 'Georgescu-Roegen versus Solow/Stiglitz', *Ecological Economics*, **22**, 261–6.

Dasgupta, P. and G. Heal (1974), 'The optimal depletion of exhaustible resources', *Review of Economic Studies*, **41** (Symposium on the Economics of Exhaustible Resources), 3–28.

Dasgupta, P.S. and G.M. Heal (1979), *Economic Theory and Exhaustible Resources*, Cambridge: Cambridge University Press.

Debreu, G. (1959), *Theory of Value: An Axiomatic Study of Economic Equilibrium*, New York: Wiley.

de Swaan Arons, J. and H.J. van der Kooi (2001), 'Towards a metabolic society: a thermodynamic view', *Green Chemistry*, **3** (4), G53–G55.

Dewulf, J., J.M. Mulder, M.M.D. van den Berg, H. Van Langenhove, H.J. van der Kooi and J. de Swaan Arons (2000), 'Illustrations towards quantifying the sustainability of technology', *Green Chemistry*, **2** (3), 108–14.

Faber, M. (1985), 'A biophysical approach to the economy: entropy, environment and resources', in W. van Gool and J.J.C. Bruggink (eds), *Energy and Time in the Economic and Physical Sciences*, Amsterdam: North Holland, pp. 315–35.

Faber, M., F. Jöst and R. Manstetten (1995), 'Limits and perspectives on the concept of sustainable development', *Economie Appliquée*, **48**, 233–51.

Faber, M., R. Manstetten and J. Proops (1996), *Ecological Economics: Concepts and Methods*, Cheltenham: Edward Elgar.

Faber, M., H. Niemes and G. Stephan ([1983] 1995), *Entropy, Environment and Resources: An Essay in Physico-Economics*, 2nd edn, Heidelberg: Springer.

Faber, M. and J. Proops (1985), 'Interdisciplinary research between economists and physical scientists: retrospect and prospect', *Kyklos*, **38**, 599–616.

Faber, M. and J. Proops (1990), *Evolution, Time, Production and the Environment*, Heidelberg: Springer.

Faber, M., J. Proops and S. Baumgärtner (1998), 'All production is joint production – a thermodynamic analysis', in S. Faucheux, J. Gowdy and I. Nicolaï (eds), *Sustainability and Firms. Technological Change and the Changing Regulatory Environment*, Cheltenham: Edward Elgar, pp. 131–58.

Falk, G. and W. Ruppel (1976), *Energie und Entropie. Eine Einführung in die Thermodynamik*, Heidelberg: Springer.

Freeman, A.M. (1993), *The Measurement of Environmental and Resource Values: Theory and Measurement*, Washington DC: Resources for the Future.

Georgescu-Roegen, N. (1951), 'Some properties of a generalized Leontief model', in T.C. Koopmans (ed.), *Activity Analysis of Production and Allocation*, New York: Wiley, pp. 165–73.

Georgescu-Roegen, N. (1971), *The Entropy Law and the Economic Process*, Cambridge MA: Harvard University Press.

Georgescu-Roegen, N. (1975), 'Energy and economic myths', *Southern Economic Journal*, **41**, 347–81.

Georgescu-Roegen, N. (1979), 'Energy analysis and economic valuation', *Southern Economic Journal*, **45**, 1023–58.

Gray, L.C. (1913), 'The economic possibilities of conservation', *Quarterly Journal of Economics*, **27**, 497–519.

Gray, L.C. (1914), 'Rent under the assumption of exhaustibility', *Quarterly Journal of Economics*, **28**, 466–89.

Hanley, N. and C.L. Spash (1993), *Cost-Benefit Analysis and the Environment*, Cheltenham: Edward Elgar.

Hannon, B. (1973), 'An energy standard of value', *American Academy of Political Science Annual*, **410**, 139–53.

Hannon, B. (1979), 'Total energy cost in ecosystems', *Journal of Theoretical Biology*, **56**: 279–93.

Hannon, B., R. Costanza and R.A. Herendeen (1986), 'Measures of energy cost and value in ecosystems', *Journal of Environmental Economics and Management*, **13**, 391–401.

Hinderink, P., H.J. van der Kooi and J. de Swaan Arons (1999), 'On the efficiency and sustainability of the process industry', *Green Chemistry*, **1** (6), G176–G180.

Hotelling, H. (1931), 'The economics of exhaustible resources', *Journal of Political Economy*, **39**, 137–75.

Huang, K. (1987), *Statistical Mechanics*, 2nd edn, New York: Wiley.

Inada, K.I. (1963), 'On a two-sector-model of economic growth: comments and a generalization', *Review of Economic Studies*, **30**, 119–27.

Kåberger, T. and B. Månsson (2001), 'Entropy and economic processes: physics perspectives', *Ecological Economics*, **36**, 165–79.

Khalil, E.L. (1990), 'Entropy law and exhaustion of natural resources: is Nicholas Georgescu-Roegen's paradigm defensible?', *Ecological Economics*, **2**, 163–78.

Kneese, A.V., R.U. Ayres and R.C. d'Arge (1972), *Economics and the Environment: A Materials Balance Approach*, Washington DC: Resources for the Future.

Kondepudi, D. and I. Prigogine (1998), *Modern Thermodynamics. From Heat Engines to Dissipative Structures*, New York: Wiley.

Koopmans, T.C. (1951), 'Alternative proof of the substitution theorem for Leontief models in the case of three industries', in T.C. Koopmans (ed.), *Activity Analysis of Production and Allocation*, New York: Wiley, pp. 14–54.

Kümmel, R. (1989), 'Energy as a factor of production and entropy as a pollution indicator in macroeconomic modelling', *Ecological Economics*, **1**, 161–80.

Kümmel, R., D. Lindenberger and W. Eichhorn (2000), 'The productive power of energy and economic evolution', *Indian Journal of Applied Economics*, **8**, 231–62.

Kümmel, R. and U. Schüssler (1991), 'Heat equivalents of noxious substances: a pollution indicator for environmental accounting', *Ecological Economics*, **3**, 139–56.

Kümmel, R., W. Strassl, A. Grosser and W. Eichhorn (1985), 'Technical progress and energy dependent production functions', *Journal of Economics*, **45**, 285–311.

Kurz, H.D. and N. Salvadori (2003), 'Fund-flow versus flow-flow in production theory: reflections on Georgescu-Roegen's contribution', *Journal of Economic Behavior and Organization*, **51**, 487–505.

Landau, L.D. and E. Lifshitz (1980), *Statistical Physics*, Volume 1, Oxford: Pergamon.

Lozada, G.A. (1991), 'A defense of Nicholas Georgescu-Roegens's paradigm', *Ecological Economics*, **3**, 157–60.

Lozada, G.A. (1995), 'Georgescu-Roegens's defence of classical thermodynamics revisited', *Ecological Economics*, **14**, 31–44.

Mayumi, K. (2001), *The Origins of Ecological Economics: The Bioeconomics of Georgescu-Roegen*, London: Routledge.

Mayumi, K. and J.M. Gowdy (eds) (1999), *Bioeconomics and Sustainability: Essays in Honor of Nicholas Georgescu-Roegen*, Cheltenham: Edward Elgar.

Nakićenović, N., P.V. Gilli and R. Kurz (1996), 'Regional and global exergy and energy efficiencies', *Energy*, **21**, 223–37.

Norgaard, R.B. (1986), 'Thermodynamic and economic concepts as related to resource-use policies: synthesis', *Land Economics*, **62**, 325–8.

Odum, H.T. (1971), *Environment, Power and Society*, New York: Wiley.

Ozdogan, S. and M. Arikol (1981), 'Energy and exergy analysis of selected Turkish industries', *Energy*, **18**, 73–80.

Patterson, M.G. (1998), 'Commensuration and theories of value in ecological economics', *Ecological Economics*, **25**, 105–25.

Perrings, C. (1987), *Economy and Environment: A Theoretical Essay on the Interdependence of Economic and Environmental Systems*, Cambridge: Cambridge University Press.

Pethig, R. (2003), 'The "materials balance approach" to pollution: its origin, implications and acceptance', *Discussion Paper 105–03*, University of Siegen.

Pigou, A.C. (1912), *Wealth and Welfare*, London: Macmillan.

Pigou, A.C. (1920), *The Economics of Welfare*, London: Macmillan.

Prigogine, I. (1962), *Introduction to Non-Equilibrium Thermodynamics*, New York: Wiley.

Prigogine, I. (1967), *Thermodynamics of Irreversible Processes*, New York: Interscience.

Proops, J. (1985), 'Thermodynamics and economics: from analogy to physical functioning', in W. van Gool and J.J.C. Bruggink (eds), *Energy and Time in the Economic and Physical Sciences*, Amsterdam: North-Holland, pp. 155–74.

Proops, J. (1987), 'Entropy, information and confusion in the social sciences', *Journal of Interdisciplinary Economics*, **1**, 224–42.

Ruth, M. (1993), *Integrating Economics, Ecology and Thermodynamics*, Dordrecht: Kluwer.

Ruth, M. (1995a), 'Technology change in the US iron and steel production', *Resources Policy*, **21**, 199–214.

Ruth, M. (1995b), 'Thermodynamic constraints on optimal depletion of copper and aluminum in the United States: a dynamic model of substitution and technical change', *Ecological Economics*, **15**, 197–213.

Ruth, M. (1995c), 'Thermodynamic implications for natural resource extraction and technical change in U.S. copper mining', *Environmental and Resource Economics*, **6**, 187–206.

Ruth, M. (1999), 'Physical principles in environmental economic analysis', in J.C.J.M. van den Bergh (ed.), *Handbook of Environmental and Resource Economics*, Cheltenham: Edward Elgar, pp. 855–66.

Samuelson, P.A. (1947), *Foundations of Economic Analysis*, Cambridge MA: Harvard University Press.

Samuelson, P.A. (1951), 'Abstract of a theorem concerning substitutability in open Leontief models', in T.C. Koopmans (ed.), *Activity Analysis of Production and Allocation*, New York: Wiley, pp. 142–6.

Schaeffer, R. and R.M. Wirtshafter (1992), 'An exergy analysis of the Brazilian economy: from energy products to final use', *Energy*, **17**, 841–55.

Schumpeter, J.A. (1954), *History of Economic Analysis*, London: Oxford University Press.

Söllner, F. (1997), 'A re-examination of the role of thermodynamics for environmental economics', *Ecological Economics*, **22**, 175–201.

Solow, R.M. (1974), 'Intergenerational equity and exhaustible resources', *Review of Economic Studies*, **41** (Symposium on the Economics of Exhaustible Resources), 29–45.

Spash, C. (1999), 'The development of environmental thinking in economics', *Environmental Values*, **8**, 413–35.

Spreng, D. (1993), 'Possibilities for substitution between energy, time and information', *Energy Policy*, **21**, 13–23.

Stiglitz, J. (1974), 'Growth with exhaustible natural resources: efficient and optimal growth paths', *Review of Economic Studies*, **41** (Symposium on the Economics of Exhaustible Resources), 123–52.

Szargut, J., D.R. Morris and F.R. Steward (1988), *Exergy Analysis of Thermal, Chemical, and Metallurgical Processes*, New York: Hemisphere Publishing.

Townsend, K.N. (1992), 'Is the entropy law relevant to the economics of natural resource scarcity? Comment', *Journal of Environmental Economics and Management*, **23**, 96–100.

Turner, R.K. (1999), 'Environmental and ecological economics perspectives', in J.C.J.M. van den Bergh (ed.), *Handbook of Environmental and Resource Economics*, Cheltenham: Edward Elgar, pp. 1001–33.

Wall, G. (1987), 'Exergy conversion in the Swedish society', *Resources and Energy*, **9**, 55–73.

Wall, G. (1990), 'Exergy conversion in the Japanese society', *Energy*, **15**, 435–44.

Wall, G., E. Sciubba and V. Naso (1994), 'Exergy use in the Italian society', *Energy*, **19**, 1267–74.

Williamson, A.G. (1993), 'The second law of thermodynamics and the economic process', *Ecological Economics*, **7**, 69–71.

Young, J.T. (1991), 'Is the entropy law relevant to the economics of natural resource scarcity?', *Journal of Environmental Economics and Management*, **21**, 169–79.

Young, J.T. (1994), 'Entropy and natural resource scarcity: a reply to the critics', *Journal of Environmental Economics and Management*, **26**, 210–13.

Zeh, H.D. (2001), *The Physical Basis of the Direction of Time*, 4th edn, Berlin: Springer.

Zemansky, M.W. and R.H. Dittman (1997), *Heat and Thermodynamics: An Intermediate Textbook*, 7th edn, New York: McGraw-Hill.

7. Multi-Criteria Evaluation

Giuseppe Munda

7.1 INTRODUCTION

Sustainable development is a multidimensional concept, including socio-economic, ecological, technical and ethical perspectives. In making sustainability policies operational, basic questions to be answered are sustainability of *what and whom*? As a consequence, sustainability issues are characterized by a high degree of conflict. The main objective of this chapter is to show that multiple-criteria decision analysis is an adequate approach for dealing with sustainability conflicts. To achieve this objective, lessons, learned from both theoretical arguments and empirical experience, are reviewed. Guidelines of 'good practice' are also suggested. Section 7.2 introduces basic concepts of multi-criteria decision theory. Section 7.3 deals with the relationships between complex systems theory, sustainability issues and multi-criteria evaluation. Section 7.4 proposes the concept of 'social' multi-criteria evaluation (SMCE) as a possible useful public choice framework for sustainability decisions. In Section 7.5 the open modelling problem of the choice of adequate mathematical aggregation procedures is discussed in depth. Finally some conclusions are derived.

7.2 THE NATURE OF MULTI-CRITERIA EVALUATION

We start the discussion on multi-criteria evaluation with a simple everyday example. Imagine standing in front of a shop and looking at a set of identically-priced jackets. What will be the next step? Probably to enter the shop and ask for the *price*. At this point, we have two possibilities: to leave the shop because we think that the price is too high, or to accept the price as a reasonable one. In the second case, we still need to choose the jacket we want from the original set (of, e.g., ten jackets). Thus, probably we are going to try on the jackets and see which one *fits better aesthetically*. Let us assume that we are still undecided among four of the jackets, though we are sure we do not like the other six. How do we choose among the remaining four jackets?

At this stage, perhaps we shall use the criterion *colour*. Let us imagine we are still undecided between two jackets. Probably now we will look at the *quality of the textile composition* and we shall finally choose the one with the higher quality. This is an example of a selection of a final alternative by using the *lexicographic model*.

This method refers to the procedure used to put in order the words in a dictionary, the first letter playing the role of the first criterion, the second letter, the second criterion, and so on. To use this method, the decision-maker must give a total strict order on the criteria:

$$1 > 2 > ... > i > ... > m \qquad\qquad (7.1)$$

where g_1 would be the most important criterion and g_m the least important. In the lexicographic model, all actions are first ranked by means of the first criterion, then if some items are equally ranked, these are further explored by means of the second criterion, and soon. Lexicographic ordering usually leads to a straightforward selection of the most preferred alternative; however, most of the information collected on alternatives will not play a role in the decision process. This example allows us to draw some conclusions.

First, most people often use such a decision process, even if not with these criteria or with this order. Thus, humans frequently use multi-criteria evaluation without any formal knowledge of it; we could say that this is an accurate behavioural assumption.

Second, does the order of criteria have any influence on the final alternative selected? Yes, certainly. If one starts with the criterion 'quality' instead of 'price', the selected jacket probably would be the most expensive one. This shows that when using various criteria, humans do not necessarily attach to them the same weight. In the case of the lexicographic model, in principle just the first criterion could be enough to select the final solution (i.e., if only one jacket has the price we are willing to pay). This implies that its weight is much higher than any other criterion used in the selection process. This is the reason why the first criterion is sometimes called the 'dictator'. Clearly, then, the order of consideration of criteria determines their relative weights.

Third, what happens in our example if we do not like the overall properties of the selected jacket? Probably we will start the process again; e.g., changing the order of criteria (i.e., their weight), or accept to pay a higher price. Again, this is something that probably we have experienced, and which shows that what really matters is the *learning process*, and not the final alternative selected. The latter is *constructed* by means of the decision process and not discovered as a global optimum.

Finally, does the lexicographic method allow for any compensability among the various criteria considered? Intuitively, compensability refers to the possibility that some low criterion scores can be compensated by other very high criterion scores. For example, an overall student evaluation can be based on the principle that a very bad score in mathematics (e.g.; a mark of two on a 0–10 scale) can be compensated by a ten in literature, and thus the student can pass the final evaluation. This evaluation system is a completely compensatory one. Alternatively, a system can be based on the principle that a student has to be 'good enough' in all of the subjects, and a two in mathematics cannot be compensated by any other score, however high it is. This second evaluation system would be a non-compensatory (or partial compensatory) one. Compensability, then, requires that the various criteria scores can interact among themselves; if no interaction is possible, no compensability can exist. Since in a lexicographic method the evaluation criteria are not considered simultaneously, this procedure is completely non-compensatory.

Compensability is a very important concept when multi-criteria evaluation is applied to economic-environmental policies. In fact in evaluating a project, if we consider that the equivalent of a score of two in mathematics could be a very bad environmental impact, and that of ten in literature a very good economic impact, it is clear that allowing or not for compensability, and to what degree, is the real issue in sustainability policies. To look for compromises implies that no-dictator must exist. That is, all of the dimensions relevant in a policy problem have to be used simultaneously and not in a lexicographic order, since otherwise some social dimensions will have a much higher weight *a priori*. Thus, for example, a legislative system which accepts that a financial analysis of projects has to be done before the evaluation of their environmental impacts, is, indeed, prioritizing the economic dimension with respect to the environmental one.

In empirical evaluations of public projects and publicly provided goods, multi-criteria decision theory seems to be an appropriate policy tool, since it allows the taking into account of a wide range of assessment criteria (e.g., environmental impact, distributional equity, and so on) and not simply profit maximization, as a private economic agent would do (Arrow and Raynaud, 1986; Martinez-Alier et al., 1998). As a tool for conflict management, multi-criteria evaluation has demonstrated its usefulness in many environmental policy and management problems (e.g., Beinat and Nijkamp, 1998; Janssen and Munda, 1999; Munda, 1995; Nijkamp et al., 1990; Romero and Rehman, 1989).

From an operational point of view, the major strength of multicriteria methods is their ability to revolve questions characterized by various conflicting evaluations, thus allowing an integrated assessment of the problem at hand. A typical multicriteria problem (with a discrete number of alternatives) may be described in the following way:

A is a finite set of n feasible actions (or alternatives); m is the number of different points of view or evaluation criteria g_i ($i = 1, 2, \ldots, m$) considered relevant in a decision problem, where the action a is evaluated to be better than action b (both belonging to the set A) according to the i-th point of view if $g_i(a) > g_i(b)$.

In this way a decision problem may be represented in a tabular or matrix form. Given the sets A (of alternatives) and G (of evaluation criteria), and assuming the existence of n alternatives and m criteria, it is possible to build an $n \times m$ matrix P, called the evaluation or impact matrix, whose typical element is p_{ij} ($i = 1, 2, \ldots, m; j = 1, 2, \ldots, n;$ see Table 7.1) and represents the evaluation of the j-th alternative by means of the i-th criterion. The impact matrix may include quantitative, qualitative or both types of information.

Table 7.1   Example of an impact matrix

Criteria	Alternatives			
	a_1	a_2	a_3	a_4
g_1	$g_1(a_1)$	$g_1(a_2)$	.	$g_1(a_4)$
g_2	$g_2(a_1)$	$g_2(a_2)$	.	$g_2(a_4)$
.	.	.	.	.
.	.	.	.	.
.	.	.	.	.
g_6	$g_6(a_1)$	$g_6(a_2)$	.	$g_6(a_4)$

In general, in a multicriteria problem, there is no solution optimizing all of the criteria at the same time, and therefore *compromise solutions* have to be found. In order to address contemporary issues, economics needs to expand its empirical relevance by introducing more and more realistic (thus more complex) assumptions into its models. One of the most interesting research directions in the field of public economics is the attempt to introduce political constraints, interest groups and collusion effects explicitly (e.g., Laffont, 2000). In this context, *transparency* becomes an essential feature of public policy processes (Stiglitz, 2002).

Social multi-criteria evaluation (SMCE) has been explicitly designed to enhance transparency. As the results of an evaluation exercise depend on the way a given policy problem is *represented*, and thus the assumptions used, the interests and values considered have to be made clear (Munda, 2004a).

7.3 THE ISSUE OF REPRESENTATING REAL COMPLEX SYSTEMS

The world is characterized by deep *complexity*. This straightforward observation has important implications for policy, in the way problems are represented and decision-making is framed. Each representation of a complex system reflects only a sub-set of its possible representations. A system is said to be complex when the relevant aspects of a particular problem cannot be captured when using a single perspective (Funtowicz et al., 1999; O'Connor et al., 1996).

To make things more difficult, systems including humans are *reflexively* complex. Reflexive systems present two specific aspects: *awareness* and *purpose*, both requiring an additional 'jump' in describing complexity. The presence of self-consciousness and purposes (*reflexivity*) means that these systems can continuously add new relevant qualities/attributes that should be considered when explaining, describing or forecasting their behaviour (i.e., human systems are learning systems).

Moreover, the existence of *different levels and scales* at which a hierarchical system can be analysed implies the unavoidable existence of non-equivalent descriptions of it (Giampietro, 1994). Even a simple 'objective' description of a geographical orientation is impossible without taking an arbitrary subjective decision on the system scale considered relevant. In fact, the same geographical place (e.g., in the USA) may be considered to be in the north, south, east or west according to the scale chosen as a reference point (the whole USA, a single state and so on) (Giampietro and Mayumi, 2000a, 2000b).

Therefore, the problem of *multiple identities* in complex systems cannot only be interpreted in terms of epistemological plurality (non-equivalent observers), but also in terms of *ontological characteristics* of the observed system (non-equivalent observations). A consequence of these deep subjectivities is that, in any normative exercise connected to a social decision problem, one has to choose an operational definition of 'value', in spite of the fact that social actors with different interests, cultural identities and goals, have different definitions of 'value' (O'Neill, 1993). That is, to reach a ranking of policy options, there is a previous need for deciding about *what is important* for different social actors, as well as *what is relevant* for the representation of the real-world entity described in the model. One should note that the representation of a real-world system depends on very strong assumptions about:

a. the *purpose* of this construction, e.g., to evaluate the sustainability of a given city,

b. the *scale* of analysis, e.g. a block inside a city, the administrative unit constituting a municipality or the whole metropolitan area, and

c. the *set* of dimensions, objectives and criteria used for the evaluation process.

A reductionist approach to building a descriptive model can be defined as the use of just *one measurable indicator* (e.g., the monetary city product per person), *one dimension* (e.g., economic), *one scale of analysis* (e.g., the Commune), *one objective* (e.g., the maximization of economic efficiency) and *one time horizon*.

An outcome of this discussion is that the political and social framework must find a place in the multi-criteria decision aid. To give an example, in Spain about forty years ago, there was an important policy criterion: security of the northern frontier with France. Nowadays, nobody even remembers the existence of this Francoist attitude towards frontiers. In fact, policy criteria are the consequence of the social and political framework existing in a given historical period. To give another example, at the moment the environmental dimension is becoming more and more important in the evaluation of projects, while this was almost irrelevant forty years ago.

In general, these methodological concerns were not considered very relevant for scientific research in the past (where the basic implicit assumption was that time was an infinite resource). On the other hand, the new nature of the policy problems faced in this third millennium (e.g., BSE or 'mad cow' disease, genetically modified organisms, etc.), imply that very often when using science for policy-making, long term consequences may exist and scientists and policy-makers are confronting issues where 'facts are uncertain, values in dispute, stakes high and decisions urgent' (Funtowicz and Ravetz, 1991, p. 140). In this case, scientists cannot provide any useful input without interacting with the rest of society, and the rest of society cannot perform any sound decision-making without interacting with the scientists. That is, the question on 'how to improve the quality of a policy process' must be put, quite quickly, on the agenda of 'scientists', 'decision-makers' and indeed the whole of society.

This extension of the 'peer community' is essential for maintaining the quality of the process of decision-making when dealing with reflexive complex systems. In relation to this objective, Funtowicz and Ravetz (1991, 1994) have developed a new epistemological framework of 'Post-Normal Science' ('post-normal' indicates a difference from the puzzle-solving exercises of normal science, in the Kuhnian sense (Kuhn, 1962)), where it is possible to deal better with two crucial aspects of science in the policy domain: *uncertainty* and *value conflict*.

7.4 SOCIAL MULTI-CRITERIA EVALUATION AS A TOOL FOR AIDING POLICY PROCESSES IN REFLEXIVE COMPLEX SYSTEMS

The previous discussion can be synthesized by using the philosophical concept of *weak comparability* (Martinez-Alier et al., 1998; O'Neill, 1993). Weak comparability implies *incommensurability*; i.e., there is an irreducible value conflict when deciding what common comparative term should be used to rank alternative actions. Remembering that the presence of multiple-identities in complex systems can be explained in terms of epistemological plurality, and in terms of ontological characteristics of the observed system, I argue that it is possible to further distinguish the concepts of social incommensurability and technical incommensurability (Munda, 2004a). *Social incommensurability* can be derived from the concepts of reflexive complexity and Post Normal Science, and refers to the existence of a multiplicity of legitimate values in society. *Technical incommensurability* comes from the multidimensional nature of complexity and refers to the issue of the representation of multiple identities in descriptive models.

If one wants to implement technical incommensurability, there is a clear need to take into account incommensurable dimensions using different scientific languages, coming from different legitimate representations of the same system. This is what Neurath (1973) called the need for an 'orchestration of sciences'. From the experience I have had in different real-world case studies, I have learnt that the use of a multi-criteria framework is a very efficient tool to make Neurath's idea operational. Here I refer to the idea of the orchestration of sciences as a combination of multi/inter-disciplinarity (multi-disciplinarity meaning each expert takes her/his part; inter-disciplinarity implies that methodological choices are discussed across the disciplines). In terms of inter-disciplinarity, the issue is to find an agreement on the set of criteria to be used; in terms of multi-disciplinarity, the issue is to propose and compute an appropriate criterion score.

To deal with social incommensurability, there is a need to consider the public participation issue. For the formation of contemporary public policies, it is hard to imagine any viable alternative to what Funtowicz and Ravetz (1991) call *extended peer communities*. They are already being created, in increasing numbers, either when the authorities cannot see a way forward, or know that without a broad base of consensus, no policies can succeed. They are called 'citizens' juries', 'focus groups', 'consensus conferences', or any one of a great variety of names; and their forms and powers are correspondingly varied. But they all have one important element in common: they assess the quality of policy proposals, including the scientific and technical component. And their verdicts all have some degree of moral force and hence political influence. Here, the quality is not merely in the verification, but also in the *creation*, as local people can imagine solutions and reformulate problems in ways that the accredited experts, with the best will in the world, do not find natural (Corral-Quintana, 2001; Corral-Quintana et al., 2001; De Marchi and Ravetz, 2001; Gowdy and O'Hara, 1996).

Historically, the first stage of the development of multi-criteria decision theory was characterized by the so-called methodological principle of *multi-criteria decision making* (MCDM). The main aim of MCDM is to elicit clear subjective preferences from a mythical decision-maker (DM) and then try to solve a well-structured mathematical decision problem, using a more or less sophisticated algorithm. In this way, a multi-criteria problem can be still presented in the form of a classical optimization problem (Keeney and Raiffa, 1976). The limitations of the classical concept of an optimum solution, and the consequential importance of the decision process, have recently been emphasized in the context of the decision sciences by authors such as Simon (1976) and Roy (1985, 1990, 1996).

According to Simon (1976), a distinction must be made between the general notion of rationality as an adaptation of available means to ends, and the various theories and models based on a rationality which is either 'substantive' or 'procedural'. This terminology can be used to distinguish between the rationality of a decision considered independently of the manner in which it is made (in the case of substantive rationality, the rationality of evaluation refers exclusively to the results of the choice) and the rationality of a decision in terms of the manner in which it is made (in the case of procedural rationality, the rationality of evaluation refers to the decision-making process itself).

Roy (1985, 1990, 1996) states that, in general, it is impossible to say that a decision is good or bad by referring only to a mathematical model: all aspects of the whole decision process which leads to a given decision also contribute to its quality and success. Thus, it becomes impossible to assess the validity of a procedure either on a notion of *approximation* (i.e., discovering pre-existing truths) or on a mathematical property of *convergence* (i.e., does the decision automatically lead, in a finite number of steps, to the optimum a*?). The final solution is more like a 'creation' than a discovery. In *Multiple-Criteria Decision Aid (MCDA)* (Roy, 1985), the principal aim is not to discover a solution, but to construct or create something which is viewed as liable to help a decision-maker either to shape, and/or to argue, and/or to transform her/his preferences, or to make a decision in conformity with her/his goals.

The need for public participation has been more and more recognized in a multi-criteria decision-aid framework. Two recent proposals have been for participatory multi-criteria evaluation (Banville et al., 1998) and social-multi-criteria evaluation (Munda, 2004a). Social multi-criteria evaluation agrees on the need for extending MCDA by incorporating the notion of the stakeholder; this is the reason why a social multi-criteria process must be as *participative* and as *transparent* as possible. However, it is further argued that participation is a *necessary* condition but not a *sufficient* one. This is the main reason why the concept of 'Social Multi-Criteria Evaluation' (SMCE) is proposed instead of 'Participative Multi-Criteria Evaluation' (PMCE) or 'Stakeholder Multi-Criteria Decision Aid' (SMCDA).

In my opinion, one should not forget that even a participatory policy process could always be conditioned by heavy value judgments. Have all the social actors the same importance (i.e., weight)? Should a socially desirable ranking be obtained on the grounds of the majority principle? Should some veto power be conceded to the minorities? Are income distribution effects important?

The main principles of Social Multi-Criteria Evaluation can be summarized as follows (Munda, 2004a):

- One should not forget that the classical schematized relationship decision-maker/analyst is indeed embedded in a social framework, which is of a crucial importance in the case of public policy.
- The combination of various participatory methods, which has been proved powerful in sociological research, becomes even more so when integrated with a multi-criteria framework (De Marchi et al., 2000).
- The use of a cyclic evaluation process allows the incorporation of the concept of learning by the scientific team in the case study tackled. It is extraordinarily important that different participatory and interaction tools are used at different points in time. This allows for continuous testing of the assumptions used.
- According to the geographical scale chosen, the relevant social actors with an interest at stake can be found with institutional analysis. Institutional analysis is an essential step to identifying possible 'stakeholders' for a participatory process.

However, besides the unavoidable mistakes that may occur in carrying out an appropriate institutional analysis, there are even stronger reasons why it is not desirable to use a purely participatory study:

- In a focus group, some powerful stakeholders may influence deeply all of the others.
- Focus groups are never meant to be a representative sample of a population. As a consequence, they can be a useful instrument to improve the knowledge of the scientific team of the institutional and social dimensions

of the problem at hand, but never a way of deriving consistent conclusions on social preferences.

- The notion of the stakeholder only recognizes relevant organized groups and not every possible social actor.
- Since decision-makers search for *legitimacy* of the decisions taken, it is extremely important that public participation or scientific studies do not become instruments of political de-responsibility. Social participation does not imply that scientists and policy-makers have no *responsibility* for policy actions defended and eventually taken. As a consequence, *ethics matters*.
- In this framework, mathematical algorithms still play an important role; i.e., to ensure that the policy rankings obtained are *consistent* with the information and the assumptions used. For this reason, multi-criteria algorithms to be used in a social context should be as simple as possible (i.e., with the minimum number of exogenous parameters) and their axiomatization should be complete and clear.

An example of the difference between MCDM, MCDA, PMCE and SMCE can be found in the determination of criterion weights. While in MCDM and MCDA frameworks, a relationship is supposed between an analyst and a decision-maker, this is no longer true in PMCE and SMCE, where there is a need to interact with the whole social framework.

A basic point of SMCE is that in society there are different legitimate values and points of view. This creates social pressure for taking into account various policy dimensions, e.g., economic, social and environmental. These dimensions are then translated, by analysts, into objectives and criteria. At this point a question arises: who should attach criterion weights and how? To answer this question we have to accept a basic assumption: *to attach weights to different criteria implies giving weights to different groups in society.* This assumption has as a main consequence that in social decision processes, weights cannot be derived as inputs coming from participatory techniques. This is *technically* very difficult (e.g.: Which elicitation method has to be used? Which statistical index is a good synthesis of the results obtained? Do average values of weights have meaning at all?), *pragmatically* not desirable (since strong conflicts among the various social actors are very probable to occur) and even *ethically* unacceptable. Let us imagine the case where a development project in the Amazon forest will affect an indigenous community with as yet little contact with other civilizations. Would it be ethically more correct to invite them to participate in a focus group, or to take into account the consequences of the project for their survival? Thus a *plurality of ethical principles* (e.g., economic development attaching more weight to the economic dimension, precautionary principle giving a bigger weight to the environmental dimension or sustainability which might imply an equal weighting of all the dimensions) seems the only consistent way to derive weights in a SMCE framework.

These reflections can be synthesized graphically, in Figure 7.1. We begin with the pragmatic solution of no criterion weighting. This approach would probably reduce conflicts in the problem-structuring step, but is it *normatively* correct? Indeed, the fact that all the criteria have the same weight does not guarantee at all that objectives, dimensions and, above all, social groups have the same weight. This would be guaranteed only under the condition that all the dimensions have the same number of criteria. This, of course, is quite unnatural and artificial, and even dangerous. Analysts could be tempted to choose the same number of criteria for each dimension, although these criteria were completely redundant. A better solution could be to give the same weight to each dimension and to split each weight among the criteria of any dimension proportionally. We arrive, then, at the conclusion that, by giving the same weight to all the criteria, the different social dimensions have different weights (since any dimension will be weighted according to its number of criteria). Conversely, *different criterion weights* can guarantee that all the *dimensions are considered equal*!

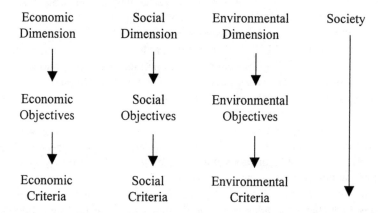

Figure 7.1 A schematized vision of the hierarchical structure of a policy problem

Thus from normative (since at least there is a clear decision to weight all the dimensions equally) and maybe also pragmatic (since this decision may reduce social conflicts) points of view, it seems better to attach weights to different criteria than not to attach them at all. But at this point one should answer another question: Why should different social dimensions be weighted equally? To answer this question, we have to remember that to give weights to different criteria implies to attach weights to different groups in society (see Figure 7.1). Can we find any normative justification for the weighting of social actors? I think that at least four different ethical justifications exist, and these are capable of being transformed into social weights:

- Political democracy
- Economic democracy
- Sustainability
- Precautionary principle

We discuss each briefly.

7.4.1 Political Democracy

The basic idea here is that the majority of a population has the right to influence decisions more than minorities. In this case, the derivation of social weights is relatively easy: each dimension should have a weight equal to the proportion of the population supporting the values represented by this dimension. This approach presents two main problems (Moulin, 1988). One is pragmatic in nature; i.e., to know the exact percentage of the population for each group can be a difficult and expensive process (for instance to use a referendum each time there is a complex decision that affects a community). The other problem is more theoretical; i.e., minorities always lose without any compensation. For these reasons, economists have proposed the concept of economic democracy.

7.4.2 Economic Democracy

The main idea here is that it is possible to avoid any type of referendum, simply because it is possible to derive people's preferences by looking at their behaviour on the market (Munda, 1996; Spash and Hanley, 1995). Moreover, in this way it is possible to know also the intensity of preference of the economic agents (while this is not possible in the political democracy, since the principle is one person, one vote) by looking at their consumer surplus and to compensate minorities by means of the Kaldor-Hicks compensation principle. There are at least two problems connected with this approach:

- Distributional issues. Very often willingness to pay depends on *ability to pay*, and not on preferences. Income distribution is, then, the basic principle one should accept to arrive at social decisions.

- There are goods and services for which markets do not exist; e.g., environmental goods. For these kind of goods and services, one should then invent artificial markets, or derive implicit markets, to obtain so-called shadow prices. The most general valuation method is contingent valuation.

7.4.3 Sustainability

This may imply that the economic, social and environmental dimensions should be taken into consideration *equally* (at least if one accepts that sustainability has three main aspects to be integrated simultaneously: economic efficiency, inter/intra generational equity, and impacts of the society on environmental quality (Munda, 1997)). As a consequence, this is the only principle under which all of the dimensions should have the same weight. One should note that, under this principle, the environmental dimension should have the same weight as the economic one, although perhaps only 5 per cent of society has some environmental concerns. One way to explain this apparent paradox is that one should accept that this 5 per cent of the population is also speaking for animals and future generations, which cannot be taken into account by either political and economic democracy principles. Another way to defend this position is that humans should behave according to a Kantian principle of universality, such that any negative impact of their actions on the planet should be avoided. Thus, even if no social group is willing to support the environmental dimension, this should anyway be weighted like the other dimensions, or even more. This last position, of a higher weight to the environmental dimension, could be defended by using the so-called precautionary principle.

7.4.4 Precautionary Principle

This maintains that in all situations where there is a simultaneous presence of uncertainty and irreversibility, prudence is the correct principle for informing social actions (Wynne, 1992). For example, in the case of global warming, due to the fact that there is no clear scientific evidence of what may happen with the present trend of greenhouse gas emissions, it is better to be prudent and to reduce these emissions now, even if the economic cost could be very high. A consequence of the adoption of this principle is that the environmental dimension has a higher weight, or that it must be operationalized by using constraints instead of criteria.

Concluding, for public policy in the third millennium, I propose the notion of 'social multi-criteria evaluation', which can be considered an approach that is:

- *Multidisciplinary*, to respect the plurality of scientific points of view.
- *Participative*, to take as many inputs as possible from the general public.
- *Transparent*, to make clear the assumptions adopted in the study.
- *Consistent*, to ensure that the results are a real consequence of the assumptions adopted.

Properties 1 to 3 are clearly dependent on the decision process; property 4 is more connected to the mathematical models used. This discussion on consistency and its mathematical meaning is the main topic of the rest of this chapter. My main effort here is an attempt to make clear which properties are desirable in a SMCE framework. Of course, in another framework (e.g., stock exchange investments) these properties could easily be irrelevant or even undesirable.

7.5 HOW TO CHOOSE AN ADEQUATE AGGREGATION CONVENTION?

In a discrete multi-criteria problem, there is a range of multi-criteria problem formulations, which may take one of the following forms (Roy, 1985, 1996):

(α) The aim is to identify one and only one final alternative.
(β) The aim is the assignment of each alternative to an appropriate predefined category, according to what one wants it to become afterwards (for instance, acceptance, rejection or delay for additional information).
(γ) The aim is to rank all feasible alternatives according to a total or partial preorder.
(δ) The aim is to describe relevant alternatives and their consequences.

Clearly, the steps required by such a process need a number of arbitrary unavoidable subjective decisions. The degree of the subjective component may be higher or lower, but it is always present. When different and conflicting evaluation criteria are taken into consideration, a multi-criteria problem is mathematically ill-defined. The consequence is that a complete axiomatization of a multi-criteria aggregation convention (i.e., a multi-criteria method is rather difficult (Arrow and Raynaud, 1986)). To deal with the problem pointed out by Arrow and Raynaud, two main approaches can be distinguished.

- The attempt to check under which specific circumstances each method could be more useful than others; i.e., the search for the right method for the right problem (e.g., Guitouni and Martel, 1998).

- The attempt to look for a complete set of formal axioms that can be attributed to a specific method (e.g., Arrow and Raynaud, 1986; Vincke, 1994).

Here, I shall try to isolate some properties that may be considered desirable for a discrete multi-criteria method in the framework of SMCE. We start with a principle that carries considerable epistemological implications: the principle that *dominated alternatives* can be ignored in an evaluation exercise, and thus only *efficient alternatives* have to be taken into account.

The concept of efficiency can easily be illustrated graphically (see Figure 7.2 which refers to a 2-criteria state space). Alternative C performs better than B in all respects, and hence C is preferred to B. The same can be said for B compared with A. Thus only alternatives C and D are 'efficient' alternatives.

It has to be noted that efficiency does not imply that every efficient solution is necessarily to be preferred above every non-efficient solution; e.g., the non-efficient alternatives A and B are preferable to the efficient alternative D if the second criterion would receive a high priority compared to the first criterion (Nijkamp et al., 1990).

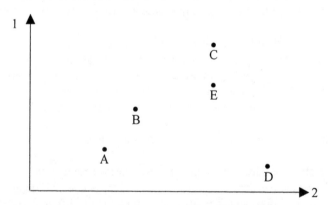

Figure 7.2   Graphical representation of efficiency in a two-dimensional case

The principle that inefficient solutions may be ignored (often presented as a simple technical step) needs the acceptance of the following assumptions:

- The assumption that all the relevant criteria have been identified needs to be accepted. If relevant criteria are omitted, there are potential opportunity costs associated with assuming that it is safe to ignore dominated alternatives.

• The assumption that only one alternative, considered the best, has to be identified needs to be accepted (α problem formulation). Since the 'second best' may have been eliminated during the technical screening, if more than one action has to be found, the elimination of the 'inefficient' action may result in an opportunity loss (one has to note that if the best action is removed from the set of feasible alternatives, then the second best becomes a member of the non-dominated set) (Bogetoft and Pruzan, 1991). If one is interested in the γ problem formulation, then dominated alternatives cannot be eliminated. It has to be noted that in economic-environmental policies, it is often much more useful to have a ranking of policy options than to select just one alternative. In fact, sometimes the first alternative in the ranking can also be the most controversial from a social point of view. Thus, in the framework of a sustainability dialectic, it may be more useful to implement the policy option that ranks second (so technically it is not too bad), but socially might reduce conflicts.

• A third problem is connected to the question: How relevant are 'irrelevant' alternatives (Zeleny, 1982)? Arrow's (1963) axiom of 'the independence of irrelevant alternatives' states that the choice made in a given set of alternatives A depends only on the ordering made with respect to the alternatives in that set. Alternatives outside A (irrelevant since the choice must be made within A) should not affect the choice inside A. Empirical experience does not generally support this axiom; thus to exclude some actions already inside A can have even less justification. However, the issue of the independence of irrelevant alternatives is particularly important and tricky when pair-wise comparisons are used.

To clarify this final point, let us imagine a football championship. To determine the winner, all of the teams have to compete pair-wise. Then we need to know the performance of each team with respect to all of the others; i.e., how many times a given team won, lost or drew. By using this information, we can finally determine who won the championship. Let us now imagine that when the championship is about to end, and team X is going to win (e.g., Barcelona), a new team Y is created (e.g., in Madrid). Would it be acceptable to allow this new team Y to play directly with X? Would the supporters of team X accept that if Y wins, then Y will also win the championship? Of course not!

This example seems to give a clear answer to our problem, but let us now imagine that instead of ranking football teams, our problem is to buy a new car. If we are on the point of buying car A and a new car Z enters the market, can we just compare A with Z, or do we have to make all the pair-wise comparisons again? Now the answer is less clear-cut. Moreover, let us imagine that the ranking at time T (without Z) ranks car A better than B and that at time $T+1$ (when Z is considered in the pair-wise comparisons) B is ranked better than A, just because Z is taken into consideration! Can this result be acceptable? To answer this question in a definitive manner is very controversial. What we can say for sure is that if pair-wise comparisons are used, then what has to be accepted is the assumption that the irrelevant alternative Z (irrelevant for the evaluation between A and B) can indeed change the relative evaluation of A and B. This phenomenon is called 'rank reversal'.

From these simple examples we can derive some conclusions:

- When pair-wise comparisons are used, this information is not sufficient to derive a consistent ranking. It is necessary also to exploit the relationships among all alternatives. As a consequence, no alternative is irrelevant.
- If the set of alternatives is dynamic (i.e., new alternatives enter the evaluation process), then all of the pair-wise comparisons have to be done again. It is not possible just to compare the new alternative with the one that was first in the ranking.
- The principle that the final ranking of all of the alternatives depends on the relationship among the whole set of alternatives, may cause the effect of rank reversal.
- Finally, a dominated action may be slightly worse than an efficient action; if indifference and/or preference thresholds are used, then the two actions could present an indifference relation (e.g., C and E in Figure 7.1). This point will be further developed later on in this chapter.

As a conclusion for this discussion, we can state then that in SMCE applications it is better to use aggregation procedures that do not exclude dominated alternatives *a priori*.

Another sensitive point is that of compensability. In synthesis, the information contained in the impact matrix, useful for solving the so-called multi-criterion problem, is:

- *Intensity of preference* (when quantitative criterion scores are present).
- *Number* of criteria in favour of a given alternative.
- *Weight* attached to each single criterion.
- *Relationship* of each single alternative with all the other alternatives.

Combinations of this information generate different aggregation conventions; i.e., manipulation rules of the available information to arrive at a preference structure. The aggregation of several criteria implies taking a position on the fundamental issue of compensability. *Compensability* refers to the existence of trade-offs; i.e., the possibility of offsetting a disadvantage on some criteria by a sufficiently large advantage on another criterion, whereas smaller advantages would not do the same. Thus a preference relation is non-compensatory if no trade-off occurs and is compensatory otherwise. The use of weights with intensity of preference gives rise to compensatory multi-criteria methods and gives the meaning of trade-offs to the weights. Conversely, the use of weights with ordinal criterion scores gives rise to non-compensatory aggregation procedures, and gives the weights the meaning of importance coefficients (Bouyssou and Vansnick, 1986; Keeney and Raiffa, 1976; Roberts, 1979).

From the previous discussion on weights in a SMCE framework, we already know that weights as trade-offs are not desirable for SMCE (since ethical positions can be translated into weights only as importance coefficients). From this point of view, ELECTRE II (Roy and Bertier, 1973) and ELECTRE III (Roy, 1978) methods are probably the most interesting (although the existence of a veto considered as intensity of preference may create some perplexities on the meaning of weights). An approach that certainly needs weights as importance coefficients is the REGIME method, when only ordinal criterion scores are used (Hinloopen et al., 1983). However, when mixed information is considered (Hinloopen and Nijkamp, 1990), weights are more likely to be considered as trade-offs rather than importance coefficients.

Moreover, compensability also has consequences for the so-called weak/strong sustainability debate (Faucheux and O'Connor, 1998). The so-called 'weak sustainability' concept states that an economy can be considered sustainable if it saves more than the combined depreciation of natural and manufactured capital. The concept of 'strong sustainability' is based on the assumption that certain sorts of natural capital are deemed critical and not readily substitutable by manufactured capital. In particular, the characterization of sustainability in terms of the 'strong' criterion, of non-negative change over time in stocks of specified natural capital, provides a strong justification for the development of non-monetary indicators of ecological sustainability, based on direct physical measurement of important stocks and flows. It is clear at this stage that non-compensatory and partial compensatory multi-criteria aggregation conventions are the only ones that may allow an implementation of the strong sustainability concept (for a deeper discussion of this point, see Martinez-Alier et al., 1998).

Let us now try to find other desirable properties for SMCE. It has been argued that the presence of qualitative information in evaluation problems concerning socio-economic and physical planning, is the rule rather than the exception (Nijkamp et al., 1990). Thus, the idea of technical incommensurability implies that there is a clear need for methods that are able to take into account information of a 'mixed' type (both qualitative and quantitative criterion scores). For simplicity, I refer to *qualitative information* as information measured on a nominal or ordinal scale, and to *quantitative information* as information measured on an interval or ratio scale. Moreover, ideally, this information should be precise, certain, exhaustive and unequivocal. But in reality, it is often necessary to use information which does not have these characteristics, so that one has to face the uncertainty of a stochastic and/or fuzzy nature present in the data (Munda et al., 1994, 1995; Munda, 1995). In conclusion, multi-criteria methods able to tackle consistently the widest types of mixed information should be considered as desirable ones. Examples of this kind of methods are REGIME (Hinloopen and Nijkamp, 1990), EVAMIX (Voogd, 1983), NAIADE (Munda, 1995) and the method by Martel and Zaras (1995).

Another important point is the issue of how deep should be the interaction with a method. To give an example, the implementation of the philosophy of 'Multi-Criteria Decision Aid' (MCDA) by means of, e.g., an ELECTRE method, leads to the need to establish a large number of *ad hoc* exogenous parameters (e.g., indifference and preference thresholds, concordance threshold, discordance thresholds, weights). According to Roy, these parameters allow the decision-maker to express her/his preferences and to learn about them. In this way, the concept of decision aid is implemented in this framework. Perhaps the PROMETHEE methods (Brans et al., 1984) are the best attempt to introduce various parameters with physical or economic interpretation for a decision-maker. I also used these suggestions in building the NAIADE method. However, it must be admitted that a large number of parameters may cause a loss of transparency and consistency in the model. I think that this approach is useful in the case of single person or very technical decisions, but it is not desirable in a social framework. In the latter case, the role of the multi-criteria method should be to guarantee the consistency between the information presented in the impact matrix and the rankings obtained without any further manipulation (at least if it is agreed that transparency is an important feature of this type of approach). For this reason, I believe that simplicity is a very desirable property for multi-criteria methods to be used in a SMCE framework. Thus, the only exogenous parameters I would suggest to introduce in a social framework is the idea of indifference and preference threshold (coming from the famous 'baldness' paradox in Greek philosophy: How many hairs has one to cut off to transform a person with hair to someone bald?).

Finally, one should note that the possibility of explicitly tackling the hierarchy of scale issue would be an interesting and desirable property. To my knowledge, the only method which explicitly deals with the hierarchy issue is the Analytic Hierarchy Process (AHP) method (Saaty, 1980). However, in the framework of SMCE, this method presents the problem of needing weights as trade-offs.

As a conclusion for this section, I think it is possible to state quite safely that a problem of all multi-criteria approaches is that there exist many different mathematical aggregation conventions (or methods). For the case of SMCE, the following considerations can be useful to select appropriate methods.

The idea of *social incommensurability* makes the following properties desirable in a social multi-criteria method:

- Multi-criteria methods must be as simple as possible to guarantee transparency.
- Weights in this framework are clearly meaningful only as importance coefficients, and not as trade-off. As a consequence, complete compensability cannot be implemented.
- Sensitivity and robustness analysis have to check the consequences on the final ranking of only some clear ethical positions, and not of all the possible combinations of weights.
- Conflict analysis procedures, explicitly looking for social compromises, should integrate a SMCE exercise.
- In a policy framework, to have a ranking of all of the alternatives is more useful than to select only one alternative; this implies that dominated alternatives cannot be excluded *a priori.*

The idea of *technical incommensurability* makes the following properties desirable in a social multi-criteria method:

- Partial compensability is an essential consistency requirement.
- Indifference and preference thresholds should be explicitly taken into account.
- Mixed information of the widest type should be addressed in a consistent way.
- Simplicity, meaning the use of as few parameters as possible, is a very desirable property.
- The hierarchical dimension of a policy problem should be explicitly considered.

As an example, I present Table 7.2, where the above cited methods are judged against the proposed desirable properties. The scale + + +/– – – is ordinal in nature (+ is more desirable than –; + + is more desirable than + and – – is less desirable than –) and subjectively determined by my knowledge of these methods. However, even if quite approximate, the information

Table 7.2 Evaluation of some multi-criteria methods

	Effective Alternatives	Compensability	Weights as Important Coefficients	Mixed Information	Simplicity	Hierarchy	γ prob. Formulation	Ind./pref. thresholds	Conflict Analysis
MAUT	– – –	– – –	– – –	+	+ + +	– – –	– – –	– – –	– – –
ELECTRE 2	+ + +	+ + +	+ +	+	– –	– – –	+ + +	+ +	– – –
ELECTRE 3	+ + +	+ + +	+ +	+	– – –	– – –	+ + +	+ +	– – –
REGIME (H,N,R, 1983)	+ + +	+ + +	+ + +	+	+ + +	– – –	+	– – –	– – –
REGIME (H,N, 1990)	+ + +	+	–	+ + +	+	– – –	+ +	– – –	– – –
NAIADE	+ + +	+ +	– – –	+ + +	– – –	– – –	+ + +	+ +	+ + +
AHP	+ + +	–	– – –	– – –	+ +	+ + +	+ +	– –	– – –
EVAMIX	+ + +	–	– –	+ + +	+ +	– – –	+ +	– – –	– – –
PROMETHEE	+ + +	+	+	+	– –	– – –	+ + +	+ + +	– – –
Martel and Zaras method	+ + +	+ + +	+	+ + +	– – –	– – –	+ + +	+ +	– – –

contained in Table 7.2 leads to an important conclusion: no one of these methods achieves all of the properties considered desirable.

For this reason, in Munda (2004b) a new multi-criteria aggregation procedure has been developed, which respects the properties desirable in a SMCE framework. Throughout the whole pair-wise comparison step, it is guaranteed that mixed information, in the form of ordinal, crisp, stochastic and fuzzy criterion scores, is tackled equivalently. Weights are never combined with intensities of preference; as a consequence, the theory guarantees that they are importance coefficients. Given that the sum of the weights is unity, the pair-wise comparisons can be synthesized in a matrix, which can be interpreted as a voting matrix. The information contained in the voting matrix is exploited to rank all alternatives in a complete pre-order, by using a Condorcet consistent rule. Following the normative tradition in political philosophy, the minority principle is introduced by means of a veto power. A vetoed alternative, the Borda looser, is found by means of the original Borda approach, implemented by using a frequency matrix.

7.6 CONCLUSIONS

In my opinion, the substantive meaning of multi-criteria evaluation in a social context is simply tolerance and democracy. Complex systems (i.e., all real-world systems) present multiple possible descriptions, and all of them are correct. Complexity is, then, a property of the appraisal process rather than a property inherent to the system itself. As a consequence, any model is the representation of reality resulting from a number of arbitrary assumptions, implying the existence of two or more different but correct representations of the same real-world system.

All of the arguments and convictions discussed in this chapter have led me to the development of the concept of Social Multi-Criteria Evaluation (SMCE), whose main principles are:

- The use of a multi-criteria framework as a very efficient tool to implement a *multi/inter-disciplinary* approach.
- *Public participation* is a necessary component, but not a sufficient one. Participation techniques are a tool for improving the knowledge of the problem at hand, and not for receiving inputs to be used uncritically in the evaluation process. Social participation does not imply a lack of responsibility for scientists and policy-makers.
- *Ethical judgements* are unavoidable components of the evaluation exercise. These judgements always influence heavily the results. As a consequence, *transparency* of the assumptions used is essential.

In this framework, of course, mathematical aggregation conventions play an important role; i.e., to ensure that the rankings of policy options obtained are *consistent* with the information and the assumptions used.

REFERENCES

Arrow, K.J. (1963), *Social Choice and Individual Values*, New York: Wiley.

Arrow, K.J. and H. Raynaud (1986), *Social Choice and Multicriterion Decision Making*, Cambridge MA: M.I.T. Press.

Banville, C., M. Landry, J.M. Martel and C. Boulaire (1998), 'A stakeholder approach to MCDA', *Systems Research and Behavioral Science*, **15**, 15–32.

Beinat, E. and P. Nijkamp (eds) (1998), *Multicriteria Evaluation in Land-Use Management: Methodologies and Case Studies*, Dordrecht: Kluwer.

Bogetoft, P. and P. Pruzan (1991), *Planning with Multiple Criteria*, Amsterdam: North-Holland.

Bouyssou, D. and J.C. Vansnick (1986), 'Noncompensatory and generalized noncompensatory preference structures', *Theory and Decision*, **21**, 251–66.

Brans, J.P., B. Mareschal and Ph. Vincke (1984), 'PROMETHEE: A new family of outranking methods in multicriteria analysis', in J.P. Brans (ed.), *Operational Research '84* , Amsterdam, Elsevier, pp. 408–21.

Corral-Quintana, S. (2001), *Una metodología integrada de exploración y comprensión de los procesos de elaboración de políticas públicas*, unpublished Ph.D. thesis, Department of Economics, University La Laguna, Spain.

Corral-Quintana, S., B. De Marchi, S. Funtowicz, G. Gallopín, A. Guimarães-Pereira and B. Maltoni (2001), *The Visions Project at the JRC*, European Commission, Joint Research Centre, Institute for the Protection and Safety of the Citizens, EUR 19926 EN (http://alba.jrc.it/visions).

De Marchi, B., S.O. Funtowicz, S. Lo Cascio and G. Munda (2000), 'Combining participative and institutional approaches with multi-criteria evaluation: an empirical study for water issue in Troina, Sicily', *Ecological Economics*, **34**, 267–82.

De Marchi, B. and J. Ravetz (2001), *Participatory Approaches to Environmental Policy*, Concerted Action EVE, Policy Research Brief, No. 10.

Faucheux, S. and M. O'Connor (eds) (1998), *Valuation for Sustainable Development: Methods and Policy Indicators*, Cheltenham: Edward Elgar.

Funtowicz, S.O. and J. Ravetz (1991), 'A new scientific methodology for global environmental issues', in R. Costanza (ed.), *Ecological Economics*, New York: Columbia University Press, pp. 137–52.

Funtowicz, S.O. and J. Ravetz (1994), 'The worth of a songbird: ecological economics as a post-normal science', *Ecological Economics*, **10**, 197–207.

Funtowicz S., J. Martinez-Alier, G. Munda and J. Ravetz (1999), *Information Tools for Environmental Policy Under Conditions of Complexity*, European Environmental Agency, Experts' Corner, Environmental Issues Series, No. 9.

Giampietro, M. (1994), 'Using hierarchy theory to explore the concept of sustainable development', *Futures*, **26** (6), 616–25.

Giampietro, M. and K. Mayumi (2000a), 'Multiple-scale integrated assessment of societal metabolism: introducing the approach', *Population and Environment*, **22** (2), 109–54.

Giampietro, M. and K. Mayumi (2000b), 'Multiple-scale integrated assessment of societal metabolism: integrating biophysical and economic representations across scales', *Population and Environment*, **22** (2), 155–210.

Gowdy, J.M. and S. O'Hara (1996), *Economic Theory for Environmentalists*, New York: Saint Lucie Press.

Guitouni, A. and J.M. Martel (1998), 'Tentative guidelines to help choosing an appropriate MCDA method', *European Journal of Operational Research*, **109**, 501–21.

Hinloopen, E., P. Nijkamp and P. Rietveld (1983), 'Qualitative discrete multiple criteria choice models in regional planning', *Regional Science and Urban Economics*, **13**, 77–102.

Hinloopen, E. and P. Nijkamp (1990), 'Qualitative multiple criteria choice analysis, the dominant regime method', *Quality and Quantity*, **24**, 37–56.

Janssen, R. and G. Munda (1999), 'Multi-criteria methods for quantitative, qualitative and fuzzy evaluation problems', in J. van den Bergh (ed.), *Handbook of Environmental and Resource Economics*, Cheltenham: Edward Elgar, pp. 837–52.

Keeney, R. and H. Raiffa (1976), *Decision with Multiple Objectives: Preferences and Value Trade-Offs*, New York: Wiley.

Kuhn, T.S. (1962), *The Structure of Scientific Revolutions*, Chicago: University of Chicago Press.

Laffont J.J. (2000), *Incentives and Political Economy*, Oxford: Oxford University Press.

Martel, J.M. and K. Zaras (1995), 'Stochastic dominance in multicriteria analysis under risk', *Theory and Decision*, **35** (1), 31–49.

Martinez-Alier, J., G. Munda and J. O'Neill (1998), 'Weak comparability of values as a foundation for ecological economics', *Ecological Economics*, **26**, 277–86.

Moulin, H. (1988), *Axioms of Co-Operative Decision Making*, Cambridge: Cambridge University Press.

Munda, G. (1995), *Multicriteria Evaluation in a Fuzzy Environment*, Heidelberg: Physica-Verlag.

Munda, G. (1996), 'Cost-benefit analysis in integrated environmental assessment: some methodological issues', *Ecological Economics*, **19**, 157–68.

Munda, G. (1997), 'Environmental economics, ecological economics and the concept of sustainable development', *Environmental Values*, **6** (2), 213–33.

Munda, G. (2004a) 'Social multi-criteria evaluation (SMCE): methodological foundations and operational consequences', *European Journal of Operational Research*, forthcoming.

Munda, G. (2004b), 'An axiomatic solution for the discrete multi-criterion problem in a public choice framework', unpublished manuscript.

Munda, G., P. Nijkamp and P. Rietveld (1994), 'Qualitative multicriteria evaluation for environmental management', *Ecological Economics*, **10**, 97–112.

Munda, G., P. Nijkamp and P. Rietveld (1995), 'Qualitative multi-criteria methods for fuzzy evaluation problems', *European Journal of Operational Research*, **82**, 79–97.

Neurath, O. (1973), *Empiricism and Sociology*, Dordrecht: Reidel.

Nijkamp, P., P. Rietveld and H. Voogd (1990), *Multicriteria Evaluation in Physical Planning*, Amsterdam: North-Holland.

O'Connor, M., S. Faucheux, G. Froger, S.O. Funtowicz and G. Munda (1996), 'Emergent complexity and procedural rationality: post-normal science for sustainability', in R. Costanza, O. Segura and J. Martinez-Alier (eds), *Getting Down to Earth: Practical Applications of Ecological Economics*, Washington D.C.: Island Press/ISEE, pp. 223–48.

O'Neill, J. (1993), *Ecology, Policy and Politics*, London: Routledge.

Roberts, F.S. (1979), *Measurement Theory with Applications to Decision Making, Utility and the Social Sciences*, London: Addison-Wesley.

Romero, C. and T. Rehman (1989), *Multiple Criteria Analysis for Agricultural Decisions*, Amsterdam: Elsevier.

Roy, B. and P. Bertier (1973), 'La méthode ELECTRE II. Une application ou media planning', in M. Ross (ed.), *Operational Research '72*, Amsterdam: North Holland, pp. 291–302.

Roy, B. (1978), 'ELECTRE III: Un algorithme de classement fondé sur une réprésentation floue des préférences en présence de critères multiples', *Cahiers du Centre d'Etudes de Recherche Opérationnelle*, **20** (1), 3–24.

Roy, B. (1985), *Méthodologie multicritère d'aide à la decision*, Paris: Economica.

Roy, B. (1990), 'Decision aid and decision making', in C.A. Bana e Costa (ed.), *Readings in Multiple Criteria Decision Aid*, Berlin: Springer-Verlag, pp. 17–35.

Roy B. (1996), *Multicriteria Methodology for Decision Analysis*, Kluwer, Dordrecht.

Saaty, T.L. (1980), *The Analytic Hierarchy Process*, New York: McGraw Hill.

Simon, H.A. (1976), 'From substantive to procedural rationality', in J.S. Latsis (ed.), *Methods and Appraisal in Economics*, Cambridge: Cambridge University Press.

Spash, C. and N. Hanley (1995), 'Preferences, information, and biodiversity preservation', *Ecological Economics*, **12**, 191–208.

Stiglitz, J.E. (2002), 'New perspectives on public finance: recent achievements and future challenges', *Journal of Public Economics*, **86**, 341–60.

Vincke, Ph. (1994), 'Recent progress in multicriteria decision-aid', *Rivista di Matematica per le scienze Economiche e Sociali*, **2**, 21–32.

Voogd, H. (1983), *Multicriteria Evaluation for Urban and Regional Planning*, London: Pion.

Wynne, B. (1992), 'Uncertainty and environmental learning: reconceiving science in the preventive paradigm', *Global Environmental Change*, **2**, 111–27.

Zeleny, M. (1982), *Multiple Criteria Decision Making*, New York: McGraw Hill.

8.   Agent-Based Models

Marco A. Janssen[1]

8.1 INTRODUCTION

Agent-based modelling (ABM)[2] is the computational study of social agents as evolving systems of autonomous, interacting agents. ABM is a tool for the study of social systems from the complex adaptive system perspective. From this perspective, the researcher is interested in how macro-phenomena are emerging from micro-level behaviour among a heterogeneous set of interacting agents (Holland, 1992). By using ABM as computational laboratories, one may test different hypotheses related to attributes of the agents, their behavioural rules, and the types of interactions, and their effect on macro-level stylized facts of the system.

An illustrative example of emergence in ecological economic systems and the use of ABM is the Bali irrigation system as studied by Lansing (1991). The irrigators have to solve a complex coordination problem. On the one hand, control of pests is most effective when all rice fields have the same schedule of rice planting. On the other hand, the terraces are hydrologically interdependent, with long and fragile systems of tunnels, canals, and aqueducts. To balance the need for coordinated fallow periods and use of water, a complex calendar system has been developed which states what actions should be done on each specific date. These actions are related to offerings to temples: from the little temples at the rice terrace level, to the temple at the village level; from the region level up to the temple of the high priest Jero Gde, the human representative of the Goddess of the Temple of the Crater Lake. This crater lake feeds the groundwater system which is the main source of water for irrigation. These offerings were collected as a counter-performance for the use of water that belonged to the gods.

The function and power of the water temples were invisible to the planners involved in promoting the Green Revolution during the 1960s. They regarded agriculture as a purely technical process. Farmers were forced to switch to the miracle rice varieties that give three harvests a year, instead of the two harvests of the traditional varieties. Farmers were stimulated by

governmental programmes which subsidized the use of fertilizers and pesticides. The farmers continued to perform their rituals, but now they no longer
coincided with the timing of rice farming activities. Soon after the introduction of the miracle rice, a plague of plant-hoppers caused huge damage to rice
production. A new variety was introduced, but then a new pest plague hit the
farmers. Furthermore, there were problems of water shortage.

During the 1980s, an increasing number of farmers wanted to switch back
to the old system, but the engineers interpreted this as religious conservatism
and resistance to change. It was Lansing (1991) who unravelled the function
of the water temples, and he was able to convince the financers of the Green
Revolution project on Bali that the irrigation was best coordinated at the level
of the water temples. Lansing built an ABM of the interactions of *subaks'*
(groups of rice farmers having adjacent fields) management strategies and the
ecosystem, and the local adaptation of *subaks* to strategies of neighbouring
subaks, and showed that for different levels of coordination, from farmer
level, up to central control, the temple level was the level of scale where
decisions could be made to maximize the production of rice (see also Lansing
and Kremer, 1994). He also showed how the coordination might have been
evolved as a result of local interactions (Lansing, 2000).

The complex irrigation systems and the role of the temples have evolved
over a long history of local adaptations, at different levels of scale. The water
temples played a significant role in the coordination of the use of water. The
problem of coordination and multi-level interaction is not unique to the Bali
irrigation example, and such interactions of social agents and their environments can be found in many social systems.

For modelling such micro-level interactions, since the early 1990s ABM
has increasingly been used in most of the social sciences (e.g., Berry et al.,
2002; Bousquet et al., 2001; Conte et al., 1997; Epstein and Axtell, 1996;
Gilbert and Doran, 1994; Gimblett, 2002; Janssen, 2002; Kohler and Gumerman, 2000; Lomi and Larsen, 2001; Macy and Willer, 2002; Parker et al.,
2003; Tesfatsion, 2001). In this chapter I shall focus on the applications of
ABM related to ecological economics. ABM of ecological economic systems
can be defined as the study of systems that are populated with heterogeneous
population of agents, who determine their interactions with other agents, and
with their environment, on the basis of internalized social norms and mental
models, internal behavioural rules and cognitive abilities, formal and informal institutional rules that affect how agents interact, individual and social
learning, etc. Three different types of agents can be distinguished:

- *Humans*, who differ in mental maps, goals, locations, and abilities, and
  also differ in scale from individuals, households up to organizations and
  nations.

- *Non-humans*, such as animals and plants.
- *Passive* agents, such as non-living entities.

We focus on the human agents, who can be represented by a rich pallet of possible behavioural rules, varying from self rational agents up to agents behaving according to psychological heuristics. Agents may continually adapt their behaviour in response to agent-agent and agent-environment interactions in an attempt to satisfy their needs.

The rest of the chapter is structured as follows. In Section 8.2 the use of ABM will be discussed in the context of other modelling approaches. A brief overview of the main methodology is given in Section 8.3. In Section 8.4 a number of applications in ecological economics are presented, and in Section 8.5 the question of the degree of complexity in modelling is discussed, and future challenges of ABM within ecological economics are mentioned. Section 8.6 closes the chapter with some conclusions.

8.2 MOTIVATIONS FOR AGENT-BASED MODELLING

Some readers may question why we need complex approaches such as ABM. Are equation-based models not sufficient? Other readers may argue that ABM is not new. My response to these queries is that it all depends on the type of questions one is interested in. For many problems, equation-based models are excellent tools to study the problem of concern, as illustrated by other chapters in this book. However, for a problem like coordination or strategic interaction, multiple agents need to be distinguished.

Traditional game theory has been very successful in addressing strategic interaction by a small number (mainly two) (types of) players, using equation-based models. Unfortunately, traditional game theory is rather restrictive: agents are required to have high cognitive abilities, the rules of the game are fixed, and the structure of the interactions is on a rigid lattice or fully random. But from empirical studies it is known that humans are boundedly rational, the rules of the game change, and social interactions have complex social structures (e.g., Gigerenzer and Selten, 2001; Janssen and Ostrom, 2002). It is no surprise that ABM has been widely applied to games since the early 1980s (e.g., Axelrod, 1984).

Indeed, models of individual units were developed long ago, such as statistical mechanics and micro-simulations. But these methods assume no interaction, or random interaction, between the agents, while a key element in ABM is the possibility of complex structures of social interactions. In some systems, the macroscale properties are sensitive to the structure of interactions between agents and social networks. In equation-based models, the agents are frequently, implicitly, assumed to be well mixed (the mean-field assumption), and thus these approaches miss the opportunity to investigate the sensitivities of the structure of interactions.

Finally, within integrated modelling of ecological economic systems, one of the key problems is how to match the scale of social and ecological dynamics (Levin, 1992; Gibson et al., 2000). By the use of agents, we derive tools that make it possible to integrate processes and interactions at different levels of scale, for agent-agent and agent-environment interactions.

8.3 ABM METHODOLOGY

Most ABMs applied within ecological economics consist of two elements: cellular automata and agents. I will now discuss briefly both elements.

8.3.1 Cellular Automata

Originally, the cellular automata (CA) approach was introduced by John von Neumann and Stanislaw Ulam at the end of the 1940s, mainly to give a reductionist model of life and self-reproduction. The *Game of Life*, invented by John Conway in 1970, popularized the CA approach (Gardner, 1970). This game consists of cells on a checkerboard, which can have two states, 'alive' and 'dead'. Time goes by in discrete steps. According to some deterministic rules, which are the same for each cell, the state of a cell in the next time step depends on its own present state and the states of all its surrounding cells in the present period. The resulting surprising complex dynamics which evolved from this simple game, attracted the attention of many people. Since the early 1970s, CA have been used by many disciplines to study complex dynamic behaviour of systems. The essential properties of a CA are:

- A regular *n*-dimensional lattice (*n* is in most cases of one or two dimensions), where each *cell* of this lattice has a discrete state.
- A dynamical behaviour, described by so called *rules*. These rules describe the state of a cell for the next time step, depending on the states of the cells in the *neighbourhood* of the cell.

The basic element of a CA is the *cell* that is represented by *states*. In the simplest case, each cell can have the binary states 1 or 0. In more complex simulations, the cells can have a greater number of distinct states. These cells are arranged in a lattice, with the most common CAs being built in one or two dimensions. The cells can change state by transition rules, which determine the state of the cells for the next time step. In cellular automata, a rule defines the state of a cell in dependence of the *neighbourhood* of the cell. The most common neighbourhoods for two-dimensional CA are given in Figure 8.1.

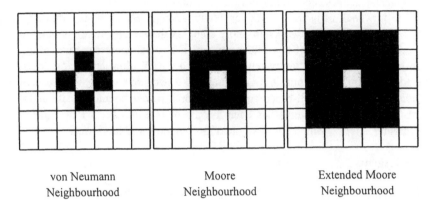

| von Neumann | Moore | Extended Moore |
| Neighbourhood | Neighbourhood | Neighbourhood |

Figure 8.1   Examples of cellular automata

The black cells are the neighbourhood cells to the centre cell. The states of these cells are used to calculate the next state of the centre cell according to the defined rule.

With regard to our interest for ecological economics, the application of CA can be rather straightforward. In fact, CA can be used to produce a dynamic Geographical Information System (GIS).[3] The lattice represents a map of a certain area, with each possible state of a cell representing a possible land use. Due to physical restrictions, cells on some locations may be restricted to a limited number of states; for example, a secondary forest cannot turn back into a primary forest. Transition rules determine when a certain land use of a cell changes into another land use. Cell changes can be influenced by local rules; for example, if a cell is a forest-cell, and if one of the neighbouring cells is on fire, then that cell turns to fire. However, global rules are also possible, since land use changes can be influenced by demand for certain land on a higher level of scale. For example, demand for extra agricultural land can be translated as changing those cells to agriculture that are the most suitable.

It must be noted that social agents can also be represented as CA. One of the earliest and best known cellular automata models of social processes is the Schelling (1971) model of neighbourhood segregation. Two types of agents are randomly distributed on a lattice, and move to empty locations if the number of in-group neighbours falls below a certain threshold. The model shows how extreme segregation tends to arise in a population that prefers diversity, as agents relocate to avoid being in the minority. In the CA approach for social processes, each cell represents an agent, which interacts with its neighbours. The state of the cells relates to different characteristics of the agents, such as social class, attitude, social orientation, etc.

A drawback of using CA for representing social agents is its simplicity. For example, social networks are more complex than the local neighbours on a lattice. The number of possible states which a social agent can take, might be too large to be efficiently represented as a CA. Within land use models, landowners may own multiple cells and make decisions on the land use of their cells. Thus, a cell-based rule that ignores parcel boundaries is inadequate. The study of agents has been a topic of research for a long time in computer science, which has developed its own tools and frameworks.

8.3.2 Agents

The architecture of agents in ABM has been much influenced by work on multi-agent systems in Artificial Intelligence (AI). Multi-agent systems research studies the behaviour of adaptive autonomous agents in the physical world (robots), or in cyberspace (software agents). The agents often consist of sensors, to derive information from the environment, and intelligent functions such as perception, planning, learning, etc.

Distributed artificial intelligence is a relatively recent development of artificial intelligence studies (Bond and Gasser, 1988). It concerns the properties of sets of intercommunicating agents, coexisting in a common environment. The aim may be to study the properties of such systems in an abstract way, to design systems of immediate practical use, or to use such a programmed multi-agent system as a model of a human or other real-world system.

Wooldridge (2002) argues that intelligent agents are able to act flexibly and autonomously. By flexibility we mean that agents are goal-directed (satisfying or maximizing their utility), reactive (responding to changes in the environment) and capable of interacting with other agents. One of the difficulties is in balancing reactive and goal-directed behaviour. Developing models with agents who have only reactive behaviour is relatively simple, and individual-based ecological modelling addresses problems by simulating non-human agents as reactive objects (e.g., DeAngelis and Gross, 1992).

However, humans combine reactive and goal-directed behaviour. Conventional economics assumes the selfish rational actor to describe individual behaviour. Although this agent model provides a good description of human behaviour in highly competitive markets, as is confirmed in experimental studies, it is not satisfactory for the description of behaviour in various decision situations of importance for ecological economics (Gintis, 2000).

For decision situations such as economic valuation and collective action, motivation, fairness and preferences play an important role, and the characteristics may vary within the population of human agents. Furthermore, decision problems related to environmental management are often so complex that it is not likely that one has full information and understanding of the problem and is able to evaluate all possible options. Models of bounded rationality have been used as an alternative in economics (Simon, 1955). Furthermore, using concepts from psychology, we are able to include dimensions of economic agents, such as emotions, motivations, and perceptions. A problem is that loosening the tight framework of the selfish rational actor leads to many possible frameworks. Within behavioural economics, there is mainly attention to models of learning that explain observed behaviour in experiments (Camerer, 2003). Others focus on fast and frugal heuristics, of how individuals make a choice in simple problems under time pressure (Gigerenzer et al., 1999).

An important agent-architecture within the multi-agent systems community is the belief-desire-intention (BDI) approach, in which decision-making depends upon the manipulation of data structures representing the beliefs, desires, and intentions of the agent. The BDI architecture is based on practical reasoning (Bratman et al., 1988), and involves two key processes: deciding what goals an agent wants to achieve (deliberation), and how an agent is going to achieve these goals (means-ends reasoning). The main idea is that an agent has limited resources to make decisions, in terms of time and knowledge. The beliefs represent information on the agent's current environment and, together with desires, in a deliberation process filter the range of possible options to a set of intentions. The intentions represent the focus on actions of the agents, though due to changes in the environment (affecting beliefs), the intentions may change.

Another important integrated approach in ABM for simulating decision-making is the *consumat* approach (Jager et al. 2000; 2002). The consumats, artificial consumers, may engage in different cognitive processes in deciding how to behave, depending on their level of need satisfaction and degree of uncertainty. Consumats having a low level of need satisfaction and a low degree of uncertainty, are assumed to deliberate, that is: to determine the consequences of all possible decisions given a fixed time-horizon in order to maximize the level of need satisfaction. Consumats having a low level of need satisfaction and a high degree of uncertainty, are assumed to socially compare. This implies the comparison of their own previous behaviour with the previous behaviour of consumats having about similar abilities, and selecting that behaviour which yields a maximal level of need satisfaction. When consumats have a high level of need satisfaction, but also a high level of uncertainty, they will imitate the behaviour of other similar consumats. Finally, consumats having a high level of need satisfaction and a low level of uncertainty, simply repeat their previous behaviour. After the consumption of opportunities, a new level of need satisfaction will be derived, and changes will occur regarding their abilities, opportunities and the social and physical environment, which will affect the consumption in succeeding time steps. As a consequence, agents may switch between heuristics in a dynamic environment that affects their satisfaction and uncertainty, and may mimic the behaviour of others only when they are uncertain.

A scheme of a simple model of two agents interacting with each other and their environment is given in Figure 8.2, which provides the simplest description of ABM applied to ecological economics. Agents derive information from the environment, that informs the perception they have about the state of the environment. Based on the goals and attributes of the agents, they make decisions about what actions to perform, and these actions affect the environment. The agents can interact indirectly, for example by affecting the common resource, or directly by communication. This communication might be used to exchange information about possible strategies, knowledge about the resource and agreements on how to solve collective action problems.

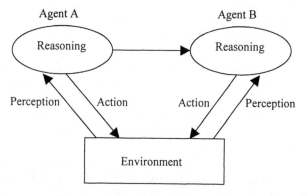

Figure 8.2   *A scheme of cognitive interactions between two agents and their environment*

The main dilemma concerning the architecture of agents with regard to the study of ecosystem management, is the degree of complexity embodied in the agent. Since the roots of agent research lie in computer science, the agents are often designed for certain tasks (smart software agents to assist the limited human agent), but do not necessarily represent theoretical insights from behavioural science. Within ecological economics, the techniques of multi-agent systems are combined, together with concepts from sociology, psychology and economics, to design more comprehensive agents from a social science point of view.

8.4 AGENT-BASED MODELLING IN ECOLOGICAL ECONOMICS

I shall now describe the main areas within ecological economics where ABM has been applied and provide some of the key references.

8.4.1 Evolution of Cooperation

One of the key problems in science is the evolution of cooperation. Cooperation has been explained when the social agents are generically related, and/or interact repeatedly. The question of when social agents cooperate relates to a number of important issues in ecological economics, especially to the question of institutional configurations for common resources and public goods. Ostrom (1990) shows that there are many empirical cases where local communities have developed institutions to deal with social dilemmas. These examples show that people have the capacity to organize themselves to achieve much better and more cooperative outcomes than is predicted by conventional theory (Ostrom, 1990). Furthermore, laboratory experiments have been performed which show that communication is a crucial factor to stimulate cooperative behaviour, and the ability of the participants to determine their own monitoring and sanctioning system, is critical for sustaining cooperative behaviour (Ostrom et al., 1994). Note that the experiments show that the type of communication can have significant effects on the results.

The reason these factors are important is not precisely known, but the hypothesis is that it relates to the development of mutual trust during interactions between resource appropriators. ABM can contribute to a better understanding of the factors that stimulates such self-governance. The irrigation system of Bali, as discussed at the beginning of this chapter, is an example of the use of ABM to understand self-governance. Another relevant paper is Janssen and Ostrom (2002), who study the conditions that are needed for a population of agents voluntarily to restrict their own behaviour, to avoid the collapse of a resource in the longer term. They show that when agents are able to evolve mutual trust relationships, a proposed rule on restricted use of the resource will be accepted, since they trust others will, in general, also follow the rule.

There is a substantial literature on the use of ABM in the management of common-pool resources. Bousquet et al. (1998, 2001, 2002) developed a modelling platform, CORMAS, dedicated to the study of common-pool resources by ABM, and performed many applications.[4] In their applications they work together with the local stakeholders, often in Africa and Asia, to develop ABM for practical natural resource management problems. Deadman (1999) compared his ABM with experimental data of common-pool resource experiments, and Jager et al. (2000) tested how different theories of decision-making affect the state of the common resource.

8.4.2 Diffusion Processes

Diffusion processes are important for understanding what determines the spread of innovations in a population. Such innovations might be the use of a new environmentally friendly product, a technology to reduce waste, or norms about green consumption. Diffusion processes often replicate the observed stylized fact of an S-shaped curve of cumulated adopters of the innovation. In fact, the increasing number of adopters is, in essence, the diffusion process. The growth of new products is a complex process, which typically consists of a large body of agents interacting with each other over a long period of time. Traditional analytical models described diffusion processes at the market level, but in recent years ABM has become used as an alternative model. One approach is based on cellular automata, where the individuals interact with their neighbours, and transition rules determine how neighbours affect the awareness or adoption of an innovation (e.g., Weisbuch, 2000; Goldenberg and Efroni, 2001); others address more realistic network structures (e.g., Valente, 1995; Abrahamson and Rosenkopf, 1997).

Applications of ABM to diffusion problems within ecological economics are rare. An interesting example is Berger (2001), who studied the diffusion of agricultural technologies, based on the concept of different types of adapters (early and late), applied to an agricultural region in Chile. Another application is by Deffuant et al. (2002), who simulate the adoption of organic farming practices as a consequence of governmental policy, for an agricultural region in France. In a more theoretical study, Janssen and Jager (2002) study the diffusion of green products in a coevolution of consumers and firms, where firms try to make products that fit the demand of the consumers, and consumers have to make a choice between a limited number of products.

Within the field of evolutionary economics (e.g., Nelson and Winter, 1982), simulation models are used to simulate innovation, diffusion and learning of firms and organizations. An interesting application of ABM for ecological economics, related to industrial organizations, might be the area of industrial ecology, where different type of agents process material and energy flows in their economic activities (Axtell et al., 2001).

8.4.3 Mental Models and Learning

If agents do not have perfect knowledge of the complex ecological system, how does their mental model of the system affect their actions, and how can they learn to derive a more accurate mental representation? This problem refers to the general problem in ABM, that agents do not have perfect knowledge of the system and make their decisions based on the perception they have on the problem. These perceptions do not have to include correct representations of reality, and they may vary between agents.

A number of ABMs in the field of ecological economics have addressed this problem. Janssen and de Vries (1998) developed an ABM where agents have different mental models of the climate change problem. They simulate a learning process where agents may adjust their mental models when they are surprised by observations, and make adjustments in their decisions according to their new perception of the problem. This approach has been also applied to lake management (Carpenter et al., 1999), and rangeland management (Janssen et al., 2000).

Carpenter et al. (1999) developed a simulation model with different types of agents, to explore the dynamics of social-ecological systems. The ecosystem is a lake subject to phosphorus pollution, which flows from agriculture to upland soils, to surface waters, where it cycles between water and sediments. The ecosystem is multistable, and moves among domains of attraction depending on the history of pollutant inputs. The alternative states yield different economic benefits. Agents form expectations about ecosystem dynamics, markets, and/or the actions of managers, and choose levels of pollutant inputs accordingly. Agents have heterogeneous beliefs and/or access to information, and their aggregate behaviour determines the total rate of pollutant input. As the ecosystem changes, agents update their beliefs and expectations about the world they co-create, and modify their actions accordingly. Carpenter et al. (1999) analyse a wide range of scenarios, and observe irregular oscillations among ecosystem states and patterns of agent behaviour, which resemble some features of the adaptive cycle of Holling (1986).

8.4.4 Land-Use and Land-Cover Change

ABM for land-use and land-cover change combine a cellular model representing the landscape of interest, with an ABM that represents decision-making entities (Parker et al., 2003). Due to the digitalization of land-use/cover data (i.e., remotely sensed imagery), and the development of Geographic Information Systems (GIS), cellular maps can be derived for analysis, and since the 1980s, cellular automata have became used to model land-use/cover over time. Human decision-making was implicitly taken into account in the transition rules, but not expressed explicitly. Sometimes the cells represent the unit of decision-making but, in most applications, the unit of decision-making and the cell do not match. The desire to include more comprehensive decision rules, and the mismatch between spatial units and units of decision-making, led to the use of ABM for land-use and land-cover change. By including agents, one can explicitly express ownership, or the property about which an agent can make decisions. An agent can make decisions on the land use in a number of cells, for example by allocating cells for deriving a portfolio of crops.

Applications on land-use and land-cover change include impact of innovations and policy on agricultural practices (Balmann, 1997; Berger, 2001; Deffuant et al., 2002), reforestation and deforestation (Hoffman et al. 2002) and urban sprawl (Torrens and Benenson, 2004). I refer to Gimblett et al. (2002) and Parker et al. (2003) for recent reviews of this area.

8.4.5 Participatory Approaches

In the spirit of adaptive management (Holling, 1978), various researchers have developed their ABMs together with the stakeholders of the problem under concern. Bousquet et al. (2002) have developed an approach, which they call 'companion modelling', that uses role games to acquires knowledge, build an ABM, validate the ABM and use it in the decision-making process (see also Barreteau, 2003). As for the participatory modelling approach, such as in practiced in systems dynamics (e.g., Costanza and Ruth, 1998), they use the model as a tool in the mediation process with stakeholders. Within the system dynamic model, agents are represented at an aggregate level, and the use of ABM makes it possible to include a broader set of interactive autonomous agents. These autonomous agents may respond to the decisions of the stakeholders in the participatory process in unexpected ways. A non-scientific example of this is the computer game SimCity where the player, the virtual mayor, has to make decisions to satisfy the citizens, the Sims.

8.5 DEGREES OF COMPLEXITY

One of the crucial questions in the field of ABM is how much model complexity is necessary to derive an understanding of emergent properties. This can be illustrated by the 'flocking fallacy'. The visually interesting flocking 'boids' that appear often on screen savers are based on three simple rules for each agent (Reynolds, 1987):

- avoid collisions with nearby flock mates,
- attempt to match velocity with nearby flock mates, and
- attempt to stay close to nearby flock mates.

Computer scientist Reynolds was interested to simulate certain patterns, and for him it was important that '... many people who view these animated flocks immediately recognize them as a representation of a natural flock, and find them similarly delightful to watch' (Reynolds, 1987, p. 26). One might derive the impression that we have now a better understanding of flocking behaviour. However, research on schooling of fish illustrates that we lack a good understanding of the micro-behaviour of fish in relation to schooling (Camazine et al., 2001, Chapter 11). Indeed, information about the behaviour of nearby neighbours is found to be a crucial factor in empirical studies, but which behavioural rules are in use is a puzzle.

Camazine et al. (2001) show that some problems in biology have recently successfully been approached by combining field work, controlled laboratory experiments and models. They stress that the models 'should be developed solely based on observations and experimental data concerning subunits of the system and their interactions' (Camazine et al., 2001, p. 70).

If we look at ABM for the study of social phenomena, we have to conclude that the fruitful combination of fieldwork, laboratory data and modelling is lacking. Looking at most formalizations of 'bounded rationality' in agent rules, they leave the impression of being developed in a rather *ad hoc* manner, from the perspective of programming rules rather than reflecting a formalization on the basis of theoretical considerations. Bounded rationality is not an excuse for using sloppy decision rules. For example, it is very interesting to study the effects of introducing an 'imitation' strategy in agents within a system. However, not considering the issues of the conditions under which the agents are likely to imitate, and which other agents they are most likely to start imitating, may yield results that do not originate from the 'psychological laws' on imitative behaviour. Key publications in social simulation, such as segregation by Schelling (1971), and the evolution of cooperation by Axelrod (1984), could explain macro-phenomena, by assuming simple logical rules for the behaviour of the agents. However, like the flocking 'boids', the behavioural rules are not validated by empirical research. I do not seek to diminish the importance of the contributions of Schelling and Axelrod, which are evidently milestones and stimulated much work to test variations of the models. Instead, I wish to argue that the use of ABMs should more often be based on empirically tested theoretical models of human decision-making, combined with rigorous empirical research in the field and in the laboratory. Due to the rapid growth of the use of experimental research in social science, there is a potential to develop more micro-level validated decision rules of agents.

In economics, this is successfully happening with the testing of alternative learning models on relatively simple games, where the participants converge in many rounds towards a unique mixed equilibrium (Camerer, 2003). Janssen and Ahn (2003) test different ABMs on a large set of public good and common-pool resources, which are more complex since the participants do not reach an equilibrium. Janssen and Ahn (2003) find that motivational heterogeneity and satisficing are explanatory factors that lead to a reasonable fit with the observations.

Within psychology, there is an effort to test alternative, theoretically sound, heuristics on laboratory experiments of decision-making (Gigerenzer et al., 1999). Other psychologists develop ABM that combines findings of many theories in a kind of meta-theoretical framework (Jager et al., 2002; Mosler and Brucks, 2003).

Another approach is the participatory one, as described above. By playing role games, and confronting the stakeholders with the simulations, the scientists derive valuable insights into the possible rules in use. An important question is how to design role games such that the stakeholders behave during role-playing as they do normally.

8.6 CONCLUSIONS

In this chapter a brief overview has been given of ABM and its application to ecological economics. ABM applied so far has been successfully used in various social sciences, but has been limited within ecological economics. There is a great potential for the use of ABM, especially for problems related to common use of resources, land-use and land-cover change, integrated modelling and participatory processes.

Due to the rapid developments of ABM in other disciplines, ecological economics can 'piggyback', by using theory and experimentally tested models of agents who interact with their complex environment. This might provide ecological economics with a promising tool for integrated modeling, and for testing different theories of behaviour and organization at different levels of scale.

NOTES

1. The author gratefully acknowledges support from the Center for the Study of Institutions, Population, and Environmental Change at Indiana University, through National Science Foundation grants SBR9521918 and SES0083511.
2. Also referred to as multi-agent systems, multi-agent based systems, or agent-based computational economics.

3. A Geographic Information System is a computer system for capturing, storing, checking, integrating, manipulating, analysing and displaying data related to positions on the Earth's surface.
4. See http://cormas.cirad.fr.

REFERENCES

Abrahamson, E. and L. Rosenkopf (1997), 'Social network effects on the extent of innovation diffusion: a computer simulation', *Organization Science*, **8** (3), 289–309.

Axelrod, R. (1984), *The Evolution of Cooperation*, New York: Basic Books.

Axtell, R.L., C.J. Andrews and M.J. Small (2001), 'Agent-based modeling and industrial ecology', *Journal of Industrial Ecology*, **5** (4), 10–13.

Balmann, A. (1997), 'Farm-based modelling of regional structural change', *European Review of Agricultural Economics*, **25** (1), 85–108.

Barreteau, O. (2003), 'The joint use of role-playing games and models regarding negotiation processes: characterization of associations', *Journal of Artificial Societies and Social Simulation*, **6** (2), http://jasss.soc.surrey.ac.uk/6/2/3.html.

Berger, T. (2001), 'Agent-based spatial models applied to agriculture. a simulation tool for technology diffusion, resource use changes, and policy analysis', *Agricultural Economics*, **25**, 245–60.

Berry, B.J.L., L.D. Kiel and E. Elliott (eds) (2002), 'Adapive agents, intelligence, and emergent organization: capturing complexity through agent-based modeling', *Proceedings of the National Academy of Sciences*, **99** Supplement 3, 7187–316.

Bond, A.H. and L. Gasser (eds) (1988), *Readings in Distributed Artificial Intelligence*, San Mateo CA: Morgan Kaufmann.

Bousquet, F., I. Bakam, H. Proton and C. Le Page (1998), 'Cormas: Common-Pool Resources and Multi-Agent Systems', *Lecture Notes in Artificial Intelligence*, **1416**, 826–38.

Bousquet, F., R. Lifran, M. Tidball, S. Thoyer and M. Antona (2001), 'Agent-based modelling, game theory and natural resource management issues', *Journal of Artificial Societies and Social Simulation*, **4** (2), http://jasss.soc.surrey.ac.uk/4/2/0.html.

Bousquet, F., O. Barretau, P. D'Aquino, M. Etienne, S. Boissau, S. Aubert, C. Le Page, D. Babin and J-P. Castella (2002), 'Multi-agent systems and role games: collective learning processes for ecosystem management', in M.A. Janssen (ed.), *Complexity and Ecosystem Management: The Theory and Practice of Multi-Agent Systems*, Cheltenham: Edward Elgar, pp. 248–85.

Bratman, M.E., D.J. Israel and M.E. Pollack (1988), 'Plans and resource-bounded practical reasoning', *Computational Intelligence*, **4**, 349–55.

Camazine, S., J.-L. Deneubourg, N.R. Franks, J. Sneyd, G. Theraulaz and E. Bonabeau (2001), *Self-Organization in Biological Systems*, Princeton NJ: Princeton University Press.

Camerer, C.F. (2003), *Behavioral Game Theory: Experiments in Strategic Interaction*, Princeton NJ: Princeton University Press.

Carpenter, S.R., W. Brock and P. Hanson (1999), 'Ecological and social dynamics in simple models of ecosystem management', *Conservation Ecology*, **3** (2), 4 http://www.consecol.org/vol3/iss2/art4.

Conte, R., R. Hegselmann and P. Terna (eds) (1997), *Simulating Social Phenomena*, Lecture Notes in Economics and Mathematical Systems, 456, Berlin: Springer.

Costanza, R. and M. Ruth (1998), 'Using dynamic modelling to scope environmental problems and build consensus', *Environmental Management*, 22, 183–95.

Deadman, P.J. (1999), 'Modelling individual behaviour and group performance in an intelligent agent-based simulation of the tragedy of the commons', *Journal of Environmental Management*, 56, 159–72.

DeAngelis, D.L. and L.J. Gross (eds) (1992), *Individual-Based Models and Approaches in Ecology*, New York: Chapman and Hall.

Deffuant, G., S. Huet, J.P. Bousset, J. Henriot, G. Amon and G. Weisbuch (2002), 'Agent based simulation of organic farming conversion in Allier département', in M.A. Janssen (ed.), *Complexity and Ecosystem Management: The Theory and Practice of Multi-agent Systems*, Cheltenham: Edward Elgar, pp. 158–87.

Epstein, J.M. and R. Axtell (1996), *Growing Artificial Societies: Social Science from the Bottom Up*, Cambridge MA: MIT Press

Gardner, M. (1970), 'The fantastic combinations of John Conway's new solitaire game Life', *Scientific American*, 223, 120–23.

Gibson, C., E. Ostrom and T.K. Ahn (2000), 'The concept of scale and the human dimensions of global environmental change', *Ecological Economics*, 32, 217–39.

Gigerenzer, G. and R. Selten (eds) (2001), *Bounded Rationality: The Adaptive Toolbox*, Cambridge MA: MIT Press.

Gigerenzer, G., P.M. Todd and ABC Research (1999), *Simple Heuristics That Make Us Smart*, New York: Oxford University Press.

Gilbert, N. and J.E. Doran (eds) (1994), *Simulating Societies: The Computer Simulation of Social Phenomena*, London: UCL Press.

Gimblett, H.R. (ed.) (2002), *Integrating Geographic Information Systems and Agent-Based Modeling Techniques for Simulating Social and Ecological Processes*, Oxford: Oxford University Press.

Gintis, H. (2000), 'Beyond homo economicus: evidence from experimental economics', *Ecological Economics*, 35 (3), 311–22.

Goldenberg, J. and S. Efroni (2001), 'Using cellular automata modeling of the emergence of innovations', *Technological Forecasting and Social Change*, 68, 293–308.

Hoffmann, M., H. Kelley and T. Evans (2002), 'Simulating land-cover change in South-Central Indiana: an agent-based model of deforestation and afforestation', in M.A. Janssen (ed.), *Complexity and Ecosystem Management: The Theory and Practice of Multi-Agent Systems*, Cheltenham: Edward Elgar, pp. 218–47.

Holland, J.H. (1992), 'Complex adaptive systems', *Daedalus*, 121, 17–30.

Holling, C.S. (1978), *Adaptive Environmental Assessment and Management*, London: Wiley.

Holling, C.S. (1986), 'The resilience of terrestrial ecosystems: local surprise and global change', in W.C. Clark and R.E. Munn (eds), *Sustainable Development of the Biosphere*, Cambridge: Cambridge University Press, pp. 292–317.

Jager, W., M.A. Janssen, H.J.M. De Vries, J. De Greef and C.A.J. Vlek (2000), 'Behaviour in commons dilemmas: homo economicus and homo psychologicus in an ecological-economic model', *Ecological Economics*, 35 (3), 357–79.

Jager, W., M.A. Janssen and C.A.J. Vlek (2002), 'How uncertainty stimulates overharvesting in a resource dilemma: three process explanations', *Journal of Environmental Psychology*, 22, 247–63.

Janssen, M.A. (ed.) (2002), *Complexity and Ecosystem Management: The Theory and Practice of Multi-Agent Systems*, Cheltenham: Edward Elgar.

Janssen, M.A. and H.J.M. de Vries (1998), 'The battle of perspectives: a multi-agent model with adaptive responses to climate change', *Ecological Economics*, **26** (1), 43–65.

Janssen, M.A. and W. Jager (2002), 'Stimulating diffusion of green products, co-evolution between firms and consumers', *Journal of Evolutionary Economics*, **12**, 283–306.

Janssen, M.A. and E. Ostrom (2002), 'Adoption of a new regulation for the governance of common-pool resources by a heterogeneous population', in J.M. Baland, P. Bardhan and S. Bowles (eds), *Inequality, Cooperation and Environmental Sustainability*, Princeton NJ: Princeton University Press.

Janssen, M.A. and T.K. Ahn (2003), 'Adaptation vs. anticipation on public-good games', unpublished manuscript.

Janssen, M.A., B.H. Walker, J. Langridge and N. Abel (2000), 'An adaptive agent model for analysing co-evolution of management and policies in a complex rangelands system', *Ecological Modelling*, **131**, 249–68.

Kohler, T.A. and G.J. Gumerman (eds) (2000), *Dynamics in Human and Primate Societies: Agent-Based Modeling of Social and Spatial Processes*, Oxford: Oxford University Press.

Lansing, J.S. (1991), *Priests and Programmers: Technologies of Power in the Engineered Landscape of Bali*, Princeton NJ: Princeton University Press.

Lansing, J.S. (2000), 'Anti-chaos, common property and the emergence of cooperation', in T.A. Kohler and G.J. Gumerman (eds), *Dynamics in Human and Primate Societies*, Oxford: Oxford University Press, pp. 207–24.

Lansing, J.S. and J.N. Kremer (1994), 'Emergent properties of Balinese water temple networks: co-adaption on a rugged fitness landscape', in C.G. Langton (ed.), *Artificial Life III: Studies in the Sciences of Complexity*, Reading MA: Addison-Wesley, pp. 201–23.

Levin, S.A. (1992), 'The problem of pattern and scale in ecology', *Ecology*, **73**, 1943–67.

Lomi, A. and E.R. Larsen (eds) (2001), *Dynamics of Organizations: Computational Modeling and Organization Theories*, Cambridge MA: MIT Press.

Macy, M.W. and R. Willer (2002), 'From factors to actors: computational sociology and agent-based modeling', *Annual Review of Sociology*, **28**, 143–66.

Mosler, H-J. and W. Brucks (2003), 'Integrating commons dilemma findings in a general dynamic model of cooperative behavior in resource crises', *European Journal of Social Psychology*, **33**, 119–33.

Nelson, R.R. and S.G. Winter (1982), *An Evolutionary Theory of Economic Change*, Cambridge MA: Belknap.

Ostrom, E. (1990), *Governing the Commons*, Cambridge: Cambridge University Press.

Ostrom, E., R. Gardner and J. Walker (1994), *Rules, Games and Common-Pool Resources*, Michigan: The University of Michigan Press.

Parker, D., S. Manson, M.A. Janssen, M. Hoffmann and P. Deadman (2003), 'Multi-agent systems for the simulation of land-use and land-cover change: a review', *Annals of the Association of American Geographers*, **93** (2), 313–37.

Reynolds, C.W. (1987), 'Flocks, herds, and schools: a distributed behavioral model', *Computer Graphics*, **21** (4), 25–34.

Schelling, T.C. (1971), 'Dynamic models of segregation', *Journal of Mathematical Sociology*, **1**, 143–86.

Simon, H.A. (1955), 'A behavioral model of rational choice', *Quarterly Journal of Economics*, **69**, 99–118.

Tesfatsion, L. (2001), 'Introduction to the special issue on agent-based computational economics', *Journal of Economic Dynamics and Control*, **25**, 281–93.

Torrens, P.M. and I. Benenson (2004), *Geosimulation: Modeling Urban Environments*, London: Wiley.

Valente, T.W. (1995), *Network Models of the Diffusion of Innovations*, Cresskill NJ, Hampton Press.

Weisbuch, G. (2000), 'Environment and institutions: a complex dynamical systems approach', *Ecological Economics*, **34** (3), 381–91.

Wooldridge, M. (2002), *An Introduction to MultiAgent Systems*, New York: Wiley.

9. The Environmental Kuznets Curve

David I. Stern

9.1 INTRODUCTION

This chapter has two aims: to review the literature on the environmental Kuznets curve (EKC) and to highlight the importance of good econometric practice to theory testing in ecological economics.

The environmental Kuznets curve is an hypothesized relationship between various indicators of environmental degradation and income per capita. In the early stages of economic growth, degradation and pollution increase, but beyond some level of income per capita (which will vary for different indicators) the trend reverses, so that at high income levels economic growth leads to environmental improvement. This implies that the environmental impact indicator is an inverted U-shaped function of income per capita. Typically, the logarithm of the indicator is modelled as a quadratic function of the logarithm of income. An example of an estimated EKC is shown in Figure 9.1. The EKC is named for Kuznets (1955), who hypothesized that income inequality first rises and then falls as economic development proceeds.

Econometrics is not covered elsewhere in this volume, and the EKC is a leading example of the application of econometrics in ecological economics. Econometrics has a valuable contribution to make to ecological economics but has not been used very extensively. However, it is very easy to do bad econometrics and the history of the EKC exemplifies what can go wrong. Most of the EKC literature is econometrically weak. Little or no attention has been paid to the statistical properties of the data used, e.g., serial dependence or stochastic trends in time series (exceptions include Coondoo and Dinda, 2002; Stern and Common, 2001; Perman and Stern, 2003), and few tests of model adequacy are examined or presented. The general approach has been that if a model can be estimated, and the coefficients are non-zero, then it must be a valid representation of the data. But one of the main purposes of doing econometrics is to test which apparent relationships, or 'stylized facts', are valid and which are spurious correlations.

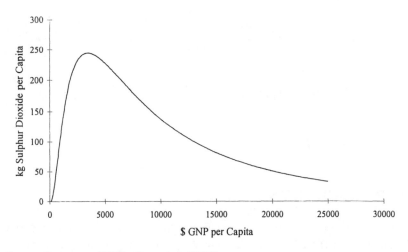

Source: Panayotou (1993); Stern et al. (1996).

Figure 9.1   Environmental Kuznets curve for sulphur emissions

For example, a Hausman test statistic can be used to choose between random effects and fixed effects models for estimating the EKC using panel data. Many EKC studies report this test statistic, which usually indicates that the random effects model cannot be estimated consistently. These researchers then, correctly, estimate the fixed effects model. But the reason that the random effects model cannot be consistently estimated is because the random effects are correlated with the explanatory variables. This suggests that there are omitted variables that are correlated with the included explanatory variables. As a result, the estimated regression parameters will be biased. Furthermore, while the fixed effects estimate is technically unbiased, it is conditional on the data used to estimate it and cannot be extrapolated to other cases.

The EKC idea only rose to prominence because few paid sufficient attention to econometric diagnostic statistics. Either the statistics were not calculated, or when they were presented, their full implications were ignored. When we do take such statistics into account and use appropriate techniques, we find that the EKC does not exist (Perman and Stern, 2003). Instead, we get a more realistic view of the effect of economic growth and technological changes on environmental quality. It seems that most indicators of environmental degradation are monotonically rising in income, though the 'income elasticity' is less than one and is not a simple function of income alone. Time related effects reduce environmental impacts in countries at all levels of income. The new (post-Brundtland) conventional wisdom that developing countries are 'too poor to be green' (Martinez-Alier, 1995) is lacking in wisdom. However, in rapidly growing middle-income countries, the scale effect, which increases pollution and other degradation, overwhelms the time effect. In wealthy countries, growth is slower, and pollution reduction efforts can overcome the scale effect. This is the origin of the apparent EKC effect.

The econometric results are supported by recent evidence that, in fact, pollution problems are being addressed and remedied in developing economies (e.g., Dasgupta et al., 2002).

This chapter follows the development of the EKC concept in approximately chronological order. No attempt is made to review or cite all studies. A number of reviews have been published, but the number of papers on the topic continues to increase rapidly. The next two sections of the chapter review in more detail the theory behind the EKC and the econometric methods used in EKC studies. The following sections review some EKC analyses and their critique. Sections 6 and 7 discuss the more important recent developments that have changed the picture that we have of the EKC. The final sections discuss an alternative approach – decomposition of emissions – and summarize the findings. The appendix contains a primer on the relevant econometric techniques for any readers to whom they are unfamiliar.

9.2 THEORETICAL BACKGROUND

The EKC concept emerged in the early 1990s with Grossman and Krueger's (1991) path-breaking study of the potential impacts of NAFTA, and Shafik and Bandyopadhyay's (1992) background study for the 1992 World Development Report. However, the idea that economic growth is necessary in order for environmental quality to be maintained or improved, is an essential part of the sustainable development argument promulgated by the World Commission on Environment and Development (1987) in *Our Common Future*.

The EKC theme was popularized by the World Bank's *World Development Report 1992* (IBRD, 1992), which argued: 'The view that greater economic activity inevitably hurts the environment is based on static assumptions about technology, tastes and environmental investments' (p. 38) and: 'As incomes rise, the demand for improvements in environmental quality will increase, as will the resources available for investment' (p. 39). However, the EKC has not been shown to apply to all pollutants or environmental impacts, and recent evidence (Dasgupta et al., 2002; Perman and Stern, 2003) challenges the notion of the EKC in general. The remainder of this section discusses the economic factors that drive changes in environmental impacts and which may be responsible for rising or declining environmental degradation over the course of economic development.

If there were no change in the structure or technology of the economy, pure growth in the scale of the economy would result in a proportional growth in pollution and other environmental impacts. This is called the scale effect. The traditional view that the economic development and environmental quality are conflicting goals reflects the scale effect alone. Proponents of the EKC hypothesis argue that:

> ... at higher levels of development, structural change towards information-intensive industries and services, coupled with increased environmental awareness, enforcement of environmental regulations, better technology and higher environmental expenditures, result in leveling off and gradual decline of environmental degradation (Panayotou, 1993).

Thus, there are both proximate causes of the EKC relationship (scale, changes in economic structure or product mix, changes in technology, and changes in input mix), as well as underlying causes, such as environmental regulation, awareness, and education, which can only have an effect via the proximate variables.

First, let us look in more detail at the proximate variables:

1. *Scale*

   The *scale* of production implies expanding production at given factor-input ratios, output mix, and state of technology. The scale effect is normally assumed to increase emissions proportionally, so that a 1 per cent increase in scale results in a 1 per cent increase in emissions. This is because, if there is no change in the input-output ratio or in technique, there has to be a proportional increase in aggregate inputs. However, there could, in theory, be scale economies or diseconomies of pollution. Some pollution control techniques may not be practical at a small scale of production, and vice versa, or may operate more or less effectively at different levels of output.

2. *Output Mix*

   Different industries have different pollution intensities. Typically, over the course of economic development the *output mix* changes. In the earlier phases of development there is a shift away from agriculture towards heavy industry which increases emissions, while in the later stages of development there is a shift from the more resource intensive extractive and heavy industrial sectors towards services and lighter manufacturing, which supposedly have lower emissions per unit of output.

3. *Input Mix*

Changes in *input mix* involve the substitution of less environmentally damaging inputs for more damaging inputs, and vice versa. Examples include substituting natural gas for coal, as well as substituting low sulphur coal for high sulphur coal. As scale, output mix, and technology are held constant, this is equivalent to moving along the isoquants of a neoclassical production function.

4. *State of Technology*

Improvements in the *state of technology* involve changes in both:

a. *Production efficiency* in terms of using less, *ceteris paribus*, of the polluting inputs per unit of output. A general increase in total factor productivity will result in less pollutant being emitted per unit of output if input mix is held constant, even though this is not necessarily an intended consequence.

b. *Emissions specific changes in process* result in less pollutant being emitted per unit of input. These innovations are directed specifically to reducing emissions.

Though any actual change in the level of the pollution must be a result of change in one of the proximate variables, those variables may be driven by changes in underlying variables in the course of economic development. A number of papers have developed theoretical models about how preferences and technology might interact to result in different time paths of environmental quality. The different studies make different simplifying assumptions about the economy. Most of these studies can generate an inverted U-shape curve of pollution intensity, but there is no inevitability about this. The result depends on the assumptions made and the value of particular parameters. Lopez (1994) and Selden and Song (1995) assume infinitely lived agents, exogenous technological change and that pollution is generated by production and not by consumption. John and Pecchenino (1994), John et al. (1995) and McConnell (1997) develop models based on overlapping generations, where pollution is generated by consumption rather than by production activities. Stokey (1998) allows endogenous technical change. It seems fairly easy to develop models that generate EKCs under appropriate assumptions. However, none of these theoretical models has been tested by fitting to actual data. Furthermore, if in fact the EKC for emissions is monotonic, as more recent evidence suggests, the ability of a model to produce an inverted U-shaped curve is not a particularly desirable property.

A description of one of the earliest such studies gives a flavour of the nature of this genre. Lopez (1994) provided a theoretical analysis of environment-growth relationships at a fairly high level of generality. In addition to the assumptions noted above, his model has two production sectors, weak separability between pollution and the conventional factors of production, constant returns to scale, quasi-fixed inputs of capital and labour, and exogenous output prices. Preferences are a function of revenue, pollution, and the output price vector. If producers pay a zero or fixed pollution price, then increases in output unambiguously result in increases in pollution in this system, irrespective of the features of the technology or preferences. However, when producers pay the social marginal cost of pollution, then the relation between emissions and income depends on the properties of the technology and preferences. If preferences are homothetic, increasing output again results in increasing pollution. However, when preferences are non-homothetic, as is likely in reality (Pollak and Wales, 1992), the response of pollution to growth depends on the elasticity of substitution in production between pollution and the conventional inputs, and the degree of relative risk aversion, i.e., the rate at which marginal utility declines with rising consumption of produced goods. This specific result depends on a CES revenue function. For other aggregators the time path could depend on further parameters. The faster the marginal utility declines, and the more substitution is possible in production, the less pollution will tend to increase with increased production. For empirically reasonable values of these two parameters, pollution may increase at low levels of income and fall at high levels – the inverted U. The role of pollution prices is critical in this model in determining the actual pattern.

9.3 ECONOMETRIC FRAMEWORK

The earliest EKCs were simple quadratic functions of the levels of income. However, economic activity inevitably implies the use of resources and by the laws of thermodynamics, use of resources inevitably implies the production of waste. Regressions that allow levels of indicators to become zero or negative are inappropriate except in the case of deforestation, where afforestation can occur. This restriction can be applied by using a logarithmic dependent variable. Some studies, including the original Grossman and Krueger (1991) paper, used a cubic EKC in levels and found an N shape EKC. But this result could due to not placing the non-negative concentrations condition on the model. The standard EKC regression model is:

$$\ln\left(\frac{E}{P}\right)_{it} = a_i \, g_t + b_1 \ln\left(\frac{GDP}{P}\right)_{it} + b_2 \ln\left(\frac{GDP}{P}\right)_{it}^2 + e_{it} \tag{9.1}$$

Here, E is emissions, P is population, and ln indicates natural logarithms. The first two terms on the RHS are intercept parameters which vary across countries or regions i and years t. The assumption is that, though the level of emissions per capita may differ over countries at any particular income level, the income elasticity is the same in all countries at a given income level. The time specific intercepts are intended to account for time varying omitted variables and stochastic shocks that are common to all countries.

The 'turning point' level of income, T, where emissions or concentrations are at a maximum, can be found using the following formula:

$$T = \exp\left(\frac{-b_1}{2b_2}\right)$$ (9.2)

The EKC can be reparameterized in the following way (omitting the time trend and subscripts):

$$\ln\left(\frac{E}{P}\right) = \mu_i + 1.5\kappa\tau^2 - \kappa\tau\ln\left(\frac{GDP}{P}\right) + 0.5\kappa\left(\ln\left(\frac{GDP}{P}\right)\right)^2 + \varepsilon$$ (9.3)

Here, τ is the natural log of the turning point in (9.2), μ_i is the log of the maximum level of emissions and κ is the second derivative of $\ln(E/P)$ with respect to $\ln(GDP/P)$ and therefore reflects the curvature of the EKC. Non-linear estimation of these actual parameters of interest and their confidence intervals has not been attempted.

Usually, the model is estimated with panel data. Most studies attempt to estimate both the fixed effects and random effects models. The fixed effects model treats the α_i and γ_t as regression parameters. In practice, the means of each variable for each country are subtracted from the data for that country, and the mean for all countries in the sample in each individual time period is also deducted from the observations for that period. Then ordinary least-squares (OLS) is used to estimate the regression with the transformed data. The random effects model treats the α_i and γ_t as components of the random disturbance. The residuals from an OLS estimate of the model with a single intercept are used to construct variances utilized in a generalized least-squares (GLS) estimate.

If there is correlation between the effects α_i and γ_t and the explanatory variables, then the random effects model cannot be estimated consistently (Mundlak, 1978; Hsiao, 1986). Only the fixed effects model can be estimated consistently. A Hausman (1978) test can be used to test for inconsistency in the random effects estimate, by comparing the fixed effects and random effects slope parameters. A significant difference indicates that the random effects model is estimated inconsistently, due to correlation between the explanatory variables and the error components. Assuming that there are no other statistical problems, the fixed effects model can be estimated consistently, but the estimated parameters are conditional on the country and time effects in the selected sample of data (Hsiao, 1986). Therefore, they cannot be used to extrapolate to other samples of data. This means that an EKC estimated with fixed effects, using only developed country data, might say little about the future behaviour of developing countries. Many studies compute the Hausman statistic and, finding that the random effects model cannot be consistently estimated, estimate the fixed effects model. But few have pondered the deeper implications of the failure of this orthogonality test.

GDP may be an integrated variable (Nelson and Plosser, 1982). Testing for integration and cointegration in panel data is a rapidly developing field. Perman and Stern (2003) employ some of these tests and find that the sulphur emissions and GDP per capita may be integrated variables. Coondoo and Dinda (2002) yield similar results for carbon dioxide emissions. If the EKC regressions do not cointegrate, then the estimates will be spurious. Very few studies have reported any diagnostic statistics for integration of the variables or cointegration of the regressions. Therefore, it is unclear what we can infer from the majority of EKC studies.

9.4 RESULTS OF EKC STUDIES

Many basic EKC models have been estimated, relating environmental impacts to income, without additional explanatory variables. However, the key features differentiating the models for different pollutants, data, etc., can be displayed by reviewing a few of the early studies, and examining a single impact in more detail. I review the contributions of Grossman and Krueger (1991), Shafik (1994) and Selden and Song (1994), and then look in more detail at studies for sulphur pollution and emissions. Many EKC studies have also been published that include additional explanatory variables. Several of these are reviewed in Stern (1998). Given the poor econometric properties of most EKC studies discussed in this chapter, and the problem of omitted variables bias when just one additional variable is tested, I do not review these studies systematically here.

To some (e.g., Lopez, 1994), the early EKC studies indicated that local pollutants were more likely to display an inverted U-shape relation with income, while global impacts, such as carbon dioxide, did not. This picture fits environmental economics theory – local impacts are internalized in a single economy or region and are likely to give rise to environmental policies to correct the externalities on pollutees before such policies are applied to globally externalized problems. As we shall see, the picture is not quite so clear-cut, even in the early studies. Furthermore, the more recent evidence on sulphur and carbon dioxide emissions shows there may be no strong distinction between the effect of income per capita on local and global pollutants. Stern et al. (1996) determined that higher turning points were found for regressions that used purchasing power parity (PPP) adjusted income relative to market exchange rates, and for studies using emissions of pollutants relative to studies using ambient concentrations in urban areas. In the initial stages of economic development, urban and industrial development tends to become more concentrated in a smaller number of cities, which also have rising central population densities. Many developing countries are characterized by a 'primate city' that dominates a country's urban hierarchy and contains much of its modern industry – Bangkok is one of the best such examples. In the later stages of economic development, urban and industrial development tends to decentralize. Additionally, the high population densities of less developed cities are gradually reduced by suburbanization. So it is possible for peak ambient pollution concentrations to fall as income rises, even if total national emissions are rising.

The first empirical EKC study was the NBER working paper by Grossman and Krueger (1991) that estimated EKCs as part of a study of the potential environmental impacts of NAFTA. They estimated EKCs for SO_2, dark matter (fine smoke) and suspended particles (SPM), using the GEMS dataset. This dataset is a panel of ambient measurements from a number of locations in cities around the world. Each regression involves a cubic function in levels (not logarithms) of PPP (Purchasing Power Parity adjusted) per capita GDP and various site-related variables, a time trend, and a trade intensity variable. The turning points for SO_2 and dark matter are at around $4,000–5,000 while the concentration of suspended particles appeared to decline even at low income levels. At income levels over $10,000–15,000 Grossman and Krueger's estimates show increasing levels of all three pollutants, though this may be an artifact of the non-logarithmic specification.

Shafik and Bandyopadhyay's (1992, later published as Shafik, 1994) study was particularly influential as the results were used in the 1992 World Development Report (IBRD, 1992). They estimated EKCs for ten different indicators: lack of clean water, lack of urban sanitation, ambient levels of suspended particulate matter, ambient sulphur oxides, change in forest area between 1961 and 1986, the annual observations of deforestation between 1961 and 1986, dissolved oxygen in rivers, fecal coliform in rivers, municipal waste per capita, and carbon emissions per capita.

They used three different functional forms: log-linear, log-quadratic and, in the most general case, a logarithmic cubic polynomial in PPP GDP per capita, as well as a time trend and site-related variables. In each case the dependent variable was untransformed. Lack of clean water and lack of urban sanitation were found to decline uniformly with increasing income, and over

Table 9.1   Sulphur EKC studies

Authors	Turning Point 1990 USD	Emis. or Concs.	PPP	Additional Variables
Panayotou, 1993	$3,137	Emis.	No	None
Shafik, 1994	$4,379	Concs.	Yes	Time trend, locational dummies
Torras and Boyce, 1998	$4,641	Concs.	Yes	Income inequality, literacy, political and civil rights, urbanization, locational dummies
Grossman and Krueger, 1991	$4,772–5,965	Concs.	No	Locational dummies, population density, trend
Panayotou, 1997	$5,965	Concs.	No	Population density, policy variables
Cole et al., 1997	$8,232	Emis.	Yes	Country dummy, technology level
Selden and Song, 1994	$10,391– 10,620	Emis.	Yes	Population density
Kaufmann et al., 1998	$14,730	Concs.	Yes	GDP/Area, steel exports/GDP
List and Gallet, 1999	$22,675	Emis.	N/A	None
Stern and Common, 2001	$101,166	Emis.	Yes	Time and country effects

time. Both measures of deforestation were found to be insignificantly related to the income terms. River quality tended to worsen with increasing income. The two air pollutants, however, conform to the EKC hypothesis. The turning points for both pollutants are found for income levels of between $3000 and $4000. Finally, both municipal waste and carbon emissions per capita increased unambiguously with rising income. The broader range of indicators examined by Shafik and Bandyopadhyay, shows a much more varied picture of the relationship between environment and development than indicated by Grossman and Krueger's more limited study.

Selden and Song (1994) estimated EKCs for four emissions series: SO_2, NO_x, SPM and CO, using longitudinal data from the World Resources Institute (1991). The data are primarily from developed countries. The

Table 9.1   Sulphur EKC studies (continued)

Authors	Data Source for Sulphur	Time Period	Countries/Cities
Panayotou, 1993	Own estimates	1987–88	55 developed and developing countries
Shafik, 1994	GEMS	1972–88	47 cities in 31 countries
Torras and Boyce, 1998	GEMS	1977–91	Unknown number of cities in 42 countries
Grossman and Krueger, 1991	GEMS	1977, '82, '88	Up to 52 cities in up to 32 countries
Panayotou, 1997	GEMS	1982–84	Cities in 30 developed and developing countries
Cole et al., 1997	OECD	1970–92	11 OECD countries
Selden and Song, 1994	WRI – primarily OECD source	1979–87	22 OECD and 8 developing countries
Kaufmann et al., 1998	UN	1974–89	13 developed and 10 developing countries
List and Gallet, 1999	US EPA	1929–94	US states
Stern and Common, 2001	ASL	1960–90	73 developed and developing countries

estimated turning points are all very high compared to the two earlier studies.

For the fixed effects version of their model, they are (points converted to 1990 US dollars using the US GDP implicit price deflator): SO_2, \$10,391; NO_x, \$13,383; SPM, \$12,275; and CO, \$7,114. This study showed that the turning point for emissions was likely to be higher than that for ambient concentrations.

Table 9.1 summarizes several studies of sulphur emissions and concentrations, listed in order of estimated income turning. Panayotou (1993) uses cross-sectional data, nominal GDP, and the assumption that the emission factor for each fuel is the same in all countries. In an exception to the rule that studies using concentrations data tend to have lower turning points than emissions based studies, this study has the lowest estimated turning point of all. With the exception of the Kaufmann et al. (1998) estimate, all turning point estimates using concentration data are less than $6,000. Kaufmann et al. used an unusual specification that includes GDP per area and GDP per area squared variables.

Among the emissions based estimates, both Selden and Song (1994) and Cole et al. (1997) use databases that are dominated by, or consist solely of, emissions from OECD countries. Their estimated turning points are $10,391 and $8,232 respectively. List and Gallet (1999) use data for 1929 to 1994 for the 50 US states. Their estimated turning point is the second highest in the table. Income per capita in their sample ranges from $1,162 to $22,462 in 1987 US dollars. This is bigger range of income levels than is found in the OECD based panels for recent decades. This suggests that including more low-income data points in the sample might yield a higher turning point. Stern and Common (2001) estimated the turning point at over $100,000. They used an emissions database produced for the US Department of Energy by ASL (Lefohn et al., 1999) that covers a greater range of income levels and includes more data points than any of the other sulphur EKC studies.

We see that the recent studies that used more representative samples of the data, find that there is a monotonic relation between sulphur emissions and income, just as there is between carbon dioxide and income. Interestingly, Dijkgraaf and Vollebergh (1998) estimate a carbon EKC for a panel data set of OECD countries, finding an inverted-U-shape EKC in the sample as a whole (as well as many signs of poor econometric behaviour). The turning point is at only 54 per cent of maximal GDP in the sample. A study by Schmalensee et al. (1995) also finds a within-sample turning point for carbon. In this case, a ten-piece spline was fitted to the data, such that the coefficient estimates for high-income countries are allowed to vary from those for low-income countries. All of these studies suggest that the differences in turning points that have been found for different pollutants may be due, at least partly, to the different samples used. The econometric reasons for this sample dependent behaviour will be discussed below.

The only robust conclusions from the EKC literature appear to be that concentrations of pollutants may decline from middle-income levels, while emissions tend to be monotonic in income. As we shall see below, emissions may decline over time in countries at many different levels of development. Given the poor statistical properties of most EKC models, it is hard to come to any conclusions about the roles of other additional variables, such as trade. Too few good-quality studies have been done of other indicators, apart from air pollution, to come to any firm conclusions about those impacts either.

9.5 THEORETICAL CRITIQUE OF THE EKC

A number of critical surveys of the EKC literature have been published (e.g., Ansuategi et al., 1998; Arrow et al., 1995; Ekins, 1997; Pearson, 1994; Stern et al., 1996; Stern, 1998). This section discusses the criticisms that were raised against the EKC on theoretical (rather than methodological) grounds.

The key criticism of Arrow et al. (1995), and others, was that the EKC model, as presented in the *1992 World Development Report* and elsewhere, assumes that there is no feedback from environmental damage to economic production, as income is assumed to be an exogenous variable. The assumption is that environmental damage does not reduce economic activity sufficiently to stop the growth process, and that any irreversibility is not too severe to reduce the level of income in the future. In other words, there is an assumption that the economy is sustainable. But, if higher levels of economic activity are not sustainable, attempting to grow quickly in the early stages of development, when environmental degradation is rising, may prove counter-productive.

It is clear that the levels of many pollutants per unit of output in specific processes have declined in developed countries over time, with increasingly stringent environmental regulations and technical innovations. However, the mix of effluent has shifted from sulphur and nitrogen oxides, to carbon dioxide and solid waste, so that aggregate waste is still high and per capita waste may not have declined. Economic activity is inevitably environmentally disruptive in some way. Satisfying the material needs of people requires the use and disturbance of energy flows and materials. Even Shafik (1994) showed that carbon dioxide emissions and municipal waste continued to increase with rising income. Therefore, an effort to reduce some environmental impacts may just aggravate other problems. Estimation of EKCs for total energy use are an attempt to capture environmental impact whatever its nature (e.g., Suri and Chapman, 1998).

Both Arrow et al. (1995) and Stern et al. (1996) argued that if there was an EKC type relationship, it might be partly or largely a result of the effects of trade on the distribution of polluting industries. The Hecksher-Ohlin trade theory suggests that, under free trade, developing countries would specialize in the production of goods that are intensive in the factors that they are endowed with in relative abundance: labour and natural resources. The developed countries would specialize in human capital and manufactured capital-intensive activities. Part of the reduction in environmental degradation levels in the developed countries, and increases in environmental degradation in middle-income countries, may reflect this specialization (Lucas et al., 1992; Hettige et al., 1992; Suri and Chapman, 1998). Environmental regulation in developed countries might further encourage polluting activities to gravitate towards the developing countries (Lucas et al., 1992).

These effects would exaggerate any apparent decline in pollution intensity with rising income along the EKC. In our finite world, the poor countries
of today would be unable to find further countries from which to import
resource intensive products as they themselves become wealthy. When the
poorer countries apply similar levels of environmental regulation, they would
face the more difficult task of abating these activities rather than outsourcing
them to other countries (Arrow et al., 1995; Stern et al., 1996). There are no
clear answers on the impact of trade on pollution from the empirical EKC
literature.

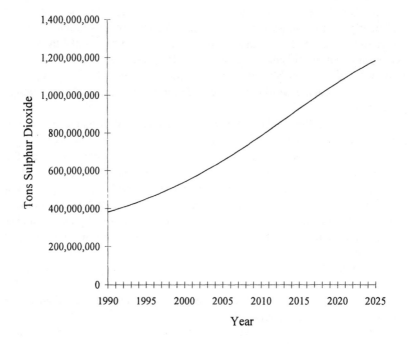

Source: Stern et al. (1996).

Figure 9.2   Projected sulphur emissions

Stern et al. (1996) argued that early EKC studies showed that a number of
indicators (SO_2 emissions, NO_x, and deforestation) peak at income levels
around the current world mean per capita income. A cursory glance at the
available econometric estimates might have led one to believe that, given
likely future levels of mean income per capita, environmental degradation
should decline from now on. This interpretation is evident in the 1992 World
Bank Development Report (IBRD, 1992). However, income is not normally

distributed, but very skewed, with much larger numbers of people below mean income per capita than above it. Therefore, it is median rather than mean income that is the relevant variable. Selden and Song (1994) and Stern et al. (1996) performed simulations which, assuming that the EKC relationship is valid, showed that global environmental degradation was set to rise for a long time to come.

Figure 9.2 presents projected sulphur emissions using the EKC in Figure 9.1 and UN and World Bank forecasts of economic and population growth. More recent estimates show that the turning point is higher or does not occur but the impression produced by the early studies in the policy, academic, and business communities, seems slow to fade.

9.6 RECENT DEVELOPMENTS

A number of studies built on the basic EKC model by introducing additional explanatory variables, intended to model underlying or proximate factors such as 'political freedom' (e.g., Torras and Boyce, 1998), output structure (e.g., Panayotou, 1997), or trade (e.g., Suri and Chapman, 1998). Stern (1998) reviews many of these papers in detail. On the whole, the included variables turn out to be significant at traditional significance levels. However, testing different variables individually is subject to the problem of potential omitted variables bias. Further, these studies do not report cointegration statistics that might tell us whether omitted variables bias is likely to be a problem. Therefore, it is not really clear what we can infer from this body of work.

Since 1998 significant developments fall into three classes:

- Empirical case study evidence on environmental performance and policy in developing countries, which is discussed in this section.
- Improved econometric testing and estimates discussed in the following section.
- Decomposition analysis, representing a new wave in the investigation of environment-development relations, discussed in Section 9.8.

Dasgupta et al. (2002) wrote a critical review of the EKC literature and other evidence on the relation between environmental quality and economic development in the *Journal of Economic Perspectives*. Dasgupta et al. (2002) provide a service by bringing a more complex view of the facts to the wider community of economists who, if they had thought about these issues, were probably familiar only with the stylized facts derived from Grossman and Krueger (1991) and IBRD (1992).

Figure 9.3 presents four alternative viewpoints regarding the nature of the emissions and income relation discussed in the article.

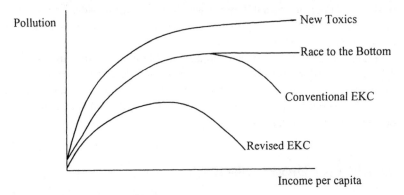

Source: Dasgupta et al. (2002); Perman and Stern (2003).

Figure 9.3   Environmental Kuznets curve: alternative views

The conventional EKC needs no further discussion. Two viewpoints argue that the EKC is monotonic. The new toxics scenario claims that, while some traditional pollutants might have an inverted U-shape curve, the new pollutants that are replacing them do not. These include carcinogenic chemicals, carbon dioxide, etc. As the older pollutants are cleaned up, new ones emerge, so that overall environmental impact is not reduced. The race to the bottom scenario posits that emissions were reduced in developed countries by outsourcing dirty production to developing countries. These countries will find it harder to reduce emissions. But also, the pressure of globalization may preclude further tightening of environmental regulation in developed countries and may even result in its loosening in the name of competitiveness.

The revised EKC scenario does not reject the inverted U-shape curve, but suggests that it is shifting downwards and to the left over time, due to technological change. This argument is already present in the 1992 World Bank Development Report (IBRD, 1992). They also review the theoretical literature and some of the econometric specification issues. But their main contribution is presenting evidence that environmental improvements are possible in developing countries, and that peak levels of environmental degradation will be lower than in countries which developed earlier.

Regulation of pollution seems to increase with income, as does enforcement, but the greatest increases happen from low to middle income levels and there would be expected to be diminishing returns to increased regulation. There is also informal or decentralized regulation in developing countries –

Coasian bargaining. Further, liberalization of developing economies over the last two decades has encouraged more efficient use of inputs and less subsidization of environmentally damaging activities – globalization is in fact good for the environment. The evidence seems to contradict the 'race to the bottom' scenario. Multinational companies respond to investor and consumer pressure in their home countries and raise standards in the countries they invest in. Further, better methods of regulating pollution, such as market instruments, are having an impact even in developing countries. Better information on pollution is available, encouraging government to regulate and empowering local communities. Those that argue that there is no regulatory capacity in developing countries seem to be wrong.

Much of Dasgupta et al.'s evidence is from China. Other researchers of environmental and economic developments in China come to similar conclusions. Gallagher (2003) finds that China is adopting European Union standards for pollution emissions from cars with an approximately eight to ten year lag. Clearly China's income per capita is far more than ten years behind that of Western Europe. Furthermore, China has reduced sulphur emissions and even carbon emissions in recent years (Streets et al., 2001).

9.7 ECONOMETRIC CRITIQUE OF THE EKC

Econometric criticisms of the EKC fall into four main categories: heteroskedasticity, simultaneity, omitted variables bias, and cointegration issues.

Stern et al. (1996) raised the issue of heteroskedasticity, which may be important in the context of cross-sectional regressions of grouped data (see Maddala, 1977). Schmalensee et al. (1995) found that regression residuals from OLS were heteroskedastic with smaller residuals associated with countries with higher total GDP and population as predicted by Stern et al. (1996). Stern (2002) estimated a decomposition model using feasible GLS. Adjusting for heteroskedasticity in the estimation significantly improved the goodness of fit of globally aggregated fitted emissions to actual emissions.

Cole et al. (1997) and Holtz-Eakin and Selden (1995) used Hausman tests for regressor exogeneity, to address directly the simultaneity issue. They found no evidence of simultaneity. In any case, simultaneity bias is less serious in models involving integrated variables than in the traditional stationary econometric model (Perman and Stern, 2003). Coondoo and Dinda (2002) test for Granger Causality between CO_2 emissions and income in various individual countries and regions. As the data are differenced to ensure stationarity, this test can address only short-run effects. The overall pattern that emerges is that causality runs from income to emissions, or there is no significant relationship in developing countries, while in developed countries causality runs from emissions to income. However, in each case the relationship is positive, so that there is no EKC type effect.

Stern and Common (2001) use three lines of evidence to suggest that the EKC is an incomplete model and that estimates of the EKC in levels can suffer from significant omitted variables bias:

- Differences between the parameters of the random effects and fixed effects models, tested using the Hausman test;
- Differences between the estimated coefficients in different subsamples; and
- Tests for serial correlation.

Table 9.2   Stern and Common (2001) key results

Region	Model	Levels				First Differences	
		Turning Points	Hausman Test	Chow F Test	ρ	Turning Points	Mean Income Elasticity
OECD	FE	$9,239			0.9109	$55,481	0.67
	RE	$9,181	0.3146 (0.8545)		0.9070		
Non-OECD	FE	$908,178			0.8507	$18,039	0.50
	RE	$344,689	14.1904 (0.0008)		0.8574		
World	FE	$101,166		10.6587 (0.0156)	0.8569	$33,290	
	RE	$54,199	10.7873 (0.0045)	4.0256 (0.0399)	0.8624		

Note: All turning points in real 1990 purchasing power parity US dollars.

Table 9.2 presents the key results from an EKC model estimated with data from 74 countries (in the World sample) over the period 1960–90.

For the non-OECD and World samples, the Hausman test shows a significant difference in the parameter estimates for the random effects and fixed effects model. This indicates that the regressors (the level and square of the logarithm of income per capita) are correlated with the country effects and time effects. As these effects model the mean effects of omitted variables that vary across countries or across time, this indicates that the regressors are probably correlated with omitted variables and the regression coefficients are biased. The OECD-only results pass this Hausman test, but this result turned out to be very sensitive to the exact sample of countries included in the subsample. As explained in Section 9.3, the fixed effects model can provide a consistent but sample dependent estimate of the parameters. Most EKC studies report significant Hausman test statistics and consequently estimate the fixed effect model. However, they do not discuss the implications of the statistic for the validity and applicability of the estimated parameters.

As expected, given the Hausman test results, the parameter estimates are dependent on the sample used, with the non-OECD estimates showing a turning point at extremely high income levels and the OECD estimates a within sample turning point (Table 9.2). As mentioned above, these results exactly parallel those for developed and developing country samples of carbon emissions. The Chow F-Test tests whether the two sub-samples can be pooled, and therefore that there is a common regression parameter vector, a hypothesis that is rejected.

The parameter ρ is the first order autoregressive coefficient of the regression residuals. This level of serial correlation indicates misspecification, either in terms of omitted variables or missing dynamics.

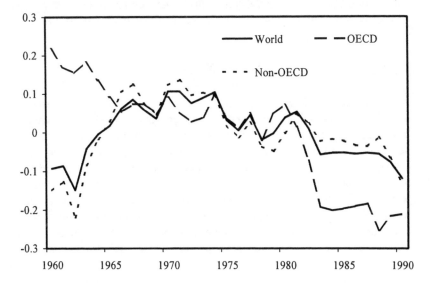

Source: Stern and Common (2001).

Figure 9.4   Time effects: first differences sulphur EKC

Perman and Stern (2003) test the data and models for unit roots and cointegration respectively. Panel unit root tests indicate that all three series – log sulphur emissions per capita, log GDP capita, and its square – have stochastic trends. Results for cointegration are less clear-cut. Around half of the individual country EKC regressions cointegrate, but many of these have parameters with 'incorrect signs'. Some panel cointegration tests indicate cointegration in all countries and some accept the non-cointegration hypothesis. But even when cointegration is found, the form of the EKC relationship varies radically across countries, with many countries having U-shaped EKCs. A common cointegrating vector in all countries is strongly rejected.

In the presence of possible non-cointegration we can estimate a model in first differences. The estimated turning points are much more similar across sub-samples (Table 9.2), although they are still significantly different, and indicate a largely monotonic EKC relationship. The estimated income elasticity is less than one (there are factors that change with income which offset the scale effect), but they are insufficiently powerful fully to overcome the scale effect.

Figure 9.4 presents the time effects from the first difference estimates. The OECD saw declining emissions holding income constant over the entire time period, though the introduction of the LRTAP agreement in the mid-1980s in Europe resulted in a larger decline. Developing countries saw rising emissions in the 1960s and declining emissions since 1973, *ceteris paribus*.

9.8 DECOMPOSING EMISSIONS

As an alternative to the EKC, an increasing number of studies carry out decompositions of emissions into the proximate sources of emissions changes described in Section 9.2. The usual approach is to utilize index numbers and detailed sectoral information on fuel use, production, emissions, etc. Stern (2002) develops an alternative econometric method, which still requires national data on fuel mix, but does not require fuel use data at an industry level. Usually, fuel use is collected on a different sectoral basis than output is measured, making index number studies impossible to implement for most countries. Antweiler et al. (2001) develop an econometric model of the effects of trade on environmental quality, which includes capital/labour abundance but no energy data.

Grossman (1995) and de Bruyn (1997) proposed the following decomposition:

$$E_{it} = \sum_{j=1}^{n} Y_{it} I_{ijt} S_{ijt} \tag{9.4}$$

Here, E_{it} is emissions in country i in year t, Y_{it} is GDP in country i in year t, I_{ijt} is the emissions intensity of sector j in country i and year t, and S_{ijt} is the share of that sector in GDP. This decomposition, therefore, attributes emissions to what Grossman calls the scale, composition (output mix), and technique effects. The latter includes the effects of both fuel mix and 'technological change', with the second breaking down into general productivity improvements, where more output is derived from a unit of input, and emissions reducing technological change, where less emissions are produced per unit of input. De Bruyn (1997) implements the decomposition for sulphur emissions in the Netherlands and Western Germany. Between 1980 and 1990 GDP grew by 26–28 per cent in the two countries, structural change on the output side contributed –4.5 per cent to emissions in Western Germany and +5.7 per cent in the Netherlands. Other effects contributed around –74 per cent in the two countries, with energy efficiency contributing 15–20 per cent and therefore energy mix and emissions specific technological change contributed a 55–60 per cent reduction in sulphur emissions.

Viguier (1999) computes his own data set for the USSR/Russia, Poland, Hungary, USA, UK, and France for 1970–94. He carries out a Divisia index decomposition of changes in emissions of SOx, NOx, and CO_2 into fuel quality, fuel mix, industrial structure, and energy intensity at the aggregate level. For sulphur emissions, specific reductions followed by changes in energy intensity seem most important. In Eastern Europe, energy intensity increased over parts of the period. Input and output structure played a minor role, though fuel mix acted to increase emissions in the US. For nitrogen and carbon, energy intensity was the most important factor.

Hilton and Levinson (1998) estimate EKCs for automotive lead emissions. Data is available on both the total consumption of gasoline and the lead content of gasoline. Hence, decomposition into scale and technical change effects is easy in this special case. The regression estimates use total lead emissions as the dependent variable for unclear reasons, and so are difficult to interpret. There is some evidence of an EKC effect in 1992, when lead content per gallon of gasoline was a declining function of income. Per capita gasoline use rises strongly with income. However, there is a wide scatter in developing countries with many low and middle-income countries having low lead contents. Before 1983 there is no evidence of an EKC type relation in the data. The inference is that there was a technological innovation that was preferentially adopted in high-income countries. As Gallagher (2003) suggests, these innovations may be adopted with a relatively short lag in developing countries.

Selden et al. (1999) carry out a decomposition of US emissions of six criteria pollutants that allows identification of all five effects identified in Section 9.2. They found that input and output mix did not contribute much to offsetting the scale effect. In fact shifts in fuel use increased some pollutants. Reductions in energy intensity were important in reducing emissions. Even so, all of these effects could not overcome even growth in emissions per capita, let alone total emissions growth. The most important factor was, therefore, specific emissions reducing technological change.

Stern (2002) uses the following econometric model to decompose sulphur emissions in 64 countries in the period 1973–90:

$$\frac{S_{it}}{P_{it}} = \gamma_i \frac{Y_{it}}{P_{it}} A_t \frac{E_{it}}{Y_{it}} \prod_{j=1}^{J} \left(\frac{y_{jit}}{Y_{it}} \right)^{\alpha_j} \sum_{k=1}^{K} \frac{e_{kit}}{E_{it}} \varepsilon_{it} \qquad (9.5)$$

Here, S is sulphur emissions and P population, and the RHS decomposes per capita emissions into the following five effects:

$\dfrac{Y_{it}}{P_{it}}$ Scale – GDP per capita.

A_t A common global time effect representing the effects of emissions specific technical progress.

$\dfrac{E_{it}}{Y_{it}}$ Energy intensity – the effect of general productivity on emissions.

$\prod_{j=1}^{J} \left(\dfrac{y_{jit}}{Y_{it}} \right)^{\alpha_j}$ Output Mix – shares of the output of different industries y in total GDP Y.

$\sum_{k=1}^{K} \dfrac{e_{kit}}{E_{it}} \varepsilon_{it}$ Input Mix – shares of different energy sources e in total energy use E.

The contribution of the five effects at the global level are given in Table 9.3.

Table 9.3   Contributions to total change in global sulphur emissions

	Weighted Logarithmic Per Cent Change
Total Change:	
Actual Emissions	28.77
Predicted Emissions	27.37
Unexplained Fraction	1.40
Decomposition:	
Scale Effect	53.78
Emissions Related Technical Change	-19.86
Energy Intensity	-10.20
Output Mix	3.77
Input Mix	-0.13

Input and output effects contributed little globally, though in individual countries they can have important effects. At the global level, the two forms of technological change reduced the increase in emissions to half of what it would have been in their absence, with emissions specific technological change lowering aggregate emissions by around 20 per cent. The residuals from the model show it to be a statistically adequate representation of the data. A nested test of this model and the EKC showed that the income-squared term in the EKC added no explanatory power to that provided by the decomposition model.

Antweiler et al. (2001) come full circle from Grossman and Krueger's (1991) study of the potential impacts of NAFTA, by applying what they describe as a decomposition model to the question of whether free trade is good for the environment. This model does not, however, attribute changes in emissions to a comprehensive set of sources. They develop a reduced form econometric model from a theoretical structural model of the demand and supply of pollution, and estimate it using the GEMS sulphur dioxide concentration data. The theoretical model allows an increase in openness to trade to have scale, compositional, and technique effects. However, the technique effect is assumed to be induced by the increase in income due to trade. This model, therefore, takes the EKC hypothesis as a given. Compositional effects are expected to differ in capital intensive and labour intensive economies. Trade is likely to increase pollution in the former and reduce it in the latter. Therefore, the capital/labour ratio is controlled for. The 'scale elasticity' is estimated to average 0.266. But this is the elasticity of concentrations to a city-based measure of GDP per square kilometre. In no way can this be a legitimate measure of scale, as urban expansion (holding GDP per square kilometre constant) is an increase in scale and, as discussed above, suburbanization and decentralization also accompany economic development. The sample mean of the technique elasticity (elasticity of concentrations with respect to GNP per capita) is −1.15. The composition elasticity (elasticity of concentrations with respect to the capital/labour ratio) is 1.01 and trade intensity has an elasticity of −0.864. Combining the effects, trade has a negative impact on emissions, but this effect is a function of income, with small or positive impacts in high-income countries and reductions in emissions in developing countries. This is because high-income countries are capital intensive and low-income countries labour intensive.

Judson et al. (1999) estimate separate EKC relations for energy consumption in each of a number of energy-consuming sectors for a large panel data set, using spline regression. This allows them to estimate different time effects in each sector and these vary substantially. Time effects show rising energy consumption over time in the household and other sectors, but flat to declining time effects in industry and construction. Technical innovations tend to introduce more energy using appliances to households and energy saving techniques to industry. The income effects add explanatory power. Income elasticities decline with rising income, but this effect is most pronounced for the households and other sector. The share of transportation tends to rise with rising income. Industry and construction has a U-shaped EKC for energy consumption.

The conclusion from all of these studies is that the main means by which emissions of pollutants can be reduced is by time related technique effects and in particular those directed specifically at emissions reduction, though productivity growth or declining energy intensity has a role to play. Though structural change and shifts in fuel composition may be important in some countries at some times, their average contribution seems less important quantitatively. Those studies that include developing countries – Judson et al. (1999), Antweiler et al. (2001), and Stern (2002) – find that these technological changes are occurring in both developing and developed countries. Innovations may first be adopted preferentially in higher income countries (Hilton and Levinson, 1998), but seem to be adopted in developing countries with relatively short lags (Gallagher, 2003). This result is in line with the evidence of Dasgupta et al. (2002) and the EKC based estimates of time effects in Stern and Common (2001) and Stern (2002).

9.9 CONCLUSIONS

The evidence presented in this chapter shows that the statistical analysis on which the environmental Kuznets curve is based is not robust. There is little evidence for a common inverted U-shaped pathway which countries follow as their income rises. There may be an inverted U-shaped relation between urban ambient concentrations of some pollutants and income though this should be tested with more rigorous time series or panel data methods. It seems unlikely that the EKC is a complete model of emissions or concentrations.

The true form of the emissions-income relationship is likely to be a mix of two of the scenarios proposed by Dasgupta et al. (2002), illustrated in Figure 9.3. The overall shape is that of their 'new toxics' EKC – a monotonic increase of emissions in income. But over time this curve shifts down. This is analogous to their 'revised EKC' scenario, which is intended to indicate that over time the conventional EKC curve shifts down. Some evidence shows that a particular innovation is likely to be adopted preferentially in high-income countries first, with a short lag before it is adopted in the majority of poorer countries. However, emissions may be declining simultaneously in low- and high-income countries over time, *ceteris paribus*, though the particular innovations typically adopted at any one time could be different in different countries.

It seems that structural factors on both the input and output side do play a role in modifying the gross scale effect, though they are less influential on the whole than time related effects. The income elasticity of emissions is likely to be less than one, but not negative in wealthy countries as proposed by the EKC hypothesis.

In slower growing economies, emissions-reducing technological change can overcome the scale effect of rising income per capita on emissions. As a result, substantial reductions in sulphur emissions per capita have been observed in many OECD countries in the last few decades. In faster growing middle-income economies, the effects of rising income overwhelmed the contribution of technological change in reducing emissions.

The research challenge now is to revisit some of the issues addressed earlier in the EKC literature, using the new decomposition models and rigorous panel data and time series statistics. For example, how can the effects of trade on emissions be modelled in the context of the decomposition model? Rigorous answers to such questions are central to the debate on globalization and the environment.

APPENDIX: ECONOMETRIC PRIMER

This chapter makes extensive use of the concept of cointegration. This appendix explains these and some other statistical concepts for readers who have a basic background in statistics but are not familiar with the recent time-series econometrics literature. Key terms are marked in bold when first defined.

Classical regression analysis makes two critical assumptions of relevance here:

1. The true residual or error term in the equation is assumed to be *covariance stationary*. This means that the error has a constant mean and variance. If this is not the case we say that this is a *spurious regression* and the results cannot be relied on.
2. All relevant variables are included in the model. If variables that are relevant and are correlated with the variables included in the regression are omitted, the estimated regression parameters will be biased and cannot be relied on. This is called *omitted variables bias*. A *biased estimator* of a parameter is one where the (statistically) expected value of the estimator is not equal to the true value of the parameter.

The regression error is not the only variable that can be stationary or non-stationary; all variables can be classified in this way. Usually also a *linear combination* (weighted sum) of these variables will also be non-stationary. The regression error term is such a linear combination. Therefore, when we carry out a regression using non-stationary variables, there is a strong possibility that the regression will be spurious.

There are two main ways in which time series variables may have a non-constant mean and therefore be non-stationary:

1. The variable may have a *deterministic time trend*. For example the variable may be a linear function of time plus a random noise term.

2. The variable may be *integrated*. Shocks to integrated variables have permanent effects – the variable 'integrates' these shocks – so that the mean is non-constant. The simplest example of an integrated variable is a random walk. In each period a random walk is equal to its value in the previous period plus a random error term. More complex processes include random walks with noise and integrated random walks. In the econometric literature, these variables are often also referred to as unit root or stochastically trending variables. A particular historical realization of an integrated process is called a *stochastic trend. Unit root tests* such as the *Augmented Dickey Fuller Test*, can determine whether variables are integrated.

Variables in either class will be correlated with each other, whether or not they are truly related. Regression analysis will show an apparent relationship but it may well be spurious.

Both these classes of variables can be made stationary. For the first class of variables, the deterministic time trend should be removed. Many integrated variables can be made stationary after *first differencing* – replacing the series with the period to period changes in the series – in which case they are termed integrated of order one or *I(1) variables*. Removing a deterministic time trend from integrated variables does not, however, render them stationary.

One response to the problem of regression involving integrated variables is to routinely difference them and then carry out the regression analysis. The resulting regression is valid as a measure of the short-run effects of the variables on each other. Differencing also reduces the correlations with omitted variables, reducing the effects of that problem too. However, important information about the long-run relation between the variables is lost, as is information about whether important variables have been omitted.

If a group of integrated variables does have a true linear causal functional relationship among themselves, then it follows that the stochastic trends present in the variables will be shared. If this is the case, a linear combination of the variables will be stationary and the parameter estimates from classical regression analysis are valid. In this case the variables are said to be *cointegrated*. If, additionally, there is no serial (time related) correlation in the residual, the traditional regression inference, such as t-statistics, applies. A group of cointegrated variables interact with each other such that there is a *long-run equilibrium* between them.

Therefore, when dealing with integrated variables, *cointegration testing* is essential. However, it is possible that two or more integrated variables are causally related but are also affected by additional integrated variables. In this case, the variables will not be cointegrated, but inclusion of the omitted variables in the model will result in cointegration. Hence, cointegration analysis is a powerful test of the possibility of omitted variables.

Therefore, cointegration analysis can be used to test the validity of supposed stylised facts, such as the EKC, when the data are time series that are integrated.

Cointegration analysis can establish statistical causality amongst integrated variables. The notion of *Granger causality* is broader and can apply to any time series. Granger causality tests examine whether past values of a variable can predict the future values of another variable given its own past history and all other relevant information.

Another test that indicates the possibility of omitted variables is the *Hausman test* for the consistency of the random effects panel regression model. *Panel data* is a dataset that has time series observations on a number of countries, firms, people, etc. The Hausman test examines whether the parameters estimated using a *fixed effects* specification differ from those estimated using a *random effects* specification. The fixed effects model assumes that the intercept term for each country or time period in the regression is a constant (but differs across countries), while the random effects model assumes that it is a random variable. The two estimates will differ when the error term in the regression is correlated with the regressors (right-hand side or explanatory variables). This violates a third crucial assumption of classical regression analysis – that there is no correlation between the error term and the regressors.

Therefore, when this assumption is violated, the random effects model parameters cannot be estimated *consistently*. The fixed effects parameters could, in theory, be estimated consistently. However, this correlation between the error and the regressors probably also indicates that variables have been omitted from the model that are correlated with those included. Therefore, the fixed parameters will be biased and cannot be relied on due to the omission of these variables. A *consistent estimator* is one where the bias of estimation is reduced by increasing the sample size.

A different version of the Hausman test can test for *simultaneity bias*. When explanatory variables are endogenous – determined by other variables in the model – they will be correlated with the true error terms, leading standard regression estimates to again be biased. Simultaneity bias can be addressed by instrumental variable or maximum likelihood estimators. When the variables are integrated, simultaneity bias is likely to be less important due to the super-consistency properties of the estimators in this case – cointegration 'trumps' simultaneity.

REFERENCES

Ansuategi, A., E.B. Barbier and C.A. Perrings (1998), 'The environmental Kuznets curve', in J.C.J.M. van den Bergh and M.W. Hofkes (eds), *Theory and Implementation of Economic Models for Sustainable Development*, Dordrecht: Kluwer.

Antweiler, W., B.R. Copeland and M.S. Taylor (2001), 'Is free trade good for the environment?', *American Economic Review*, **91**, 877–908.

Arrow, K., B. Bolin, R. Costanza, P. Dasgupta, C. Folke, C.S. Holling, B-O. Jansson, S. Levin, K-G. Mäler, C.A. Perrings and D. Pimentel (1995), 'Economic growth, carrying capacity, and the environment', *Science*, **268**, 520–21.

Cole, M.A., A.J. Rayner and J.M. Bates (1997), 'The environmental Kuznets curve: an empirical analysis', *Environment and Development Economics*, **2** (4), 401–16.

Coondoo, D. and S. Dinda (2002), 'Causality between income and emission: a country group-specific econometric analysis', *Ecological Economics*, **40**, 351–67.

Dasgupta, S., B. Laplante, H. Wang and D. Wheeler (2002), 'Confronting the environmental Kuznets curve', *Journal of Economic Perspectives*, **16**, 147–68.

de Bruyn, S.M. (1997), 'Explaining the environmental Kuznets curve: structural change and international agreements in reducing sulphur emissions', *Environment and Development Economics*, **2**, 485–503.

Dijkgraaf, E. and H.R.J. Vollebergh (1998), *Kuznets Revisited. Time-Series versus Panel Estimation: The CO_2 Case*, OFCEB Research Memorandum No. 9806, Rotterdam: Erasmus University.

Ekins, P. (1997), 'The Kuznets curve for the environment and economic growth: examining the evidence', *Environment and Planning A*, **29**, 805–30.

Gallagher, K.S. (2003), *Development of Cleaner Vehicle Technology? Foreign Direct Investment and Technology Transfer from the United States to China*, paper presented at United States Society for Ecological Economics 2nd Biennial Meeting, Saratoga Springs, May.

Grossman, G.M. (1995), 'Pollution and growth: what do we know?', in I. Goldin and L.A. Winters (eds), *The Economics of Sustainable Development*, Cambridge: Cambridge University Press, pp. 19–47.

Grossman, G.M. and A.B. Krueger (1991), *Environmental Impacts of a North American Free Trade Agreement*, National Bureau of Economic Research Working Paper 3914, Cambridge MA: NBER.

Hausman, J.A. (1978), 'Specification tests in econometrics', *Econometrica* **46**, 1251–71.

Hettige, H., R.E.B. Lucas and D. Wheeler (1992), 'The toxic intensity of industrial production: global patterns, trends, and trade policy', *American Economic Review*, **82** (2), 478–81.

Hilton, F.G.H. and A.M. Levinson (1998), 'Factoring the environmental Kuznets curve: evidence from automotive lead emissions', *Journal of Environmental Economics and Management*, **35**, 126–41.

Holtz-Eakin, D. and T.M. Selden (1995), 'Stoking the fires? CO_2 emissions and economic growth', *Journal of Public Economics*, **57**, 85–101.

Hsiao, C. (1986), *Analysis of Panel Data*, Cambridge: Cambridge University Press.

IBRD (1992), *World Development Report 1992: Development and the Environment*, New York: Oxford University Press.

John, A. and R. Pecchenino (1994), 'An overlapping generations model of growth and the environment', *Economic Journal*, **104**, 1393–410.

John, A., R. Pecchenino, D. Schimmelpfennig and S. Schreft (1995), 'Short-lived agents and the long-lived environment', *Journal of Public Economics*, **58**, 127–41.

Judson, R.A., R. Schmalensee and T.M. Stoker (1999), 'Economic development and the structure of demand for commercial energy', *The Energy Journal* **20** (2), 29–57.

Kaufmann, R.K., B. Davidsdottir, S. Garnham and P. Pauly (1998), 'The determinants of atmospheric SO_2 concentrations: reconsidering the environmental Kuznets curve', *Ecological Economics*, **25**, 209–20.

Kuznets, S. (1955), 'Economic growth and income inequality', *American Economic Review*, **49**, 1–28.

Lefohn, A.S., J.D. Husar and R.B. Husar (1999), 'Estimating historical anthropogenic global sulfur emission patterns for the period 1850-1990', *Atmospheric Environment*, **33**, 3435–44.

List, J.A. and C.A. Gallet (1999), 'The environmental Kuznets curve: does one size fit all?', *Ecological Economics*, **31**, 409–24.

Lopez, R. (1994), 'The environment as a factor of production: the effects of economic growth and trade liberalization', *Journal of Environmental Economics and Management*, **27**, 163–84.

Lucas, R.E.B., D. Wheeler and H. Hettige (1992), 'Economic development, environmental regulation and the international migration of toxic industrial pollution: 1960–1988', in P. Low (ed.), *International Trade and the Environment*, World Bank Discussion Paper No. 159, Washington DC.

Maddala, G. (1977), *Econometrics*, Singapore: McGraw Hill.

Martinez-Alier, J. (1995), 'The environment as a luxury good or "too poor to be green"', *Ecological Economics*, **13**, 1–10.

McConnell, K.E. (1997), 'Income and the demand for environmental quality', *Environment and Development Economics*, **2**, 383–99.

Mundlak, Y. (1978), 'On the pooling of time series and cross section data', *Econometrica*, **46**, 69–85.

Nelson, C.R. and C.I. Plosser (1982), 'Trends versus random walks in macroeconomic time series: some evidence and implications', *Journal of Monetary Economics*, **10**, 139–62.

Panayotou, T. (1993), *Empirical Tests and Policy Analysis of Environmental Degradation at Different Stages of Economic Development*, Working Paper WP238, Technology and Employment Programme, International Labour Office, Geneva.

Panayotou, T. (1997), 'Demystifying the environmental Kuznets curve: turning a black box into a policy tool', *Environment and Development Economics*, **2**, 465–84.

Pearson, P.J.G. (1994), 'Energy, externalities, and environmental quality: will development cure the ills it creates', *Energy Studies Review*, **6**, 199–216.

Perman, R. and D.I. Stern (2003), 'Evidence from panel unit root and cointegration tests that the environmental Kuznets curve does not exist', *Australian Journal of Agricultural and Resource Economics*, **47**, 325–47.

Pollak, R.A. and T.J. Wales (1992), *Demand System Specification, and Estimation*, New York: Oxford University Press.

Schmalensee, R., T.M. Stoker and R.A. Judson (1995), *World Energy Consumption and Carbon Dioxide Emissions: 1950-2050*, Cambridge MA: Sloan School of Management, Massachusetts Institute of Technology.

Selden, T.M. and D. Song (1994), 'Environmental quality and development: is there a Kuznets curve for air pollution?' *Journal of Environmental Economics and Environmental Management*, **27**, 147–62.

Selden, T.M. and D. Song (1995), 'Neoclassical growth, the J curve for abatement and the inverted U curve for pollution', *Journal of Environmental Economics and Environmental Management*, **29**, 162–68.

Selden, T.M., A.S. Forrest and J.E. Lockhart (1999), 'Analyzing reductions in U.S. air pollution emissions: 1970 to 1990', *Land Economics*, **75**, 1–21.

Shafik, N. (1994), 'Economic development and environmental quality: an econometric analysis', *Oxford Economic Papers*, **46**, 757–73.

Shafik, N. and S. Bandyopadhyay (1992), *Economic Growth and Environmental Quality: Time Series and Cross-Country Evidence*, Background Paper for the World Development Report 1992, The World Bank, Washington DC.

Stern, D.I. (1998), 'Progress on the environmental Kuznets curve?', *Environment and Development Economics*, **3**, 173–96.

Stern, D.I. (2002), 'Explaining changes in global sulfur emissions: an econometric decomposition approach', *Ecological Economics*, **42**, 201–20.

Stern, D.I. and M.S. Common (2001), 'Is there an environmental Kuznets curve for sulfur?', *Journal of Environmental Economics and Environmental Management*, **41**, 162–78.

Stern, D.I., M.S. Common and E.B. Barbier (1996), 'Economic growth and environmental degradation: the environmental Kuznets curve and sustainable development', *World Development*, **24**, 1151–60.

Stokey, N.L. (1998), 'Are there limits to growth?', *International Economic Review*, **39** (1), 1–31.

Streets, D.G., K. Jiang, X. Hu, J.E. Sinton, X.-Q. Zhang, S. Xu, M.Z. Jacobson and J.E. Hansen (2001), 'Recent reductions in China's greenhouse gas emissions', *Science*, **294**: 1835–37.

Suri, V. and D. Chapman (1998), 'Economic growth, trade and energy: implications for the environmental Kuznets curve', *Ecological Economics*, **25**, 195–208.

Torras, M. and J.K. Boyce (1998), 'Income, inequality, and pollution: a reassessment of the environmental Kuznets curve', *Ecological Economics*, **25**, 147–60.

Viguier, L. (1999), 'Emissions of SO_2, NO_X, and CO_2 in transition economies: emission inventories and Divisia index analysis', *Energy Journal*, **20** (2), 59–87.

World Commission on Environment and Development (1987), *Our Common Future*, Oxford: Oxford University Press.

World Resources Institute (1991), *The Transition to a Sustainable Society*, Washington DC: World Resources Institute.

Index